Free Pass

Julian Hanshaw

"You are free to be a drunkard, an idler, a coward, a backbiter, a fornicator; but you are not free to think for yourself."

–George Orwell, *Burmese Days*

"Tech companies are distracting, dividing and outraging citizens to the point where there is little basis for common ground. This is a direct threat to democracy."

–Tristan Harris, *The Social Dilemma*

"AI-powered sex robots are selling well during lockdown…"

–BusinessInsider.com, 12 Jun 2020

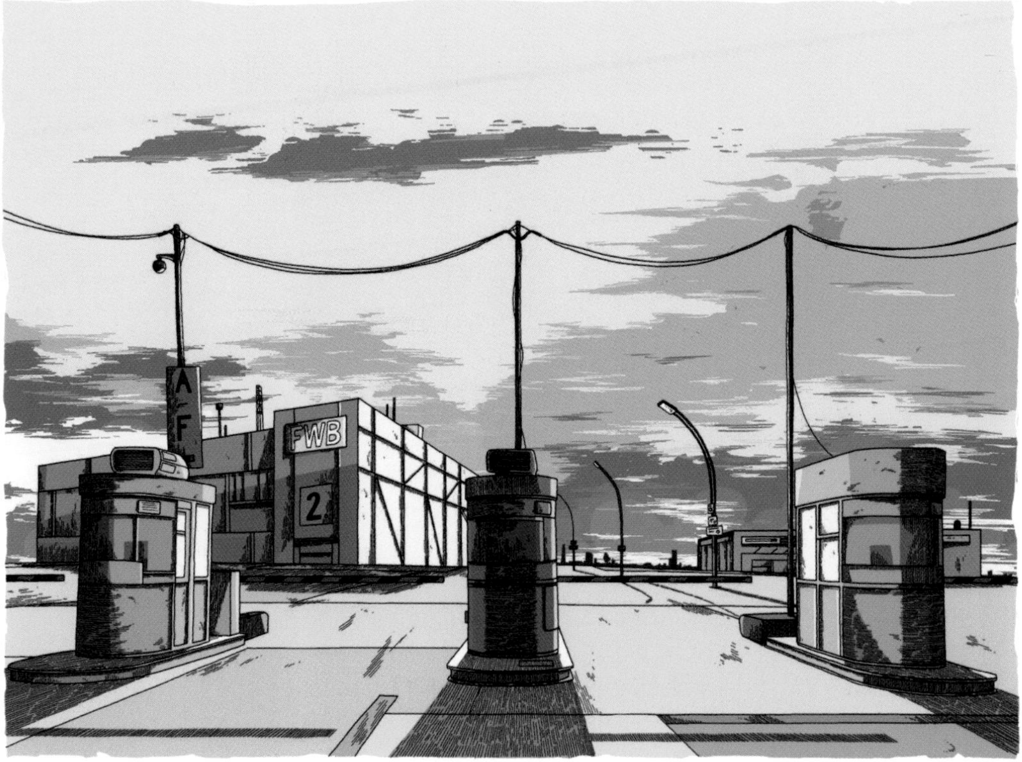
A
F
FWB
2

16 days to election.

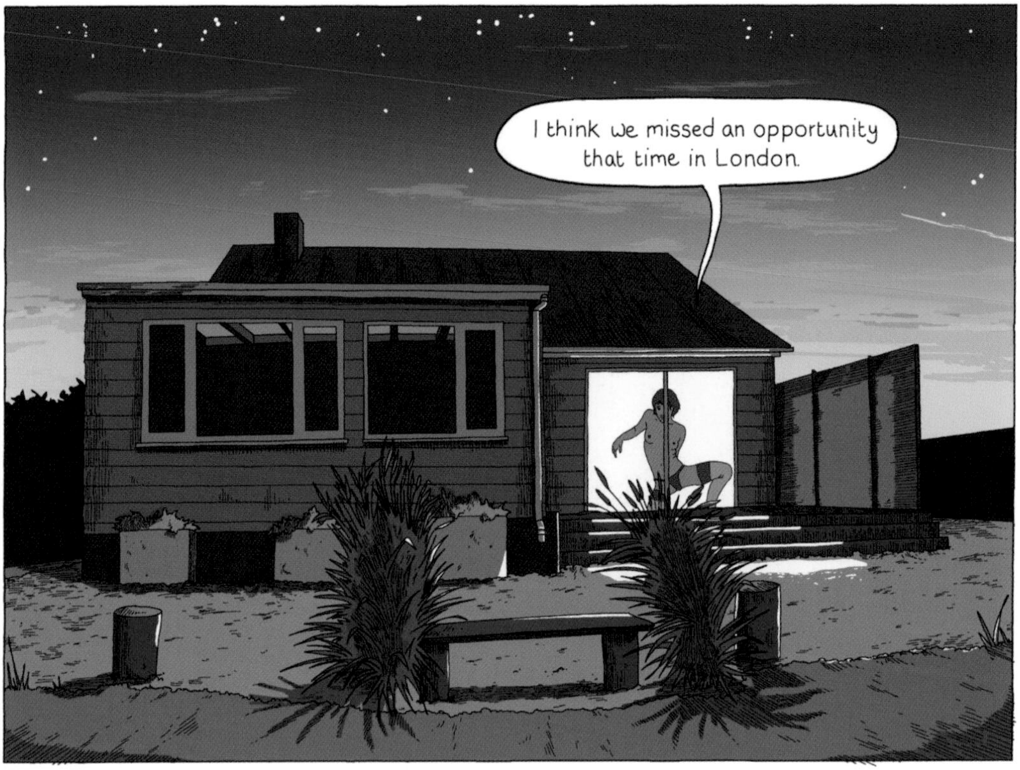
I think we missed an opportunity that time in London.

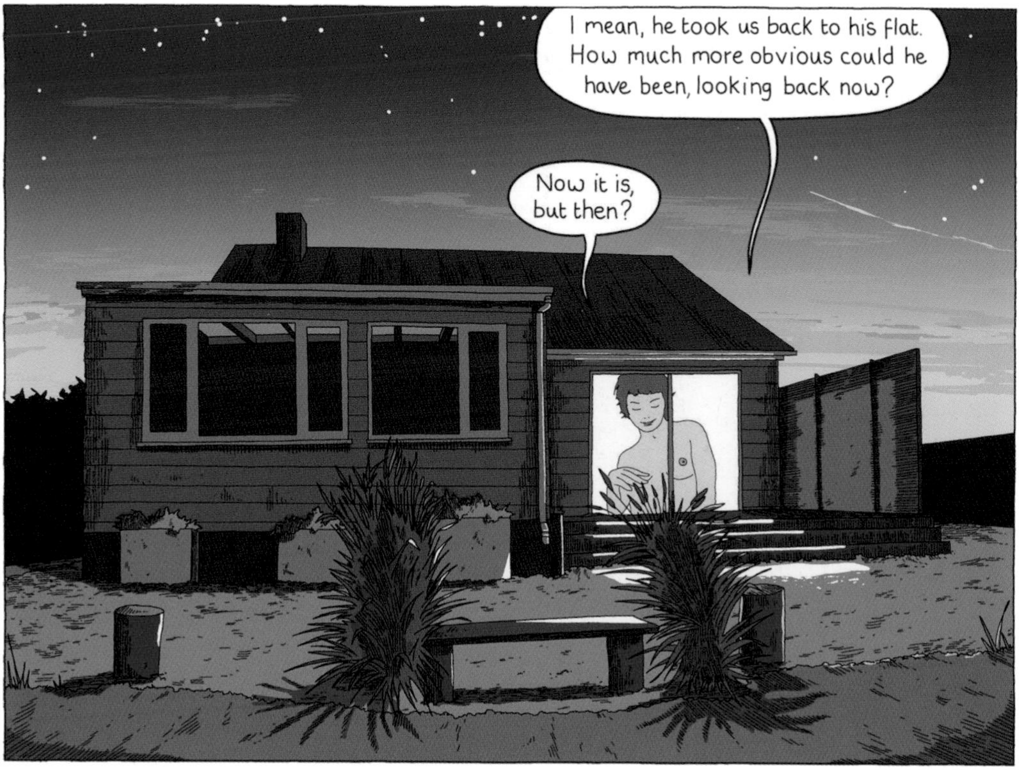
Now it is, but then?
I mean, he took us back to his flat. How much more obvious could he have been, looking back now?

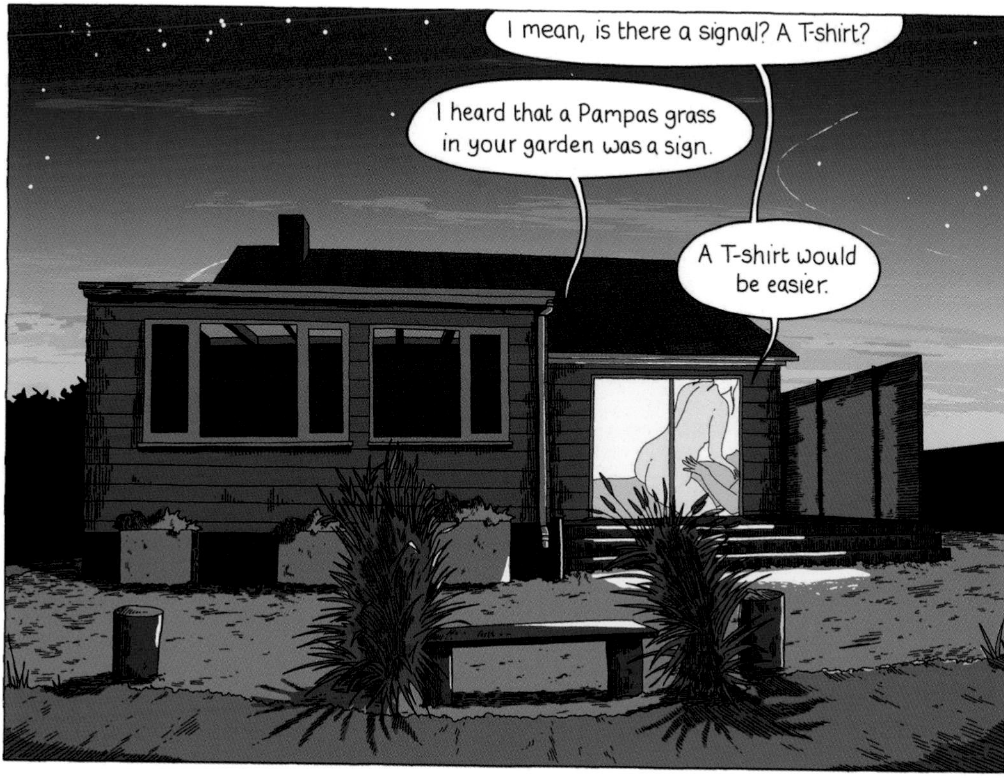
I heard that a Pampas grass in your garden was a sign.
I mean, is there a signal? A T-shirt?
A T-shirt would be easier.

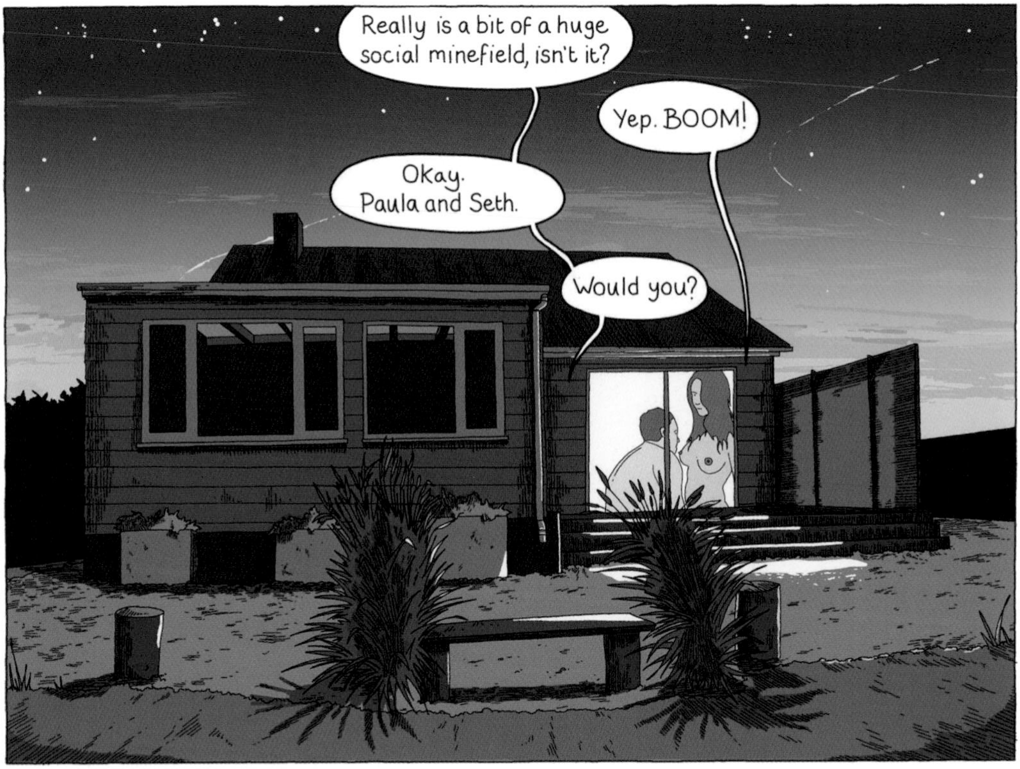
Really is a bit of a huge social minefield, isn't it?
Okay. Paula and Seth.
Would you?
Yep. BOOM!

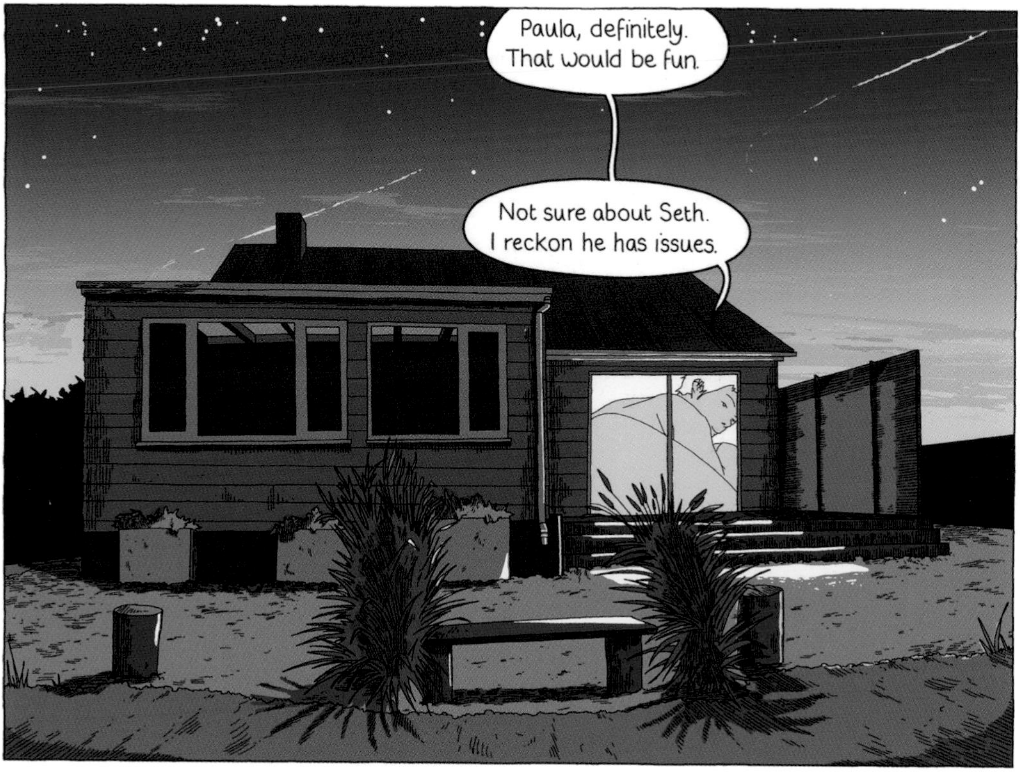
Paula, definitely. That would be fun.
Not sure about Seth. I reckon he has issues.

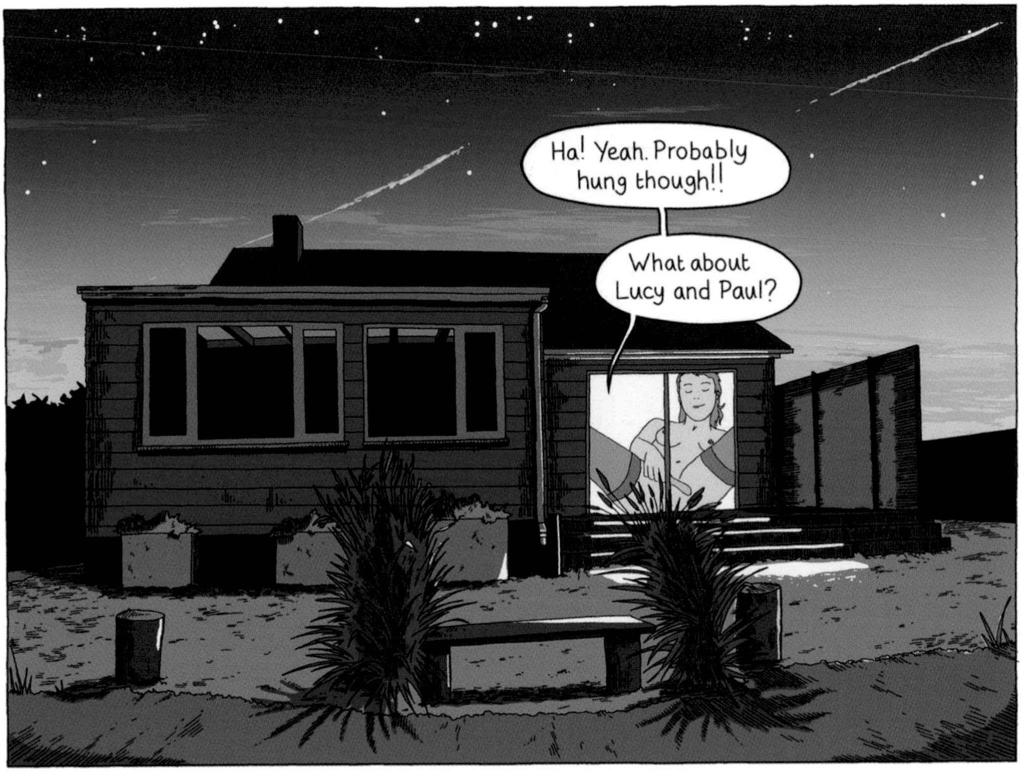
Ha! Yeah. Probably hung though!!
What about Lucy and Paul?

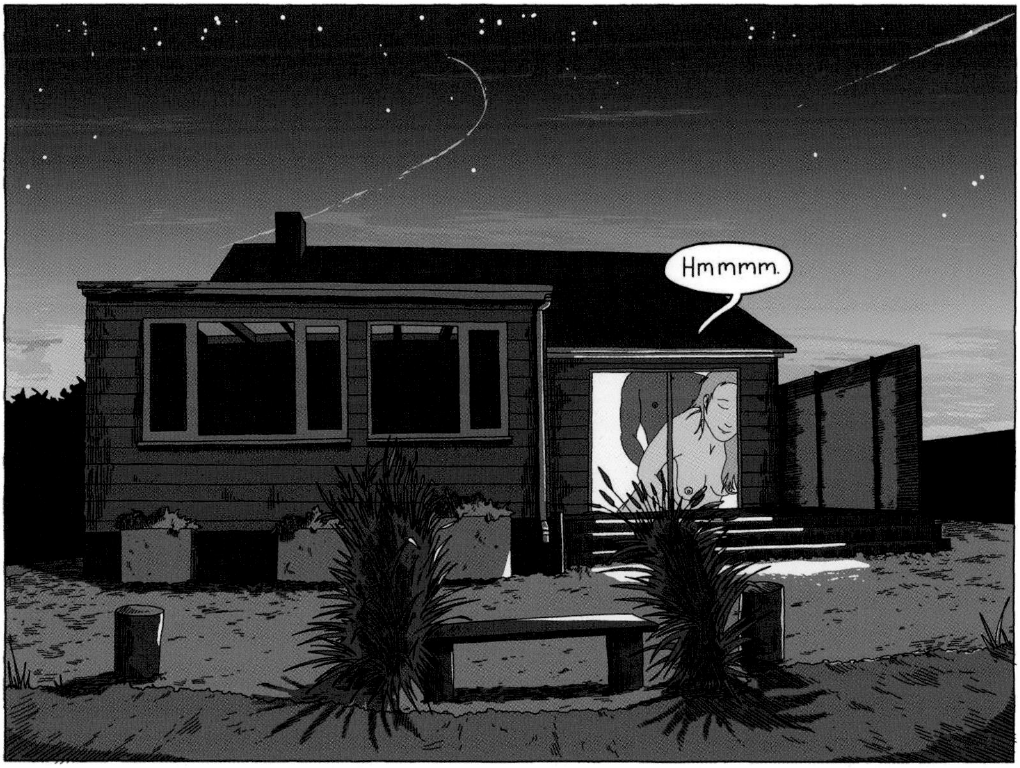
Hmmmm.

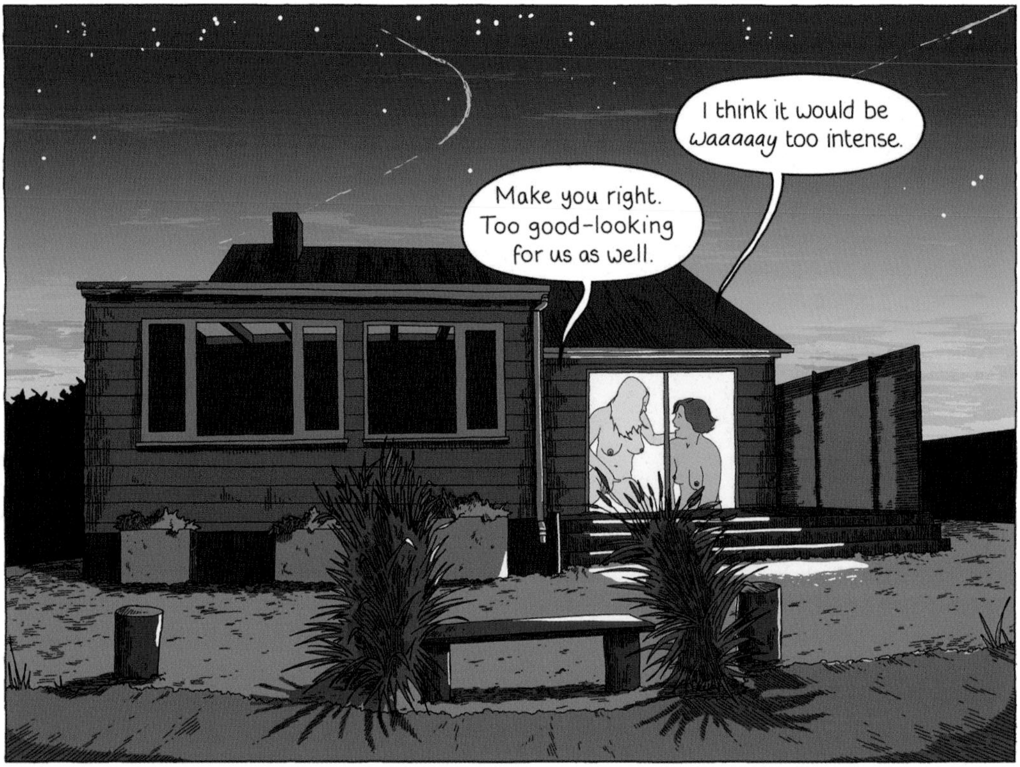
Make you right. Too good-looking for us as well.
I think it would be *waaaaay* too intense.

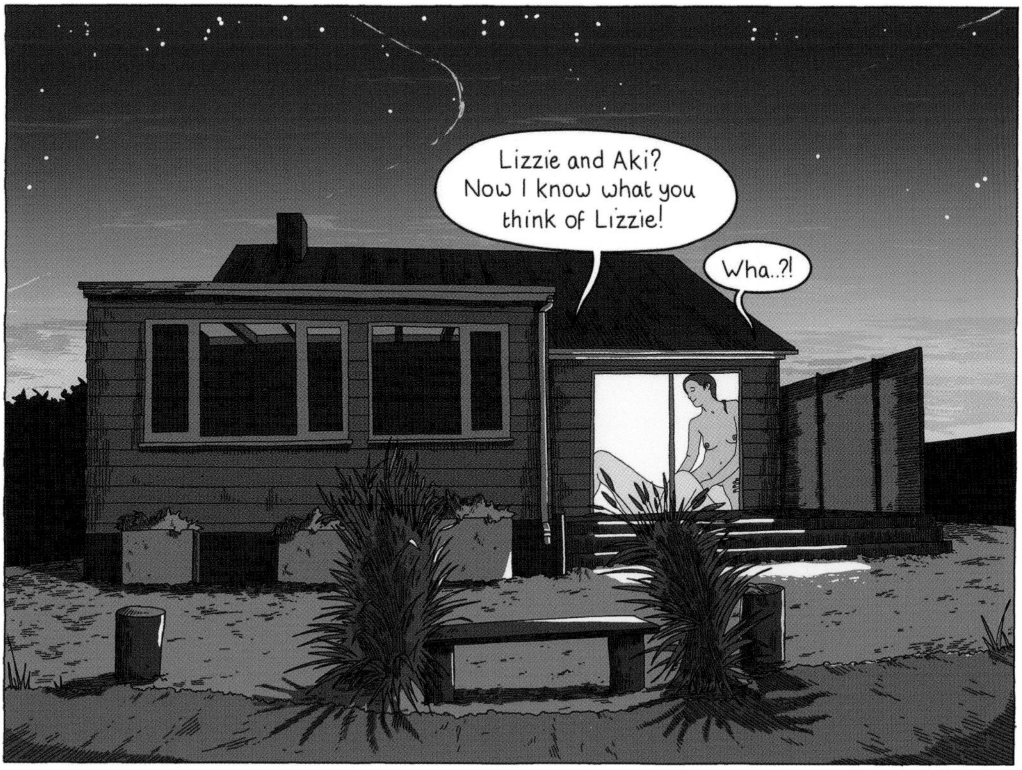
Lizzie and Aki? Now I know what you think of Lizzie!
Wha..?!

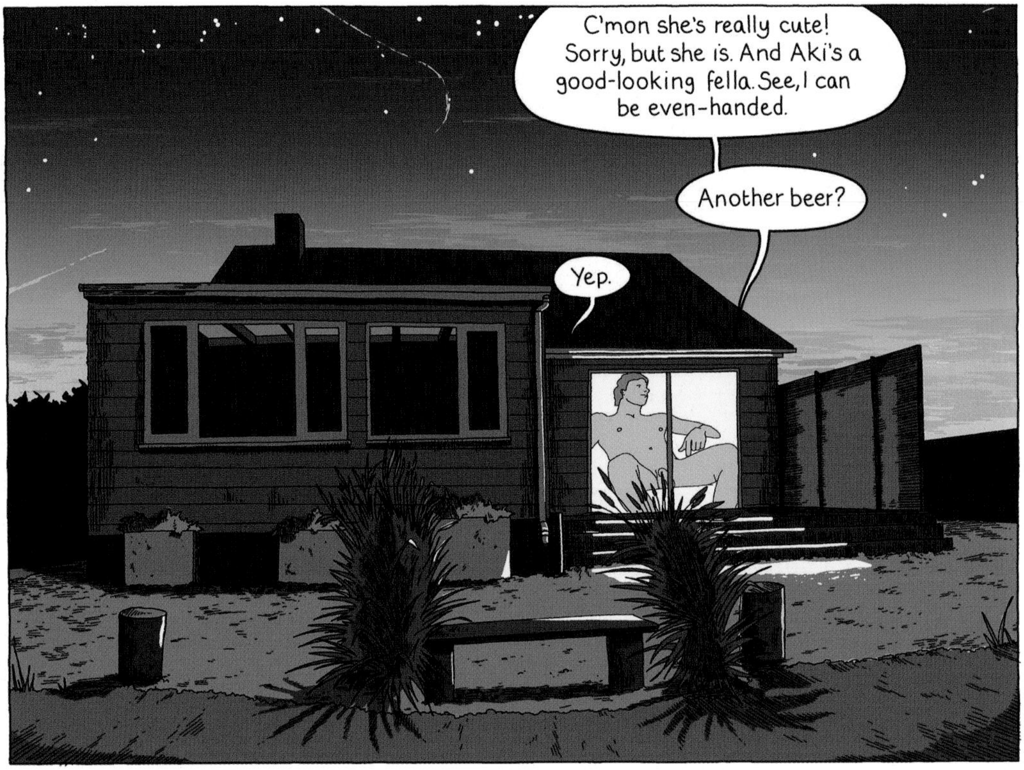
C'mon she's really cute! Sorry, but she is. And Aki's a good-looking fella. See, I can be even-handed.
Another beer?
Yep.

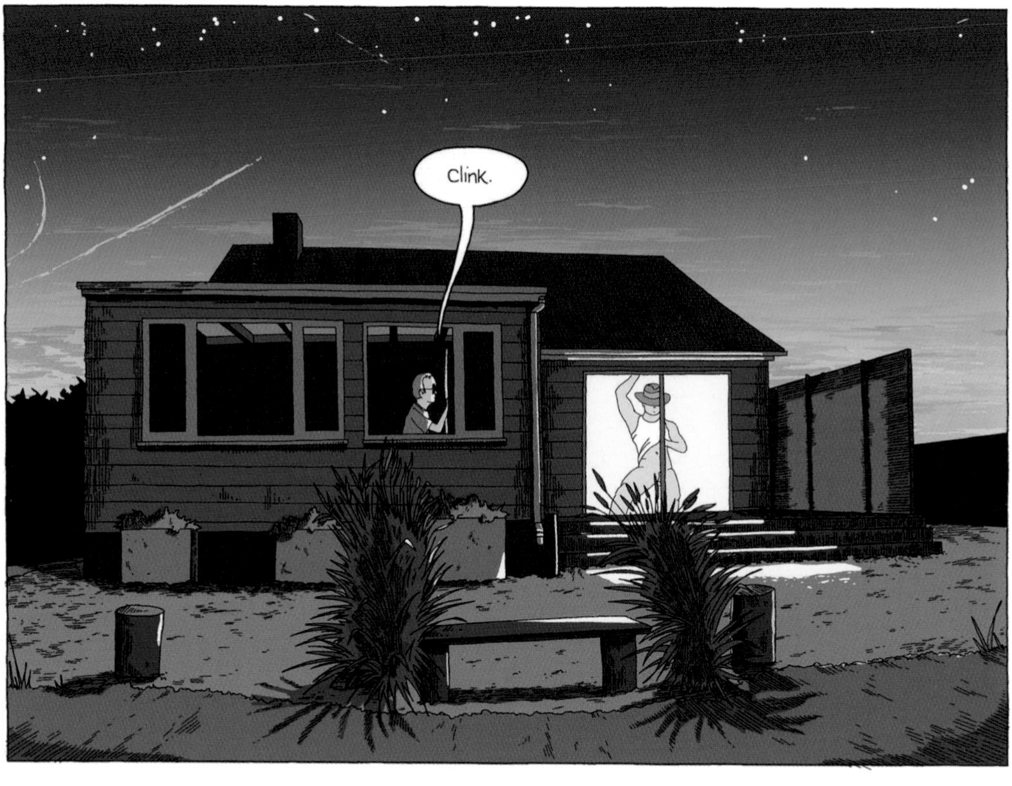
Clink.

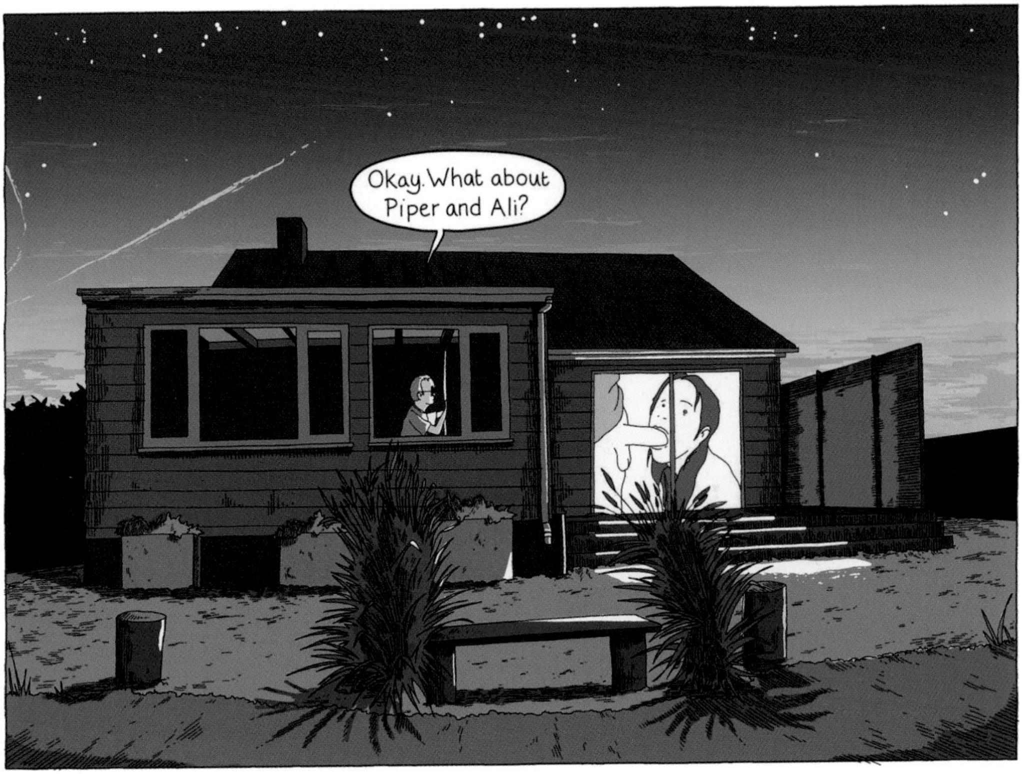
Okay. What about Piper and Ali?

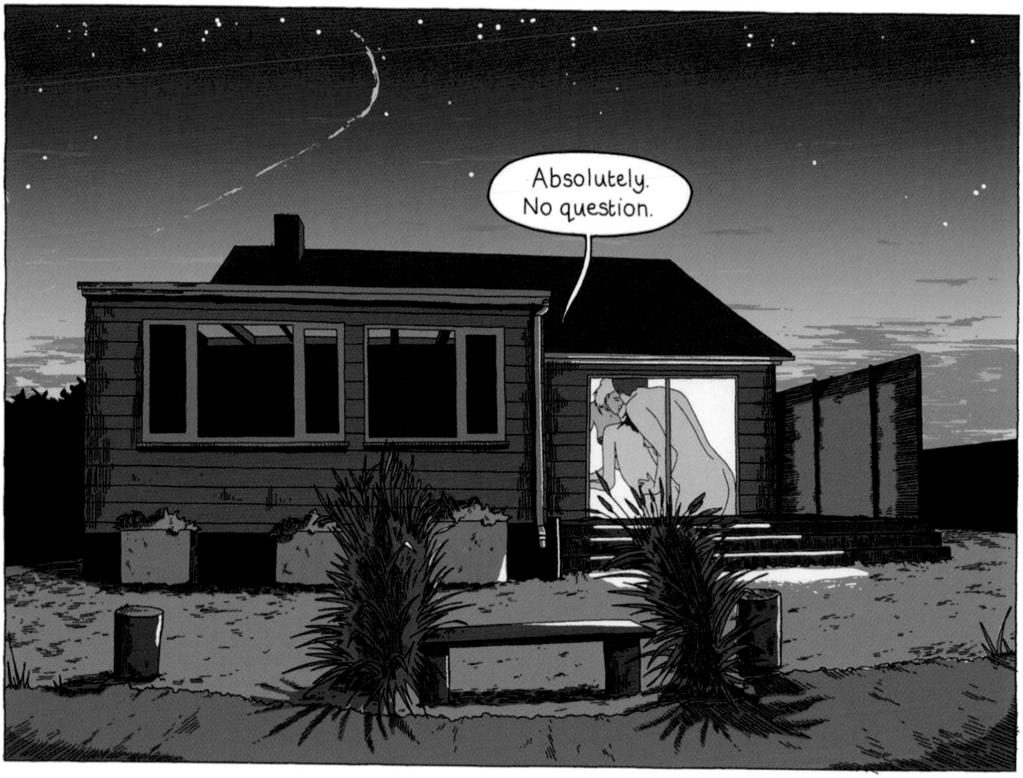
Absolutely. No question.

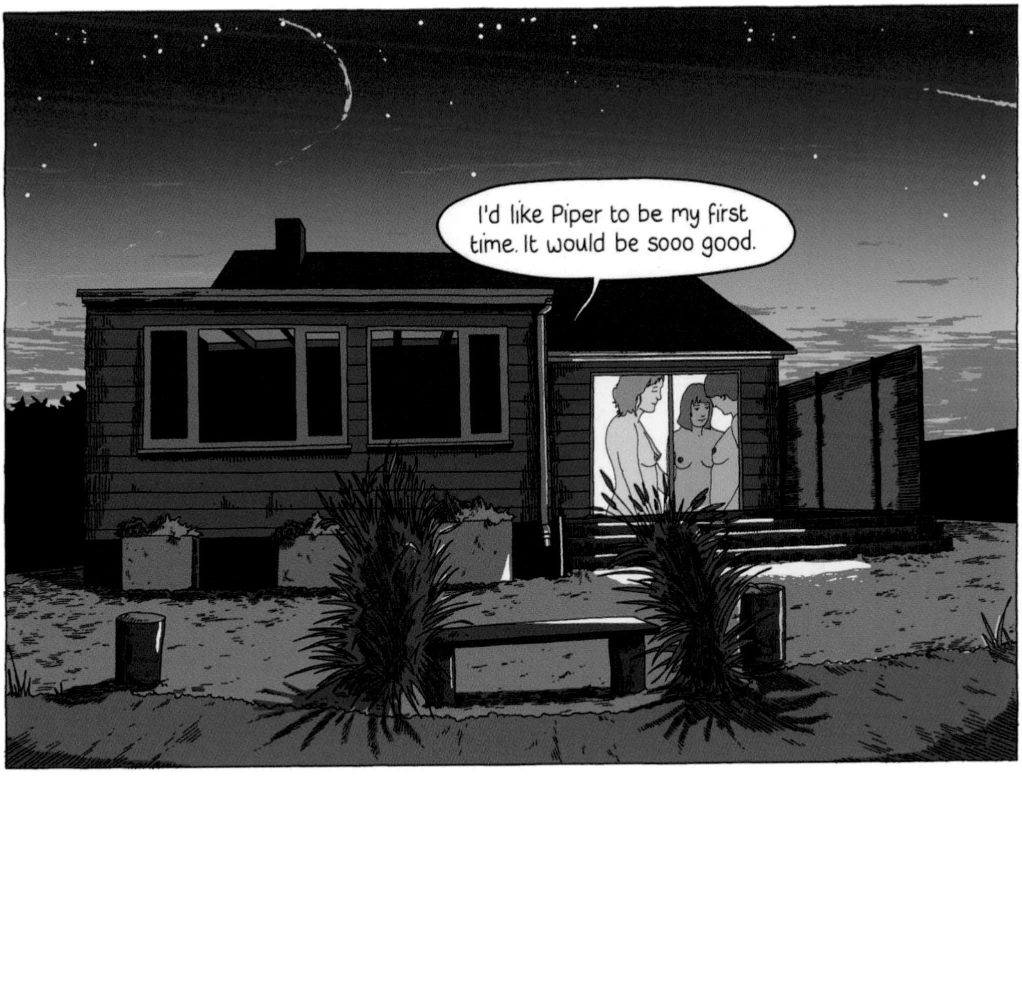
I'd like Piper to be my first time. It would be sooo good.

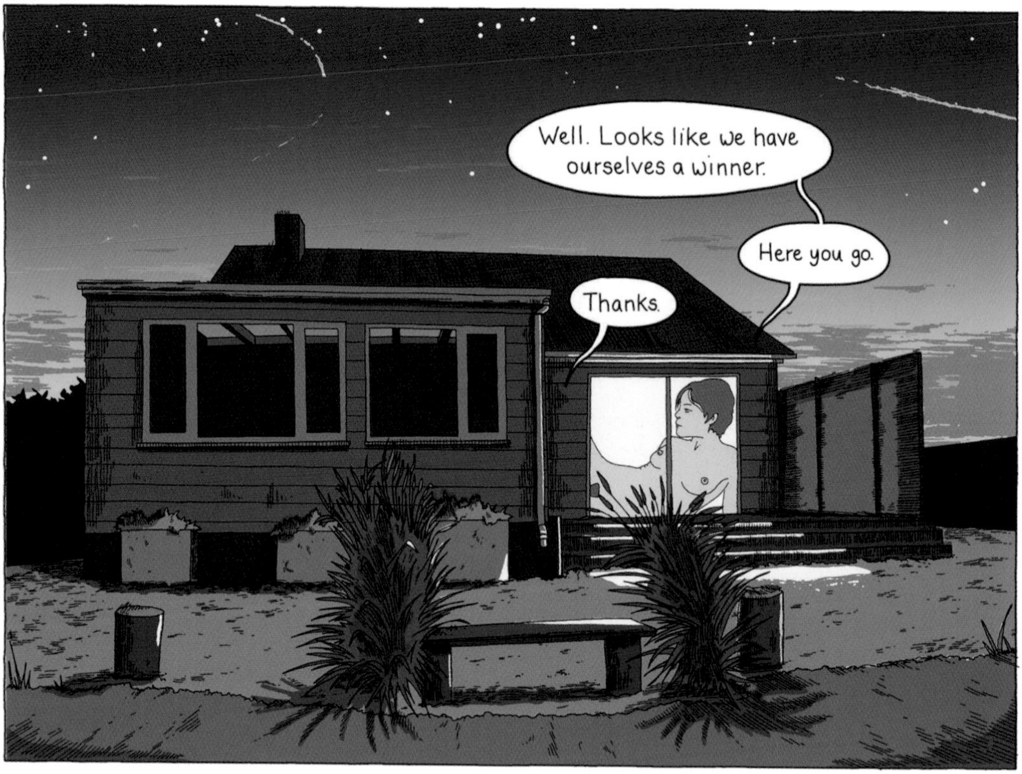
Well. Looks like we have ourselves a winner.
Here you go.
Thanks.

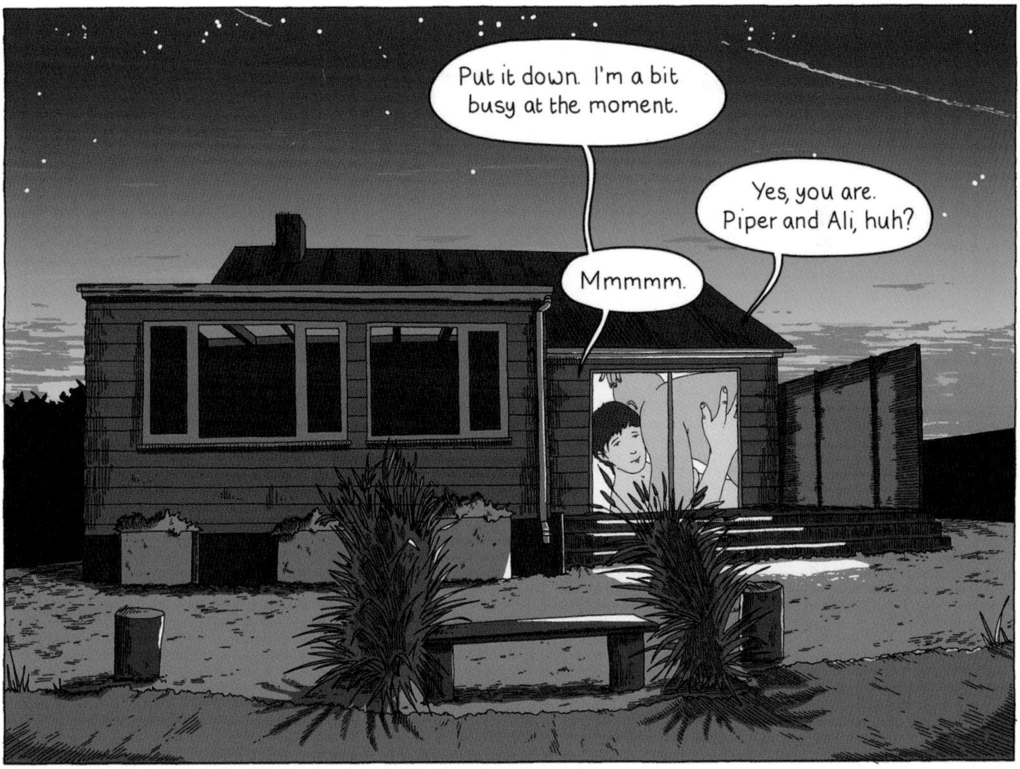
Put it down. I'm a bit busy at the moment.
Mmmmm.
Yes, you are. Piper and Ali, huh?

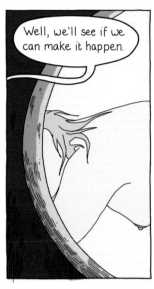

Well, we'll see if we can make it happen.

No idea how.

Do you know what a "Free Pass" is?

A what?

A "Free Pass".

Nope. What is it?

It's where...well, it's like you get a guilt-free and consequence-free chance to sleep with somebody.

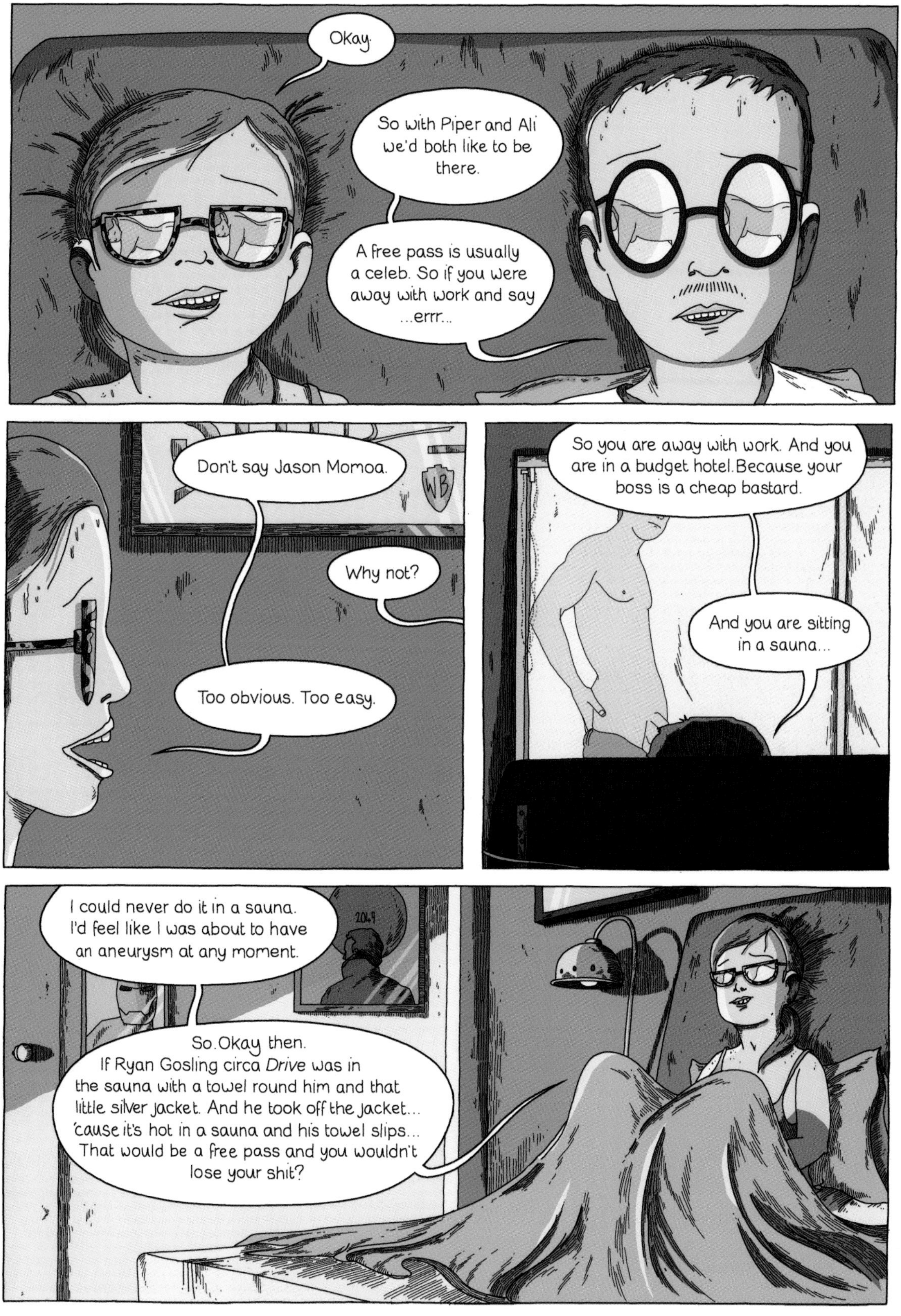
Okay.
So with Piper and Ali we'd both like to be there.
A free pass is usually a celeb. So if you were away with work and say ...errr...
Don't say Jason Momoa.
Why not?
Too obvious. Too easy.
So you are away with work. And you are in a budget hotel. Because your boss is a cheap bastard.
And you are sitting in a sauna...
I could never do it in a sauna. I'd feel like I was about to have an aneurysm at any moment.
So. Okay then. If Ryan Gosling circa *Drive* was in the sauna with a towel round him and that little silver jacket. And he took off the jacket... 'cause it's hot in a sauna and his towel slips... That would be a free pass and you wouldn't lose your shit?

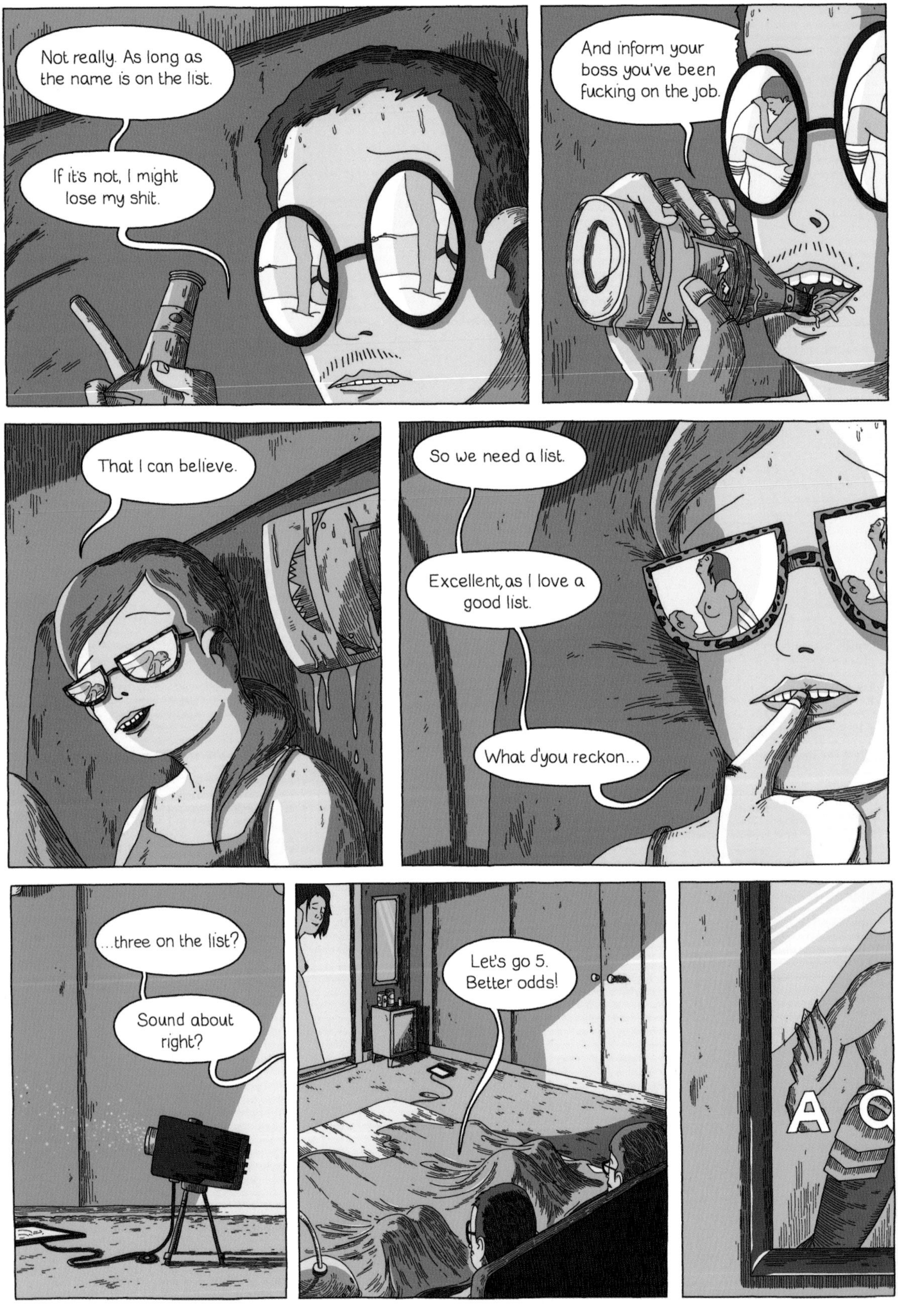
Not really. As long as the name is on the list.
If it's not, I might lose my shit.
And inform your boss you've been fucking on the job.
That I can believe.
So we need a list.
Excellent, as I love a good list.
What d'you reckon...
...three on the list?
Sound about right?
Let's go 5. Better odds!
A O

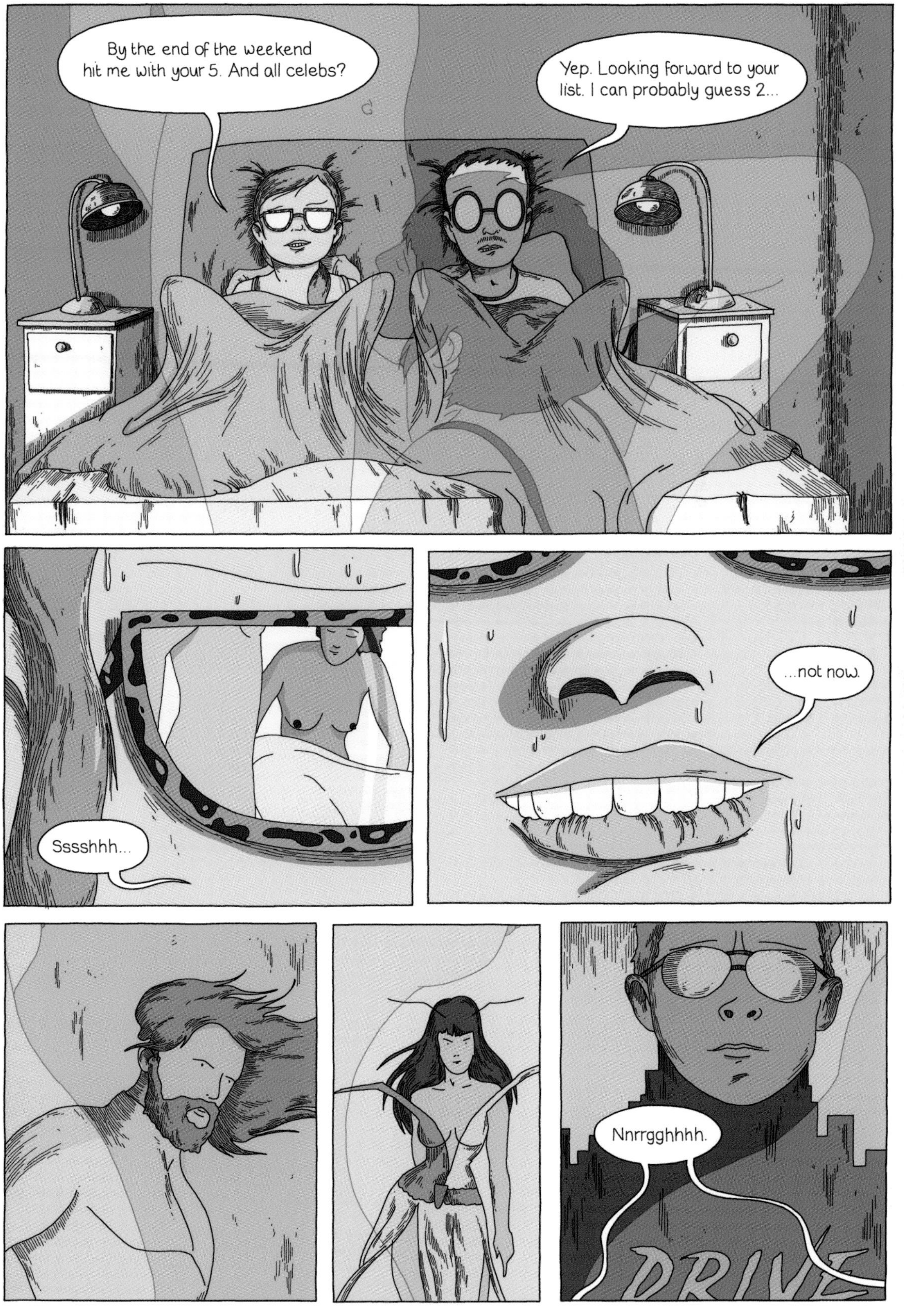
By the end of the weekend hit me with your 5. And all celebs?
Yep. Looking forward to your list. I can probably guess 2...
Sssshhh...
...not now.
Nnrrgghhhh.
DRIVE

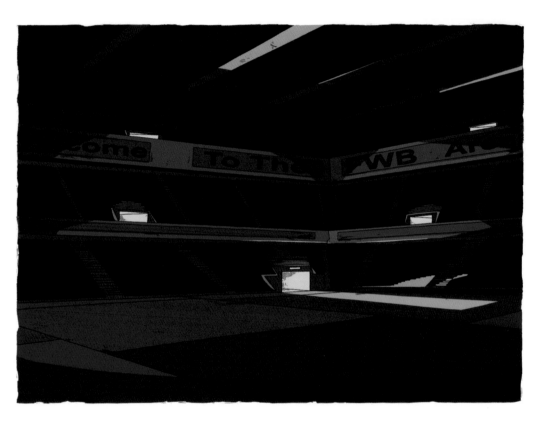

15 days to election.

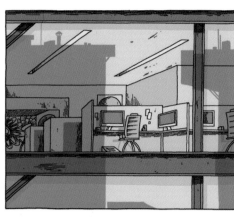

4 More Years?

BEEEP

HUCK Berninger

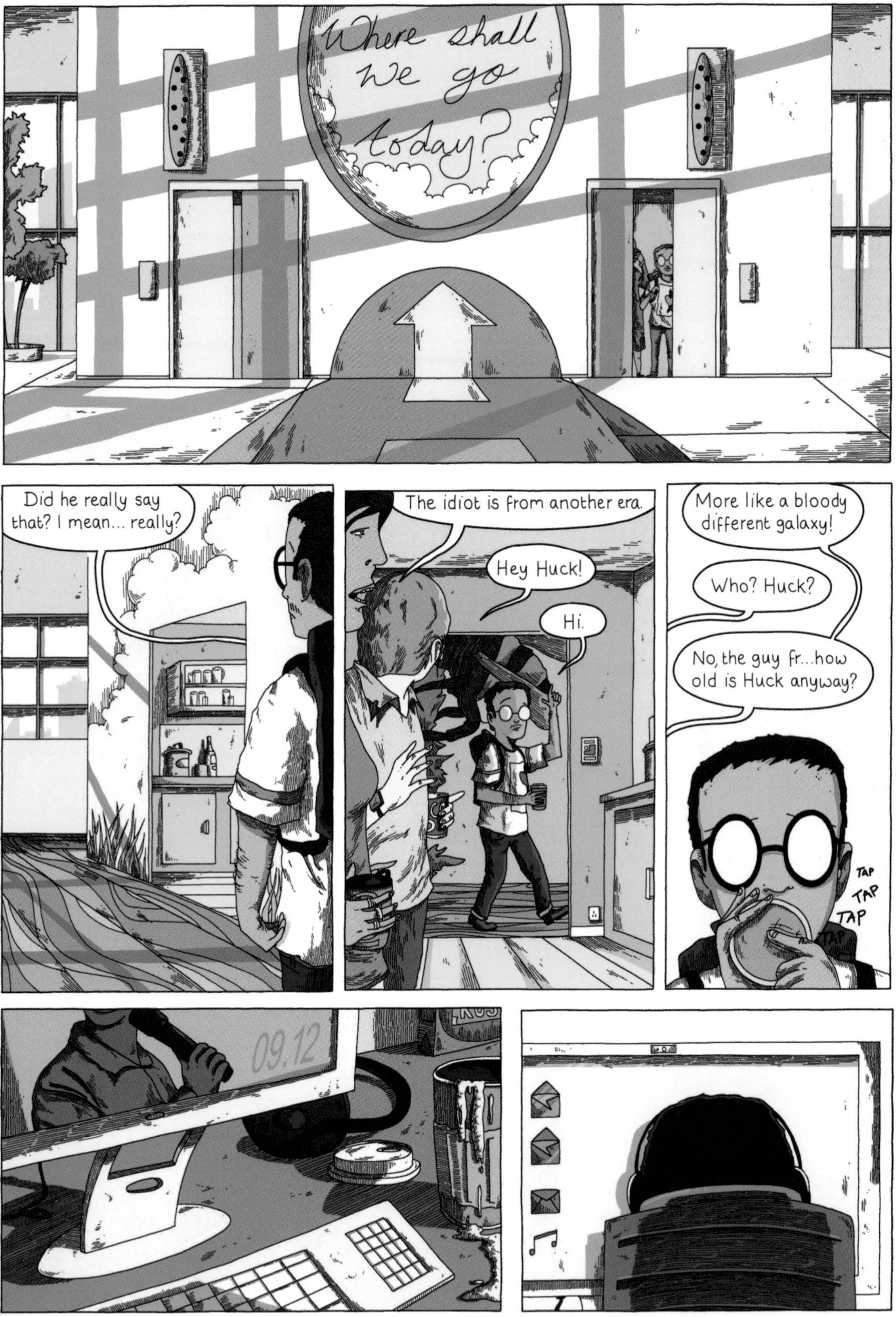
Where shall we go today?
Did he really say that? I mean... really?
The idiot is from another era.
Hey Huck!
Hi.
More like a bloody different galaxy!
Who? Huck?
No, the guy fr...how old is Huck anyway?
TAP
TAP
TAP
TAP
09.12

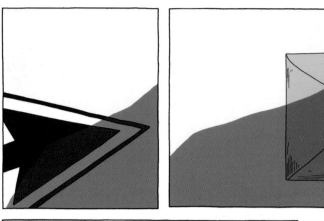

It's just a hair-line thing.

Makes me look older.

Thank you.

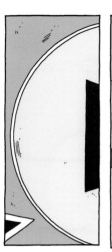

CLICK

Douglas Murr

MADNES OF CROWD

LIBRARY
🎵 Music
🎬 Movies
📺 TV Shows
📡 Podcasts   14
📶 Radio

STORE
📦 iTunes Store
✳ Purchased

"One of the strangest things in recent years is the manner in which online wars break out every single day on all of the issues I address..."

Okay. Let's see what we have here.

"...every day."

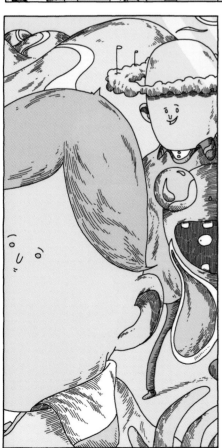

"I have to say, I really don't enjoy watching it take place."

Hi. Moderators, you need to sort this out. Only by chance I was looking at comments made below a cartoon my 6-year-old watched.

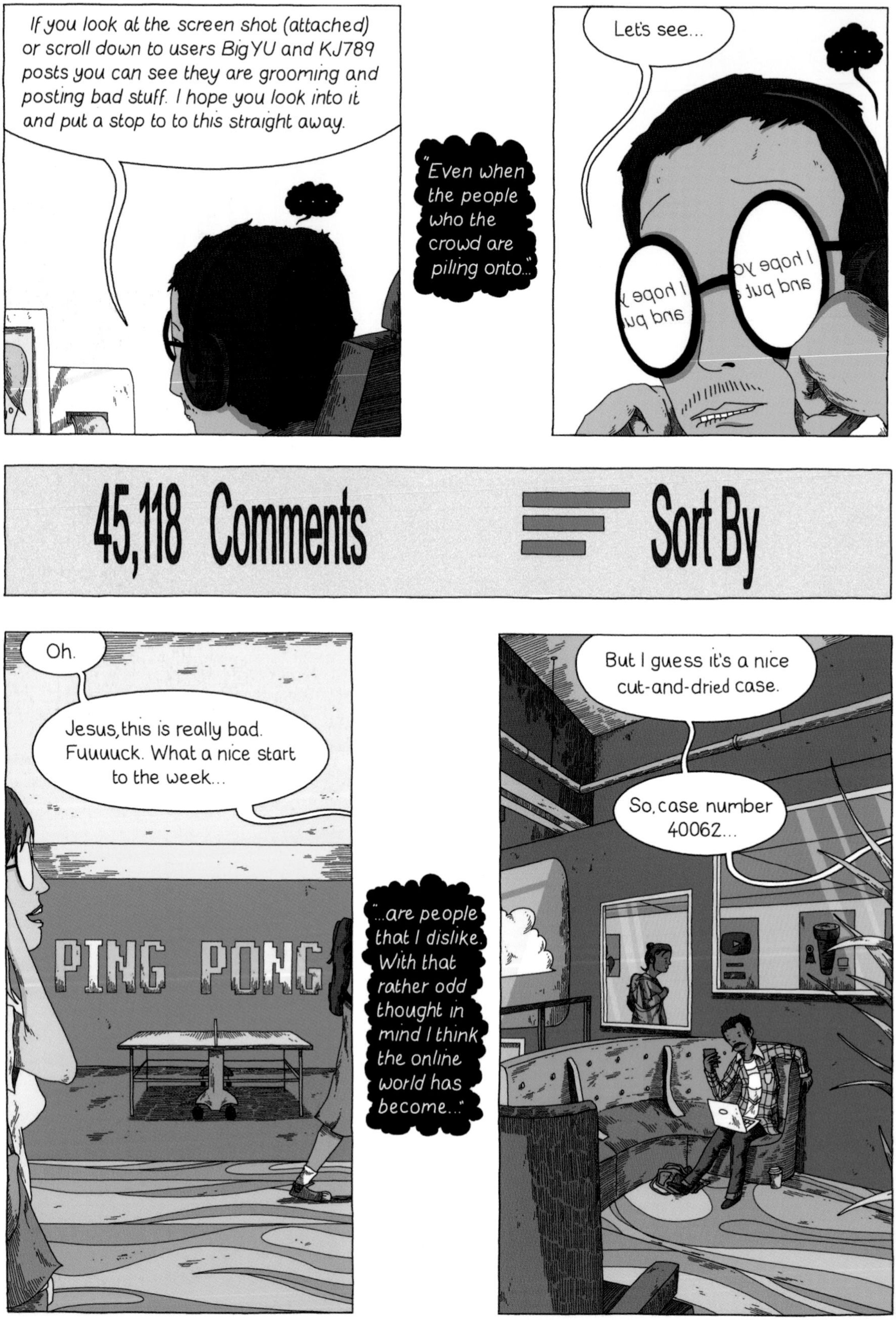
If you look at the screen shot (attached) or scroll down to users BigYU and KJ789 posts you can see they are grooming and posting bad stuff. I hope you look into it and put a stop to to this straight away.
...
"Even when the people who the crowd are piling onto..."
Let's see...
...
I hope yo and put
I hope y and pu
45,118 Comments
Sort By
Oh.
Jesus, this is really bad. Fuuuuck. What a nice start to the week...
PING PONG
"...are people that I dislike. With that rather odd thought in mind I think the online world has become..."
But I guess it's a nice cut-and-dried case.
So, case number 40062...

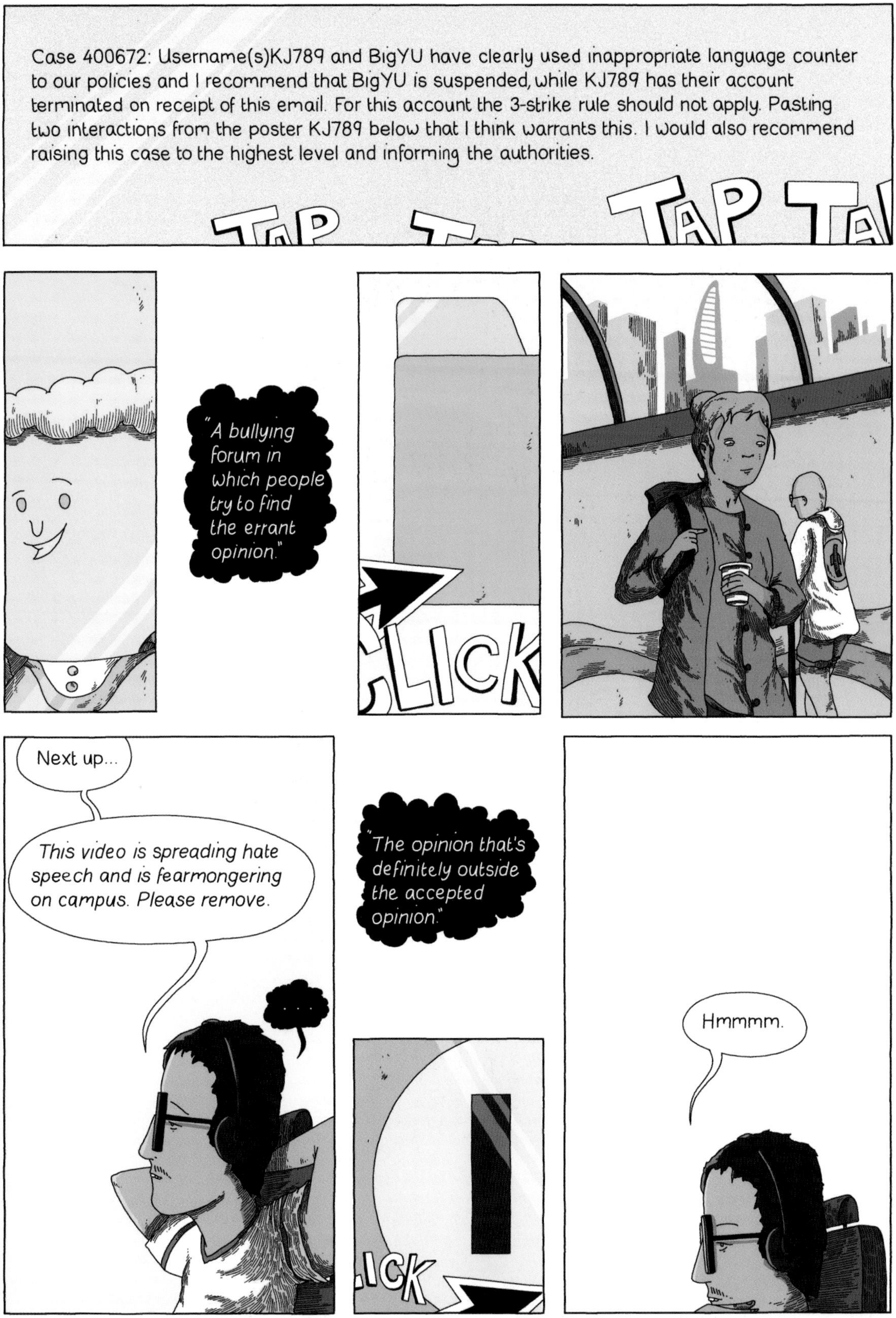
Case 400672: Username(s)KJ789 and BigYU have clearly used inappropriate language counter to our policies and I recommend that BigYU is suspended, while KJ789 has their account terminated on receipt of this email. For this account the 3-strike rule should not apply. Pasting two interactions from the poster KJ789 below that I think warrants this. I would also recommend raising this case to the highest level and informing the authorities.
TAP
TAP
"A bullying forum in which people try to find the errant opinion."
CLICK
Next up...
This video is spreading hate speech and is fearmongering on campus. Please remove.
...
"The opinion that's definitely outside the accepted opinion."
CLICK
Hmmmm.

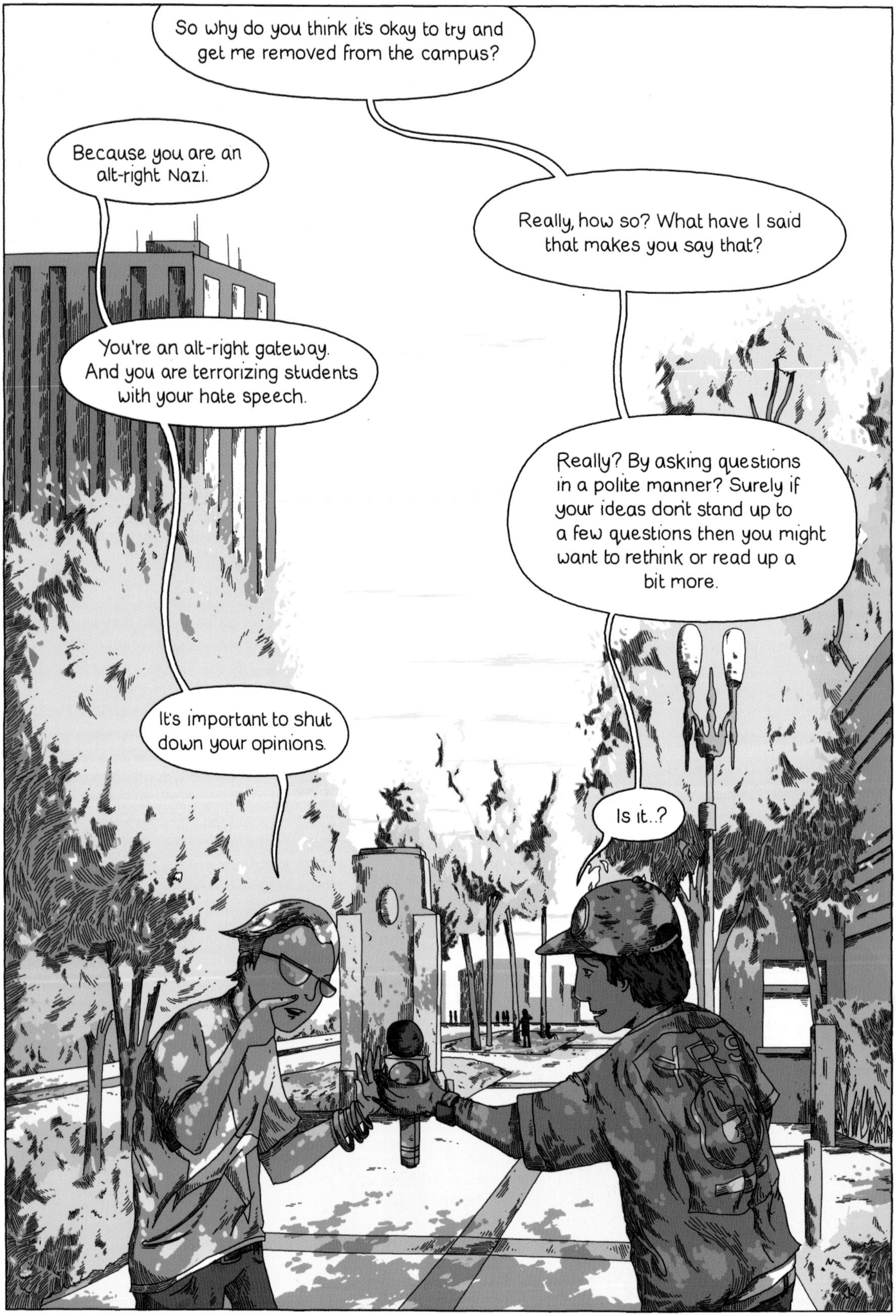
So why do you think it's okay to try and get me removed from the campus?
Because you are an alt-right Nazi.
Really, how so? What have I said that makes you say that?
You're an alt-right gateway. And you are terrorizing students with your hate speech.
Really? By asking questions in a polite manner? Surely if your ideas don't stand up to a few questions then you might want to rethink or read up a bit more.
It's important to shut down your opinions.
Is it..?

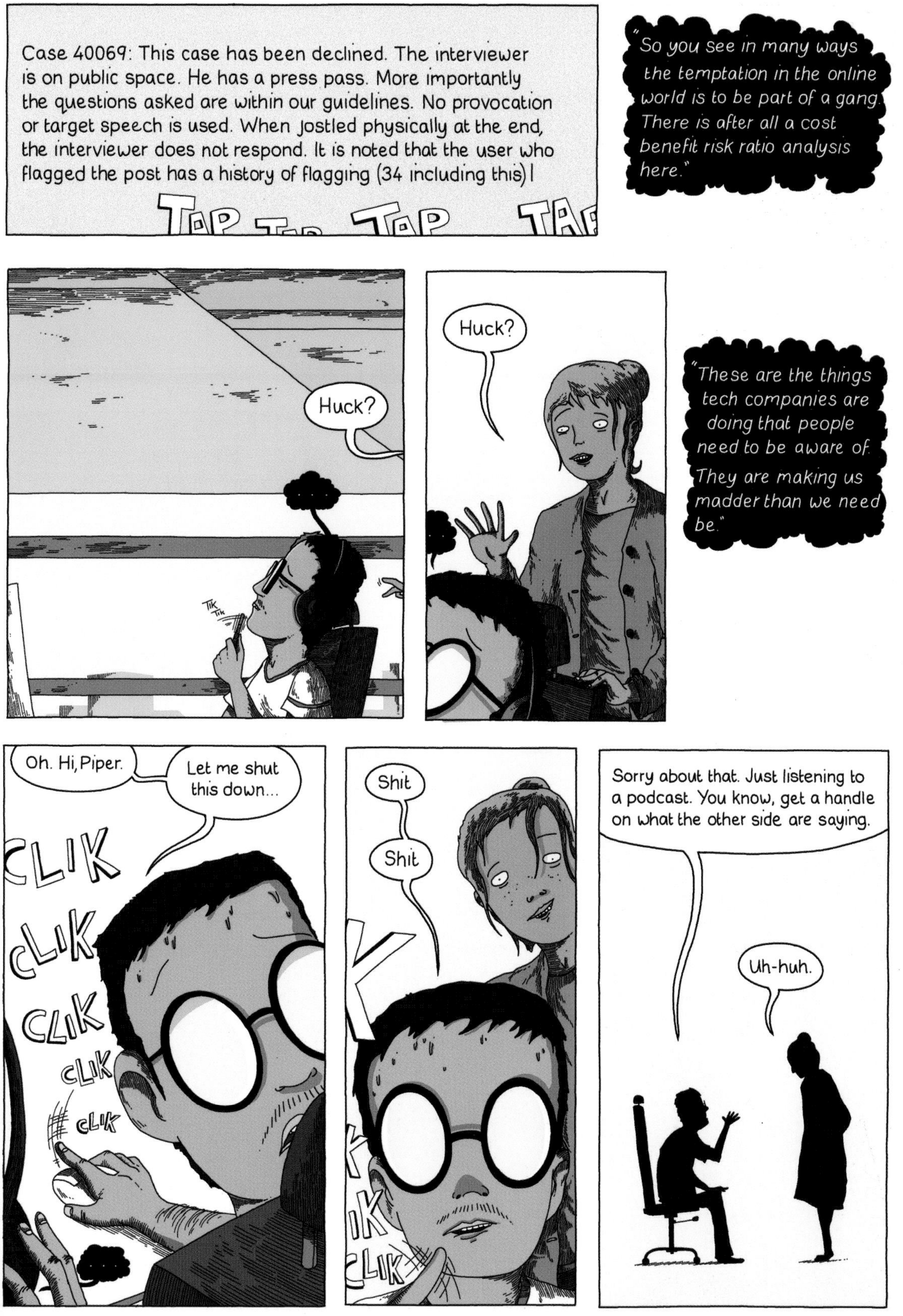
Case 40069: This case has been declined. The interviewer is on public space. He has a press pass. More importantly the questions asked are within our guidelines. No provocation or target speech is used. When jostled physically at the end, the interviewer does not respond. It is noted that the user who flagged the post has a history of flagging (34 including this)|
TAP
TAP
TAP
"So you see in many ways the temptation in the online world is to be part of a gang. There is after all a cost benefit risk ratio analysis here."
Huck?
TIK
TIK
Huck?
"These are the things tech companies are doing that people need to be aware of. They are making us madder than we need be."
Oh. Hi, Piper.
Let me shut this down...
CLIK
CLIK
CLIK
CLIK
CLIK
Shit
Shit
CLIK
Sorry about that. Just listening to a podcast. You know, get a handle on what the other side are saying.
Uh-huh.

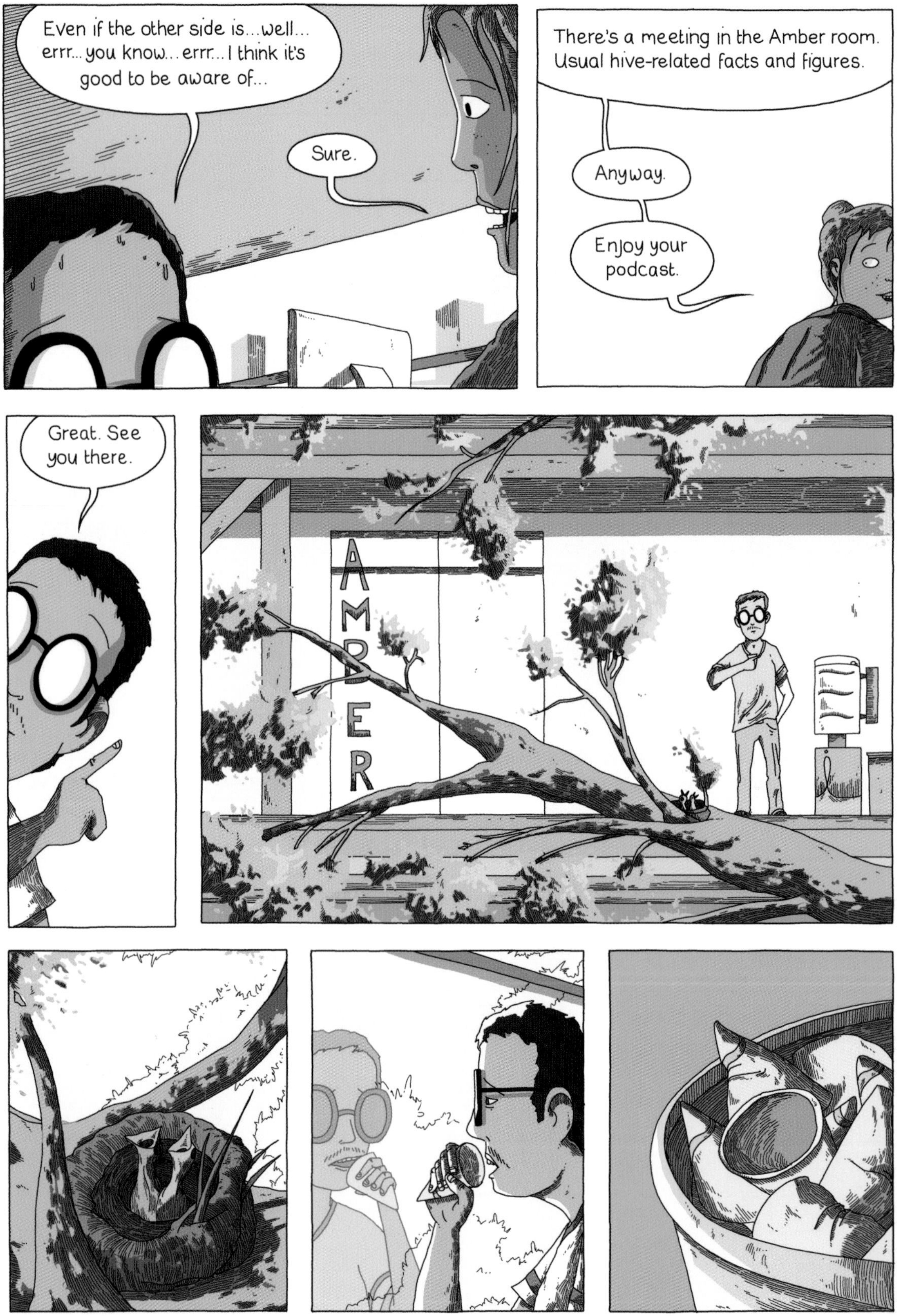
Even if the other side is... well... errr... you know... errr... I think it's good to be aware of...
Sure.
There's a meeting in the Amber room. Usual hive-related facts and figures.
Anyway.
Enjoy your podcast.
Great. See you there.
AMBER

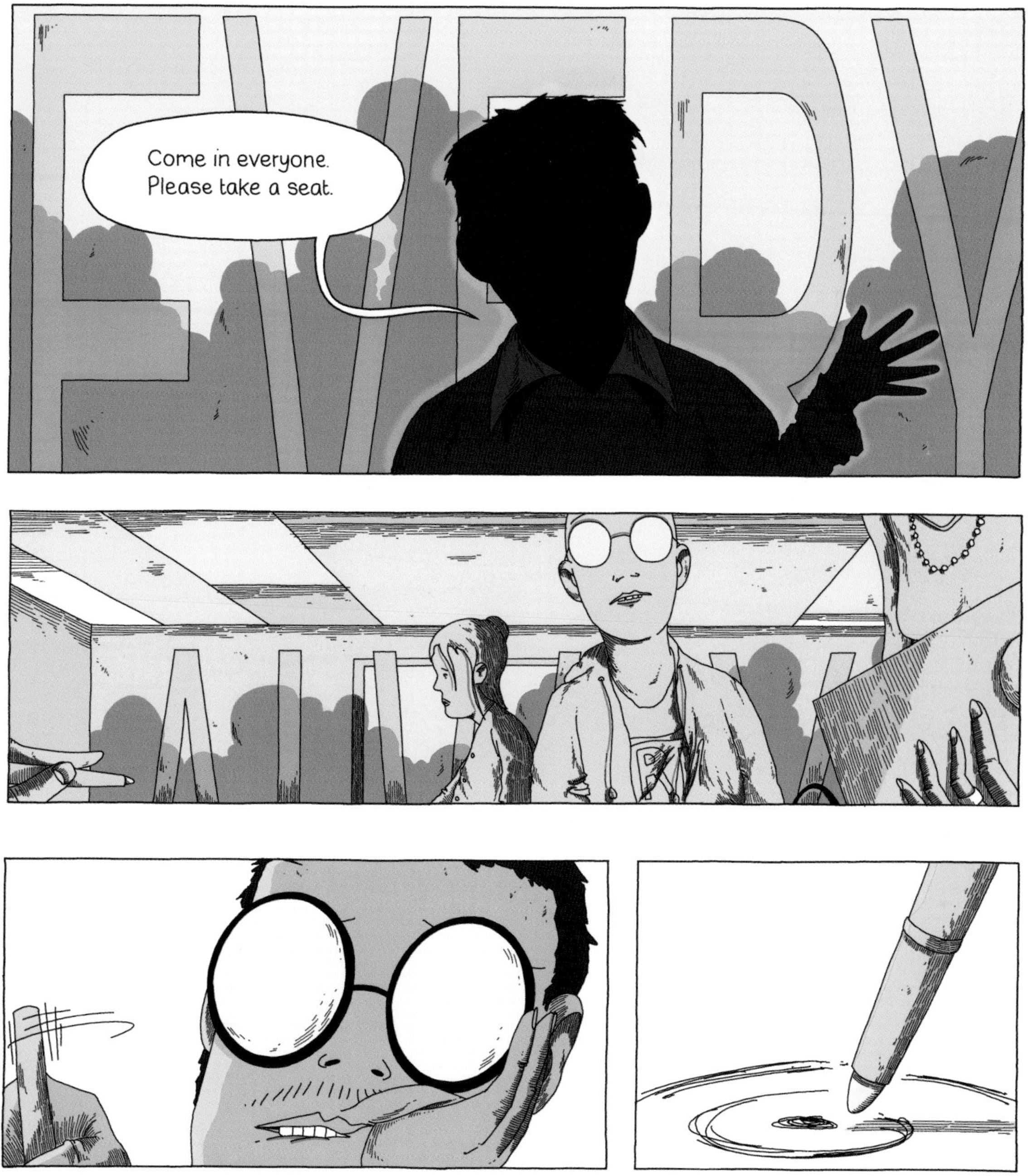
Come in everyone. Please take a seat.

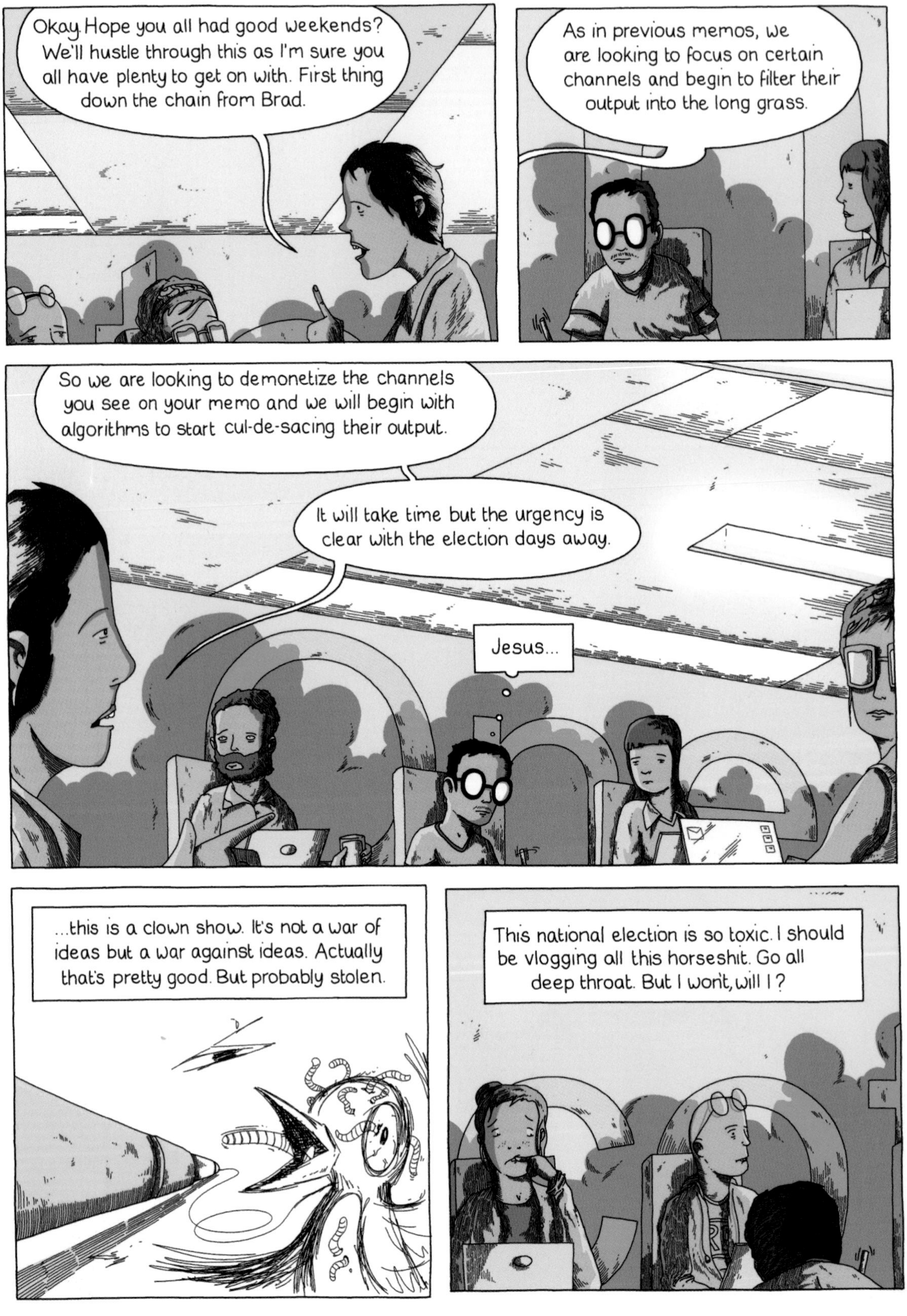
Okay. Hope you all had good weekends? We'll hustle through this as I'm sure you all have plenty to get on with. First thing down the chain from Brad.
As in previous memos, we are looking to focus on certain channels and begin to filter their output into the long grass.
So we are looking to demonetize the channels you see on your memo and we will begin with algorithms to start cul-de-sacing their output.
It will take time but the urgency is clear with the election days away.
Jesus...
...this is a clown show. It's not a war of ideas but a war against ideas. Actually that's pretty good. But probably stolen.
This national election is so toxic. I should be vlogging all this horseshit. Go all deep throat. But I won't, will I?

I'm a coward.

I mean I didn't vote for Libby but it's been okay.

And Maynard has some good ideas but she has the wacky fringe in her ear.

Who are idealist idiots.

Huck?

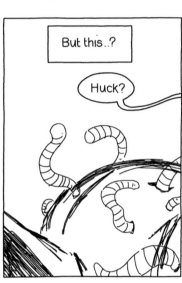

But this..?

Huck?

How are you doing number-wise in your department?

Shit.

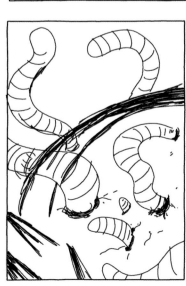

Huh?

Oh fuck.

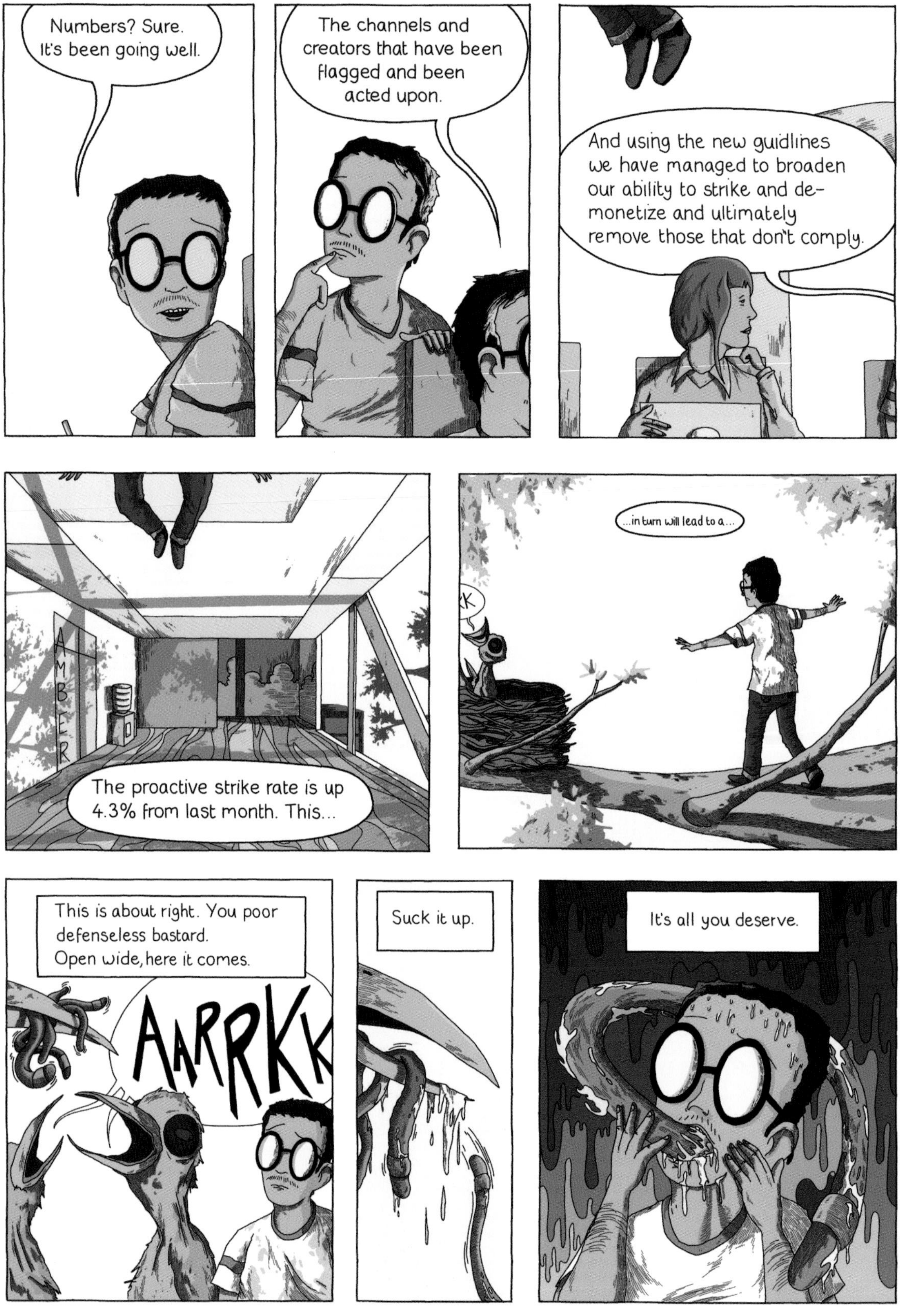
Numbers? Sure. It's been going well.
The channels and creators that have been flagged and been acted upon.
And using the new guidlines we have managed to broaden our ability to strike and de-monetize and ultimately remove those that don't comply.
AMBER
The proactive strike rate is up 4.3% from last month. This...
...in turn will lead to a...
This is about right. You poor defenseless bastard.
Open wide, here it comes.
AARRKK
Suck it up.
It's all you deserve.

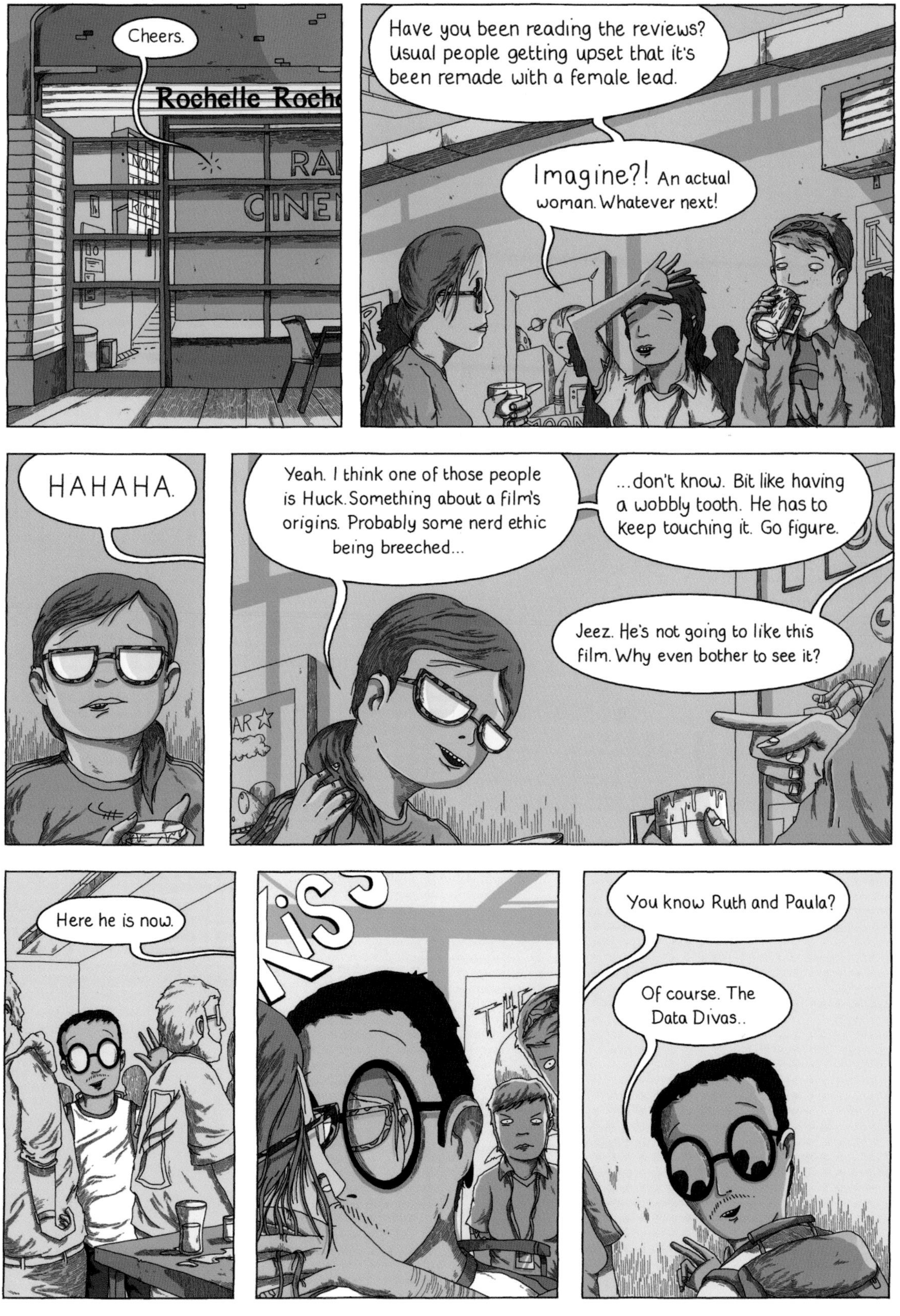
Cheers.
Rochelle Roch
RA
CINE
Have you been reading the reviews? Usual people getting upset that it's been remade with a female lead.
Imagine?! An actual woman. Whatever next!
HAHAHA.
Yeah. I think one of those people is Huck. Something about a film's origins. Probably some nerd ethic being breeched...
...don't know. Bit like having a wobbly tooth. He has to keep touching it. Go figure.
Jeez. He's not going to like this film. Why even bother to see it?
Here he is now.
KISS
You know Ruth and Paula?
Of course. The Data Divas..

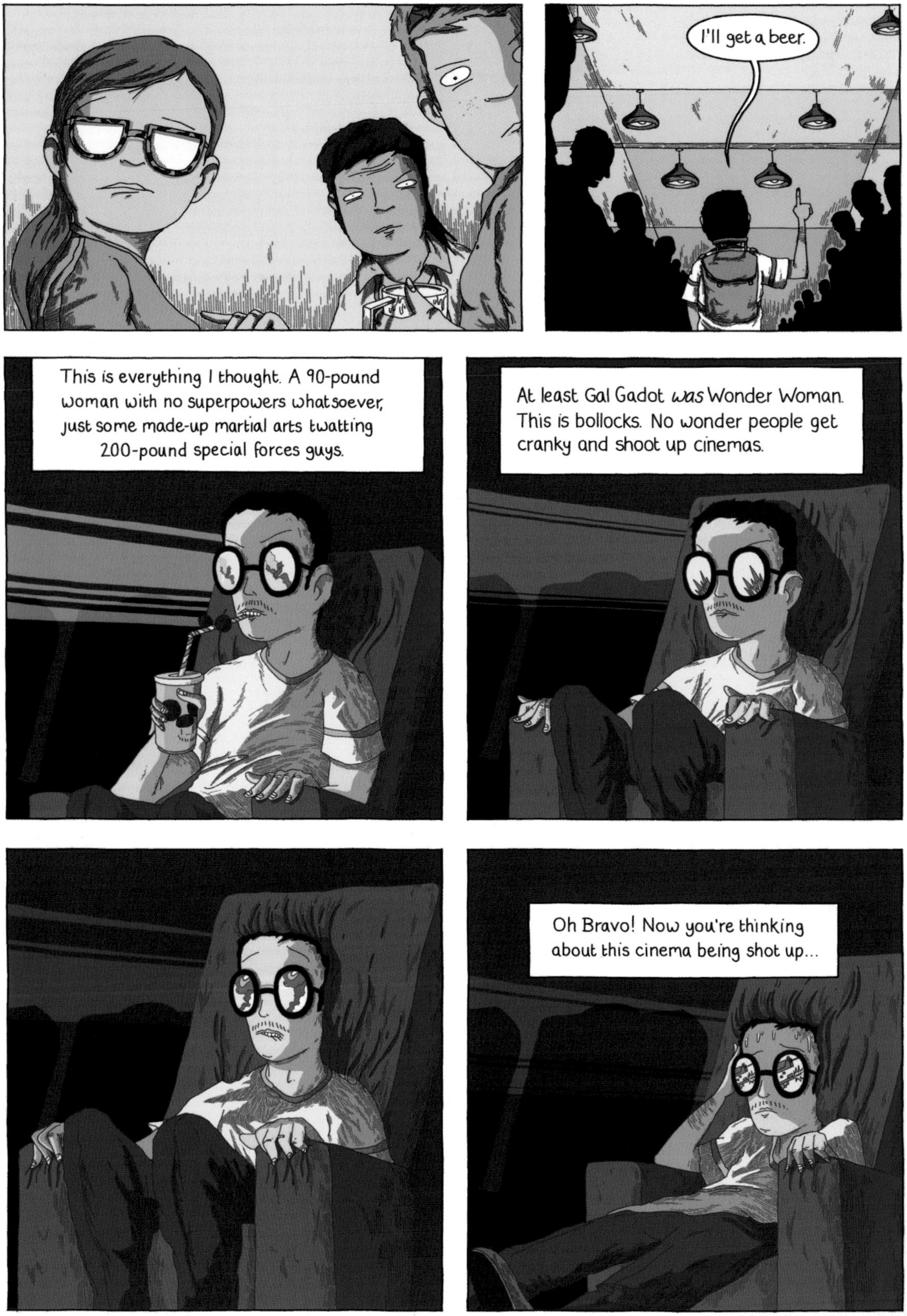
I'll get a beer.
This is everything I thought. A 90-pound woman with no superpowers whatsoever, just some made-up martial arts twatting 200-pound special forces guys.
At least Gal Gadot *was* Wonder Woman. This is bollocks. No wonder people get cranky and shoot up cinemas.
Oh Bravo! Now you're thinking about this cinema being shot up...

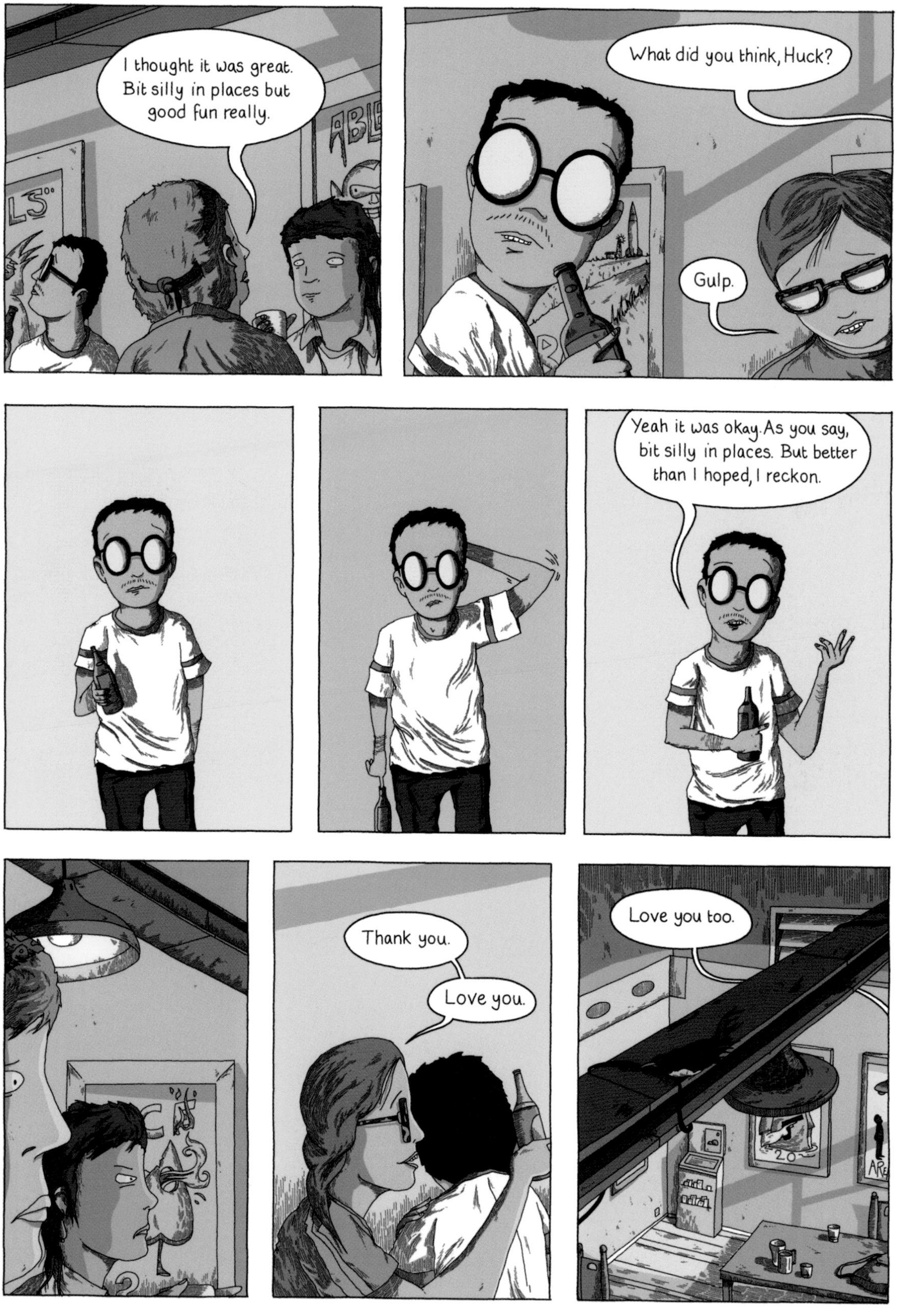
I thought it was great. Bit silly in places but good fun really.
What did you think, Huck?
Gulp.
Yeah it was okay. As you say, bit silly in places. But better than I hoped, I reckon.
Thank you.
Love you.
Love you too.

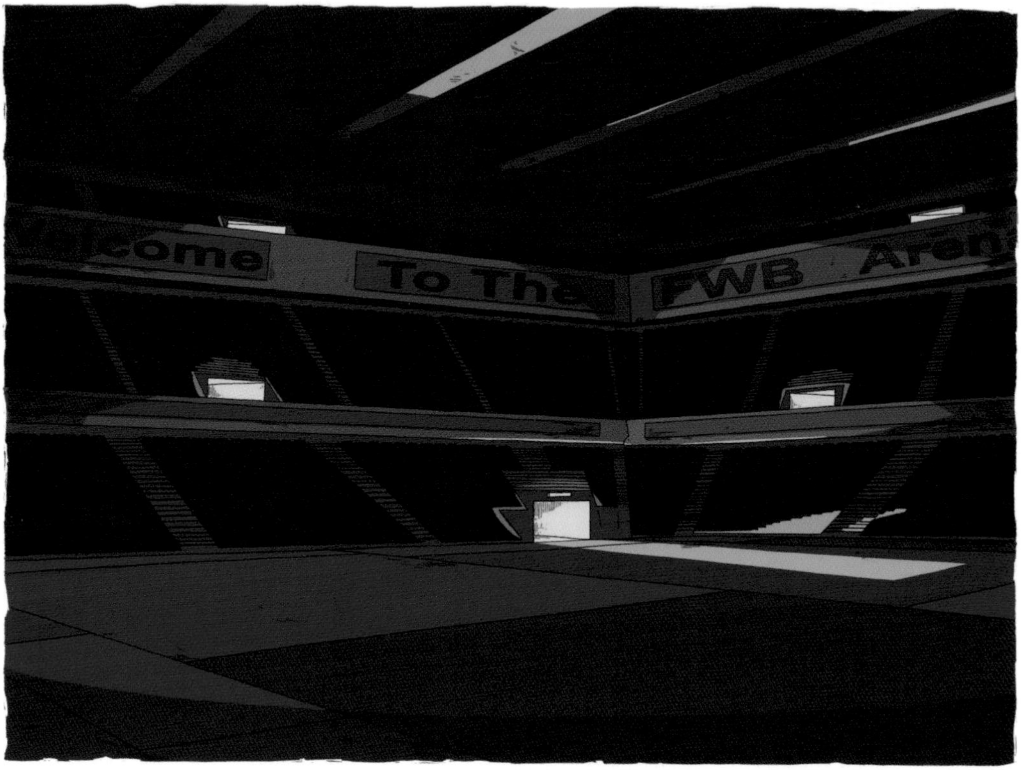
come
To The
FWB

14 days to election.

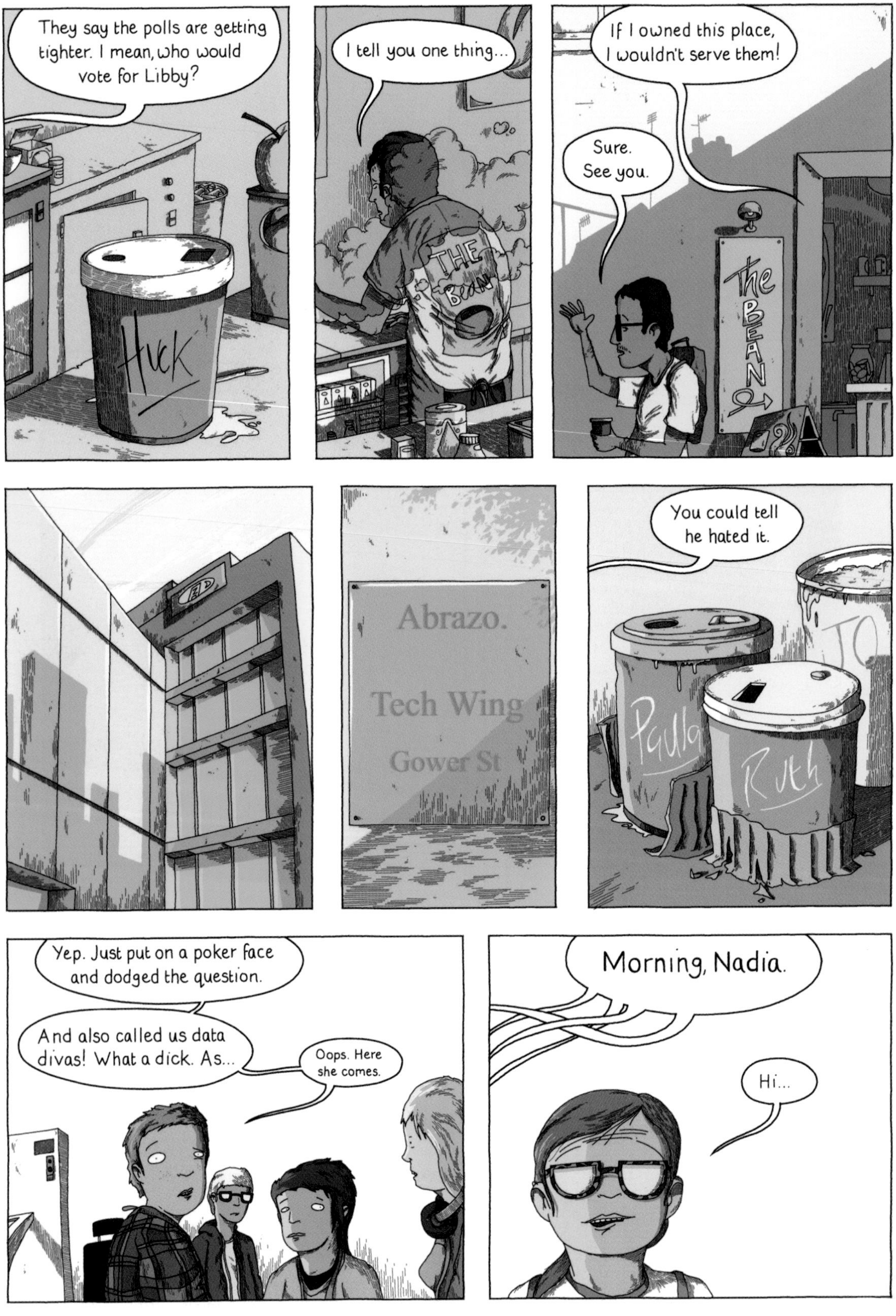
They say the polls are getting tighter. I mean, who would vote for Libby?
Huck
I tell you one thing...
THE Bean
If I owned this place, I wouldn't serve them!
Sure. See you.
The BEAN
Abrazo.
Tech Wing
Gower St
You could tell he hated it.
Paula
Ruth
Yep. Just put on a poker face and dodged the question.
And also called us data divas! What a dick. As...
Oops. Here she comes.
Morning, Nadia.
Hi...

Abrazo Offices
Cherry Park.

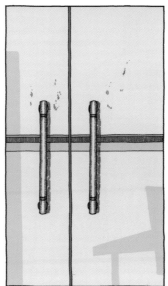

Ping.

Sent 10.16am 6/5/20

Hi Huck,
May I have a word?

Thanks
Prakash

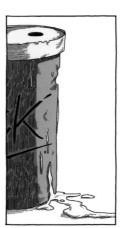

Hi, Prakash. What seems to be the trouble?

It's this report. The person here...

...is discussing how CNN and the BBC have seemingly changed the facts on the Welco incident and the creator uses this to counter it.

Things that we now consider inappropriate. But the post was changed before the rules were changed.

What should I do?

Yep. It's a little grey on some things. Sling it over and I'll look into it.

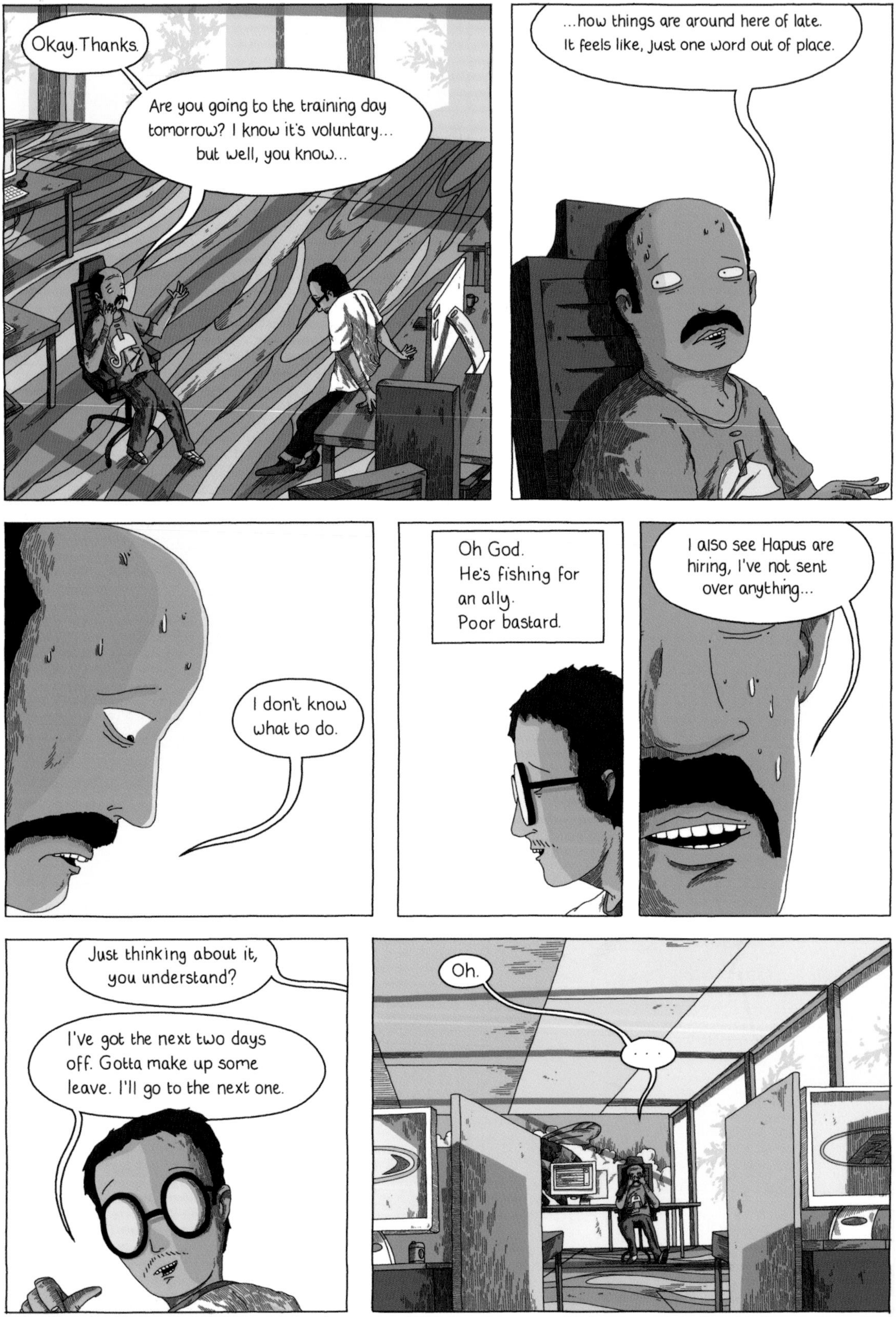
Okay. Thanks.
Are you going to the training day tomorrow? I know it's voluntary... but well, you know...
...how things are around here of late. It feels like, just one word out of place.
I don't know what to do.
Oh God. He's fishing for an ally. Poor bastard.
I also see Hapus are hiring, I've not sent over anything...
Just thinking about it, you understand?
I've got the next two days off. Gotta make up some leave. I'll go to the next one.
Oh.
. . .

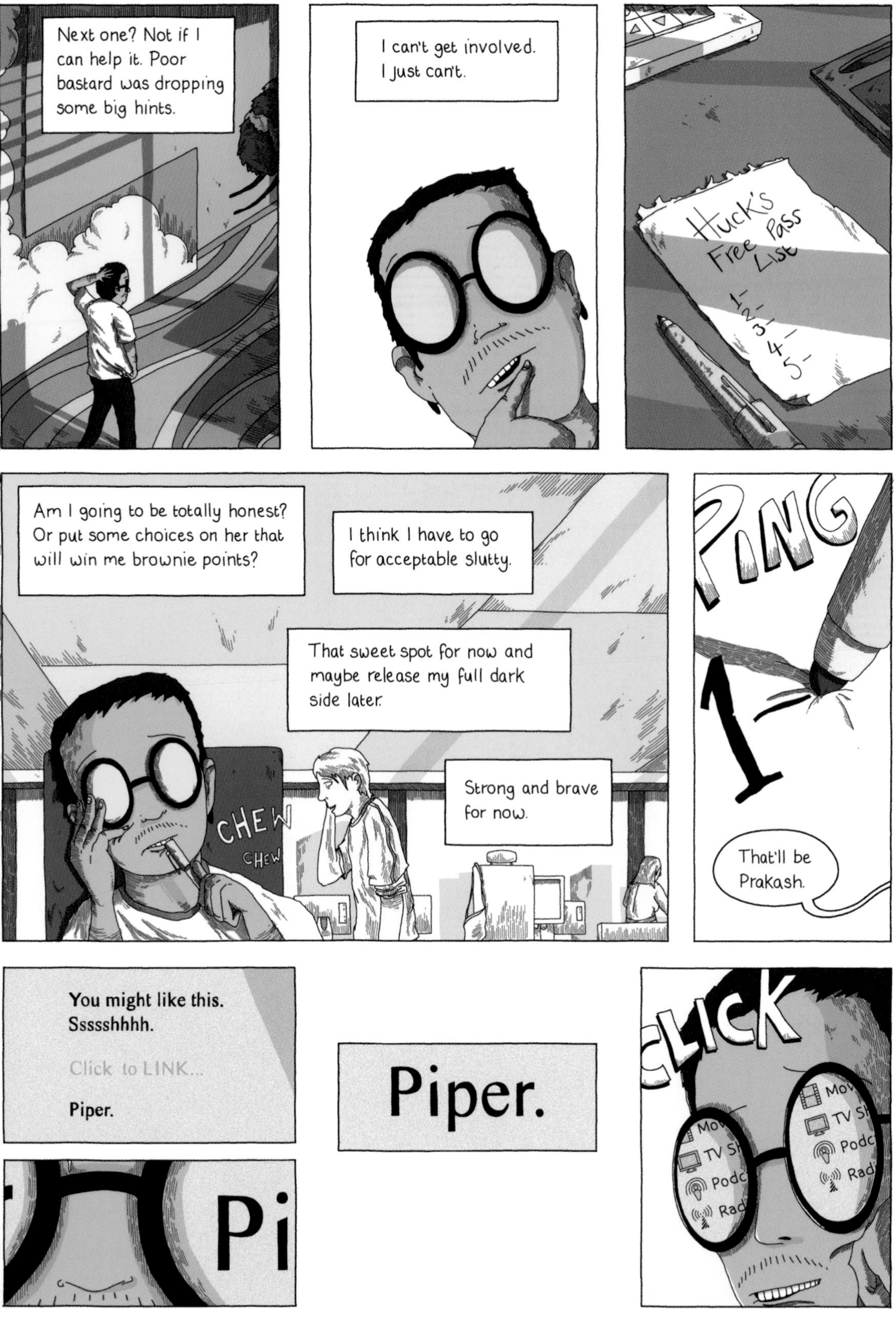
Next one? Not if I can help it. Poor bastard was dropping some big hints.
I can't get involved. I just can't.
Huck's Free Pass List
1–
2–
3–
4–
5–
Am I going to be totally honest? Or put some choices on her that will win me brownie points?
I think I have to go for acceptable slutty.
That sweet spot for now and maybe release my full dark side later.
Strong and brave for now.
CHEW
CHEW
PING
1
That'll be Prakash.
You might like this.
Ssssshhhh.
Click to LINK...
Piper.
Piper.
CLICK
Pi

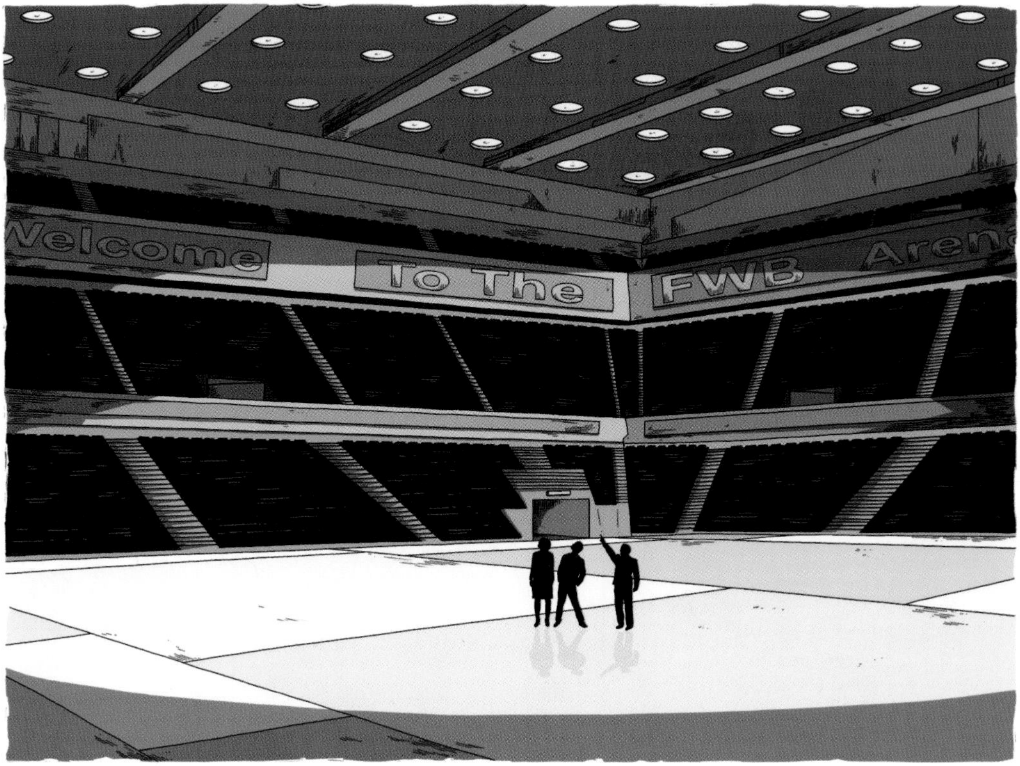
Welcome
To The
FWB
Aren

13 days to election.

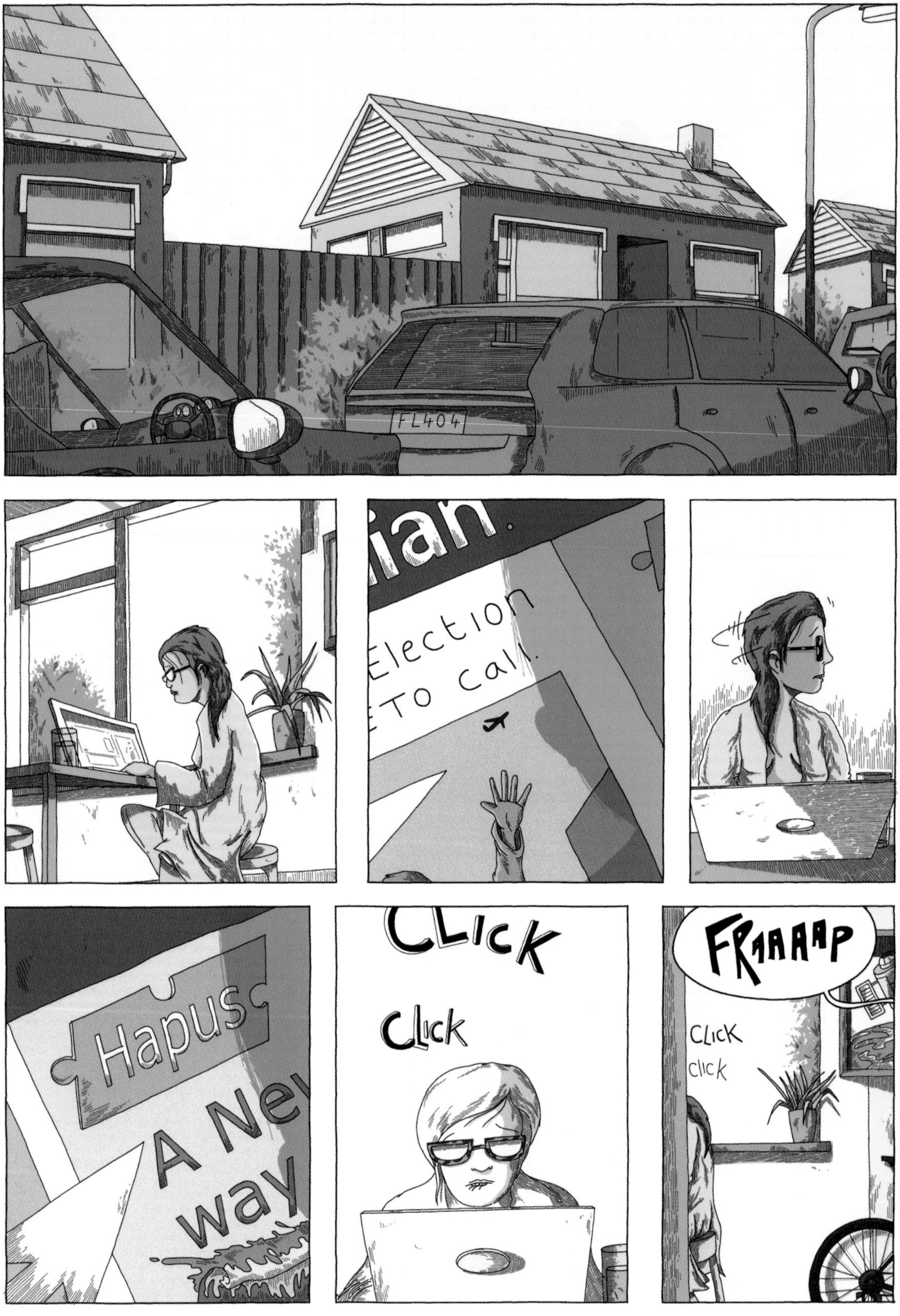
FL404
ian.
Election
TO call.
Hapus
A Ne
way
CLICK
CLICK
FRAAAAP
CLICK
click

Ah. The prince awakes.

Sleep well?

Never as good as when I have to get up for work. Then I sleep like a log, but now I'm not going to work...

So what you doing today?

Meeting Ali. And avoiding the news. That's about it.

You can't keep avoiding the news, you know?

Huck. Huck?

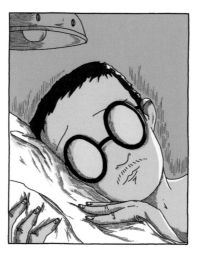

What do you know about Hapus?

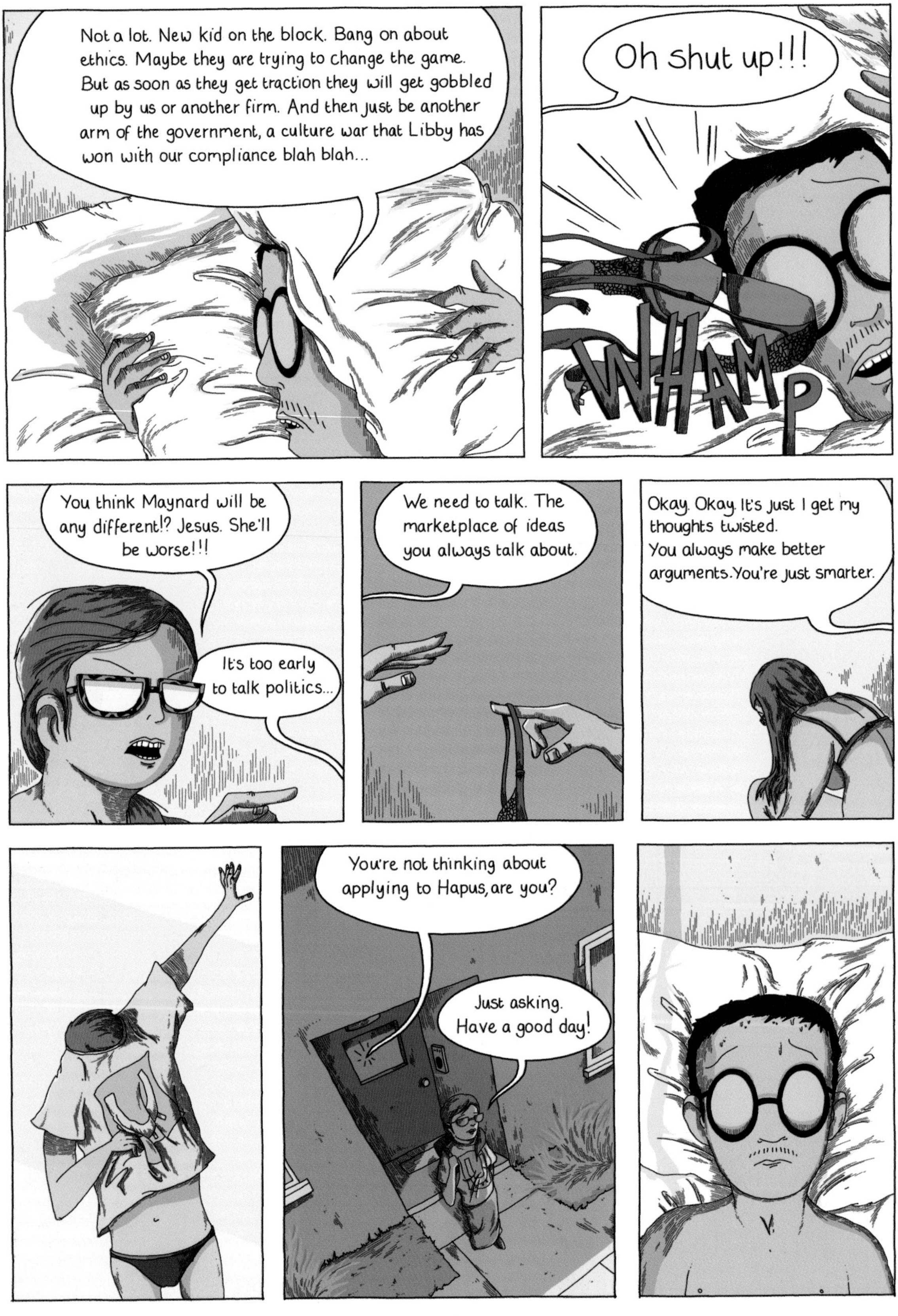
Not a lot. New kid on the block. Bang on about ethics. Maybe they are trying to change the game. But as soon as they get traction they will get gobbled up by us or another firm. And then just be another arm of the government, a culture war that Libby has won with our compliance blah blah...
Oh shut up!!!
WHAMP
You think Maynard will be any different!? Jesus. She'll be worse!!!
It's too early to talk politics...
We need to talk. The marketplace of ideas you always talk about.
Okay. Okay. It's just I get my thoughts twisted. You always make better arguments. You're just smarter.
You're not thinking about applying to Hapus, are you?
Just asking. Have a good day!

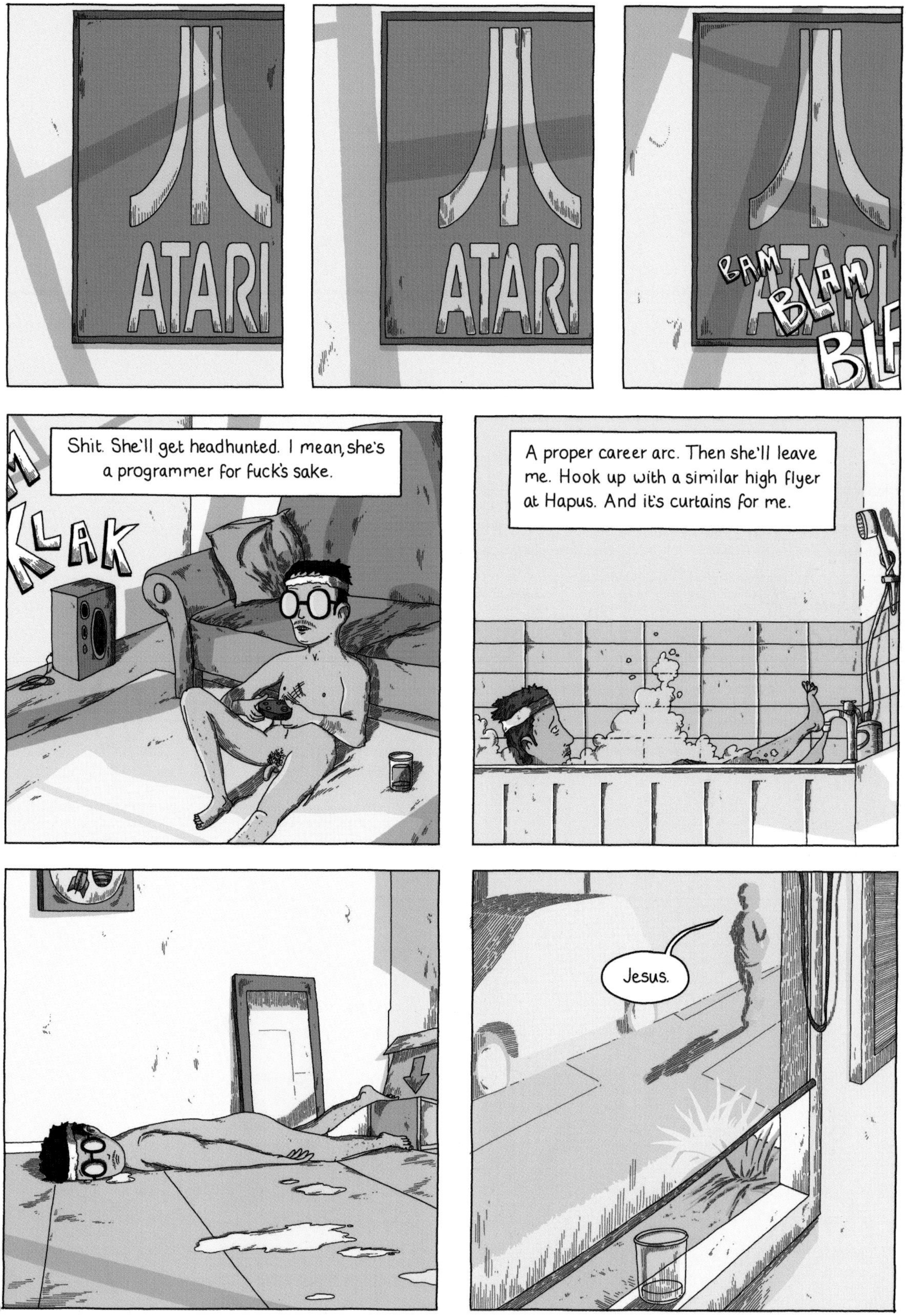
ATARI
ATARI
ATARI
BAM
BLAM
KLAK
Shit. She'll get headhunted. I mean, she's a programmer for fuck's sake.
A proper career arc. Then she'll leave me. Hook up with a similar high flyer at Hapus. And it's curtains for me.
Jesus.

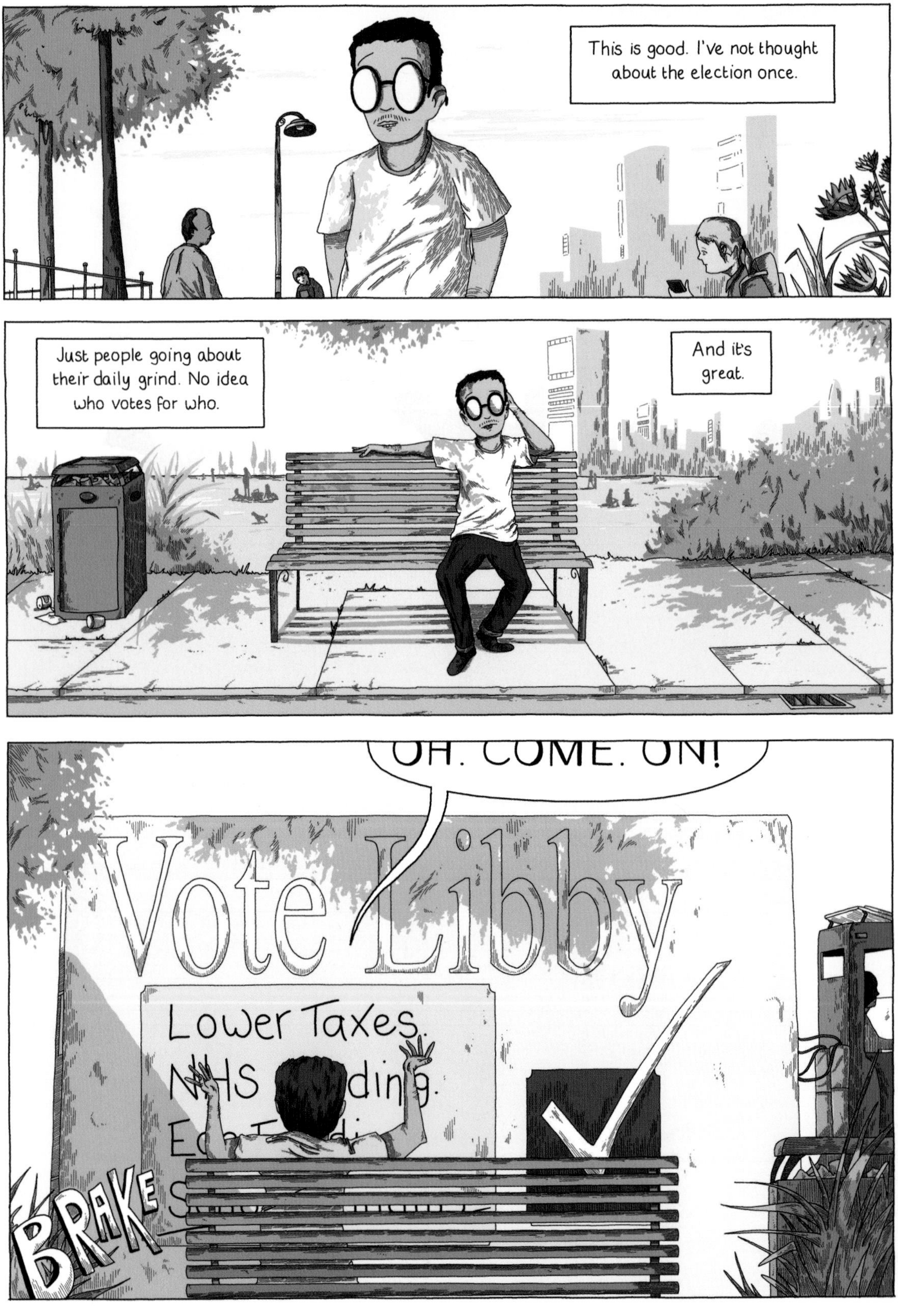
This is good. I've not thought about the election once.
Just people going about their daily grind. No idea who votes for who.
And it's great.
OH. COME. ON!
Vote Libby
Lower Taxes.
BRAKE

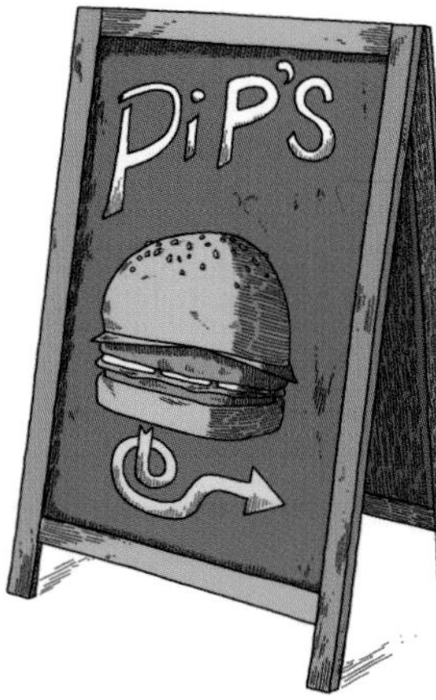
PiP'S

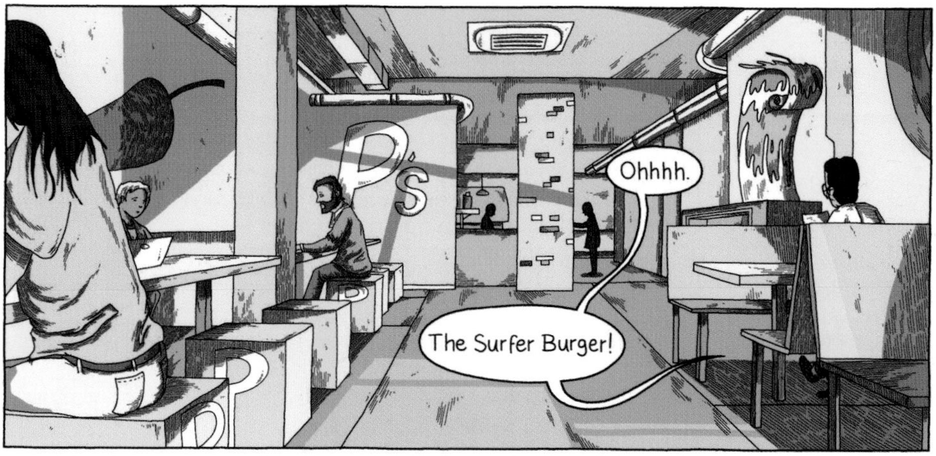
Ohhhh.
The Surfer Burger!

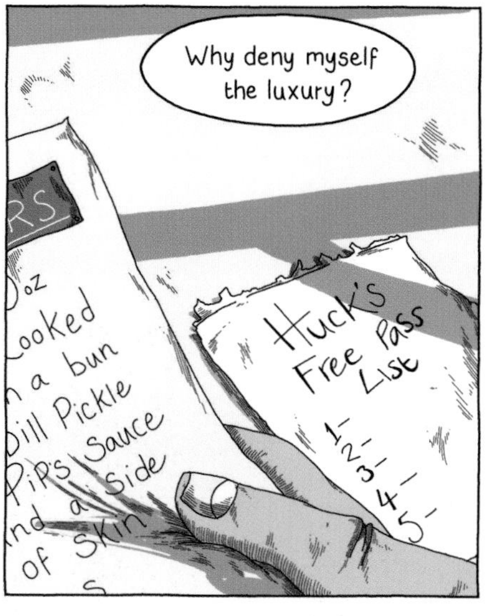
Why deny myself the luxury?
Huck's Free Pass List
1-
2-
3-
4-
5-

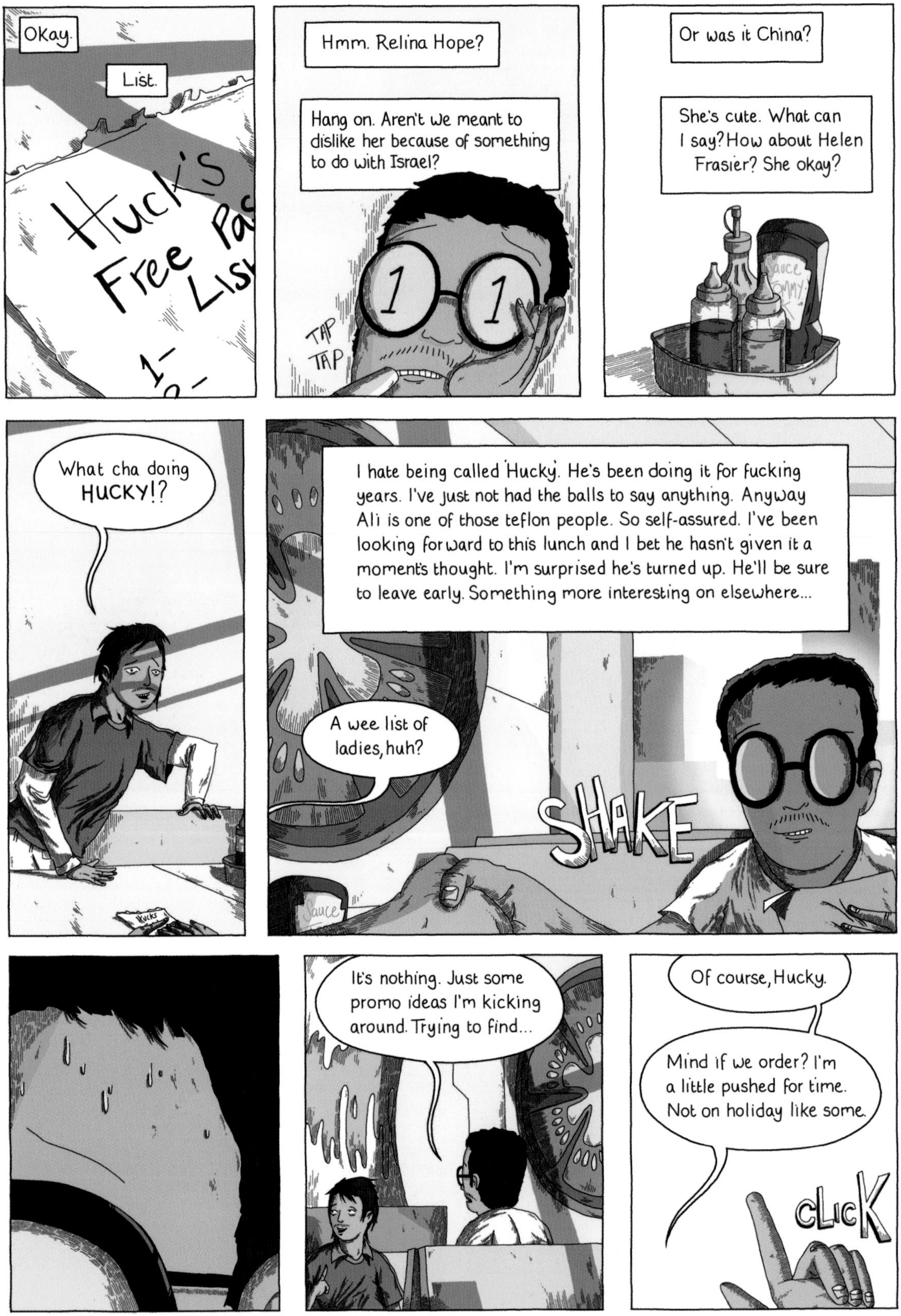

Okay.
List.
Huck's Free Pass List
1-
Hmm. Relina Hope?
Hang on. Aren't we meant to dislike her because of something to do with Israel?
1 1
TAP TAP
Or was it China?
She's cute. What can I say? How about Helen Frasier? She okay?
What cha doing HUCKY!?
I hate being called 'Hucky'. He's been doing it for fucking years. I've just not had the balls to say anything. Anyway Ali is one of those teflon people. So self-assured. I've been looking forward to this lunch and I bet he hasn't given it a moment's thought. I'm surprised he's turned up. He'll be sure to leave early. Something more interesting on elsewhere...
A wee list of ladies, huh?
SHAKE
It's nothing. Just some promo ideas I'm kicking around. Trying to find...
Of course, Hucky.
Mind if we order? I'm a little pushed for time. Not on holiday like some.
CLICK

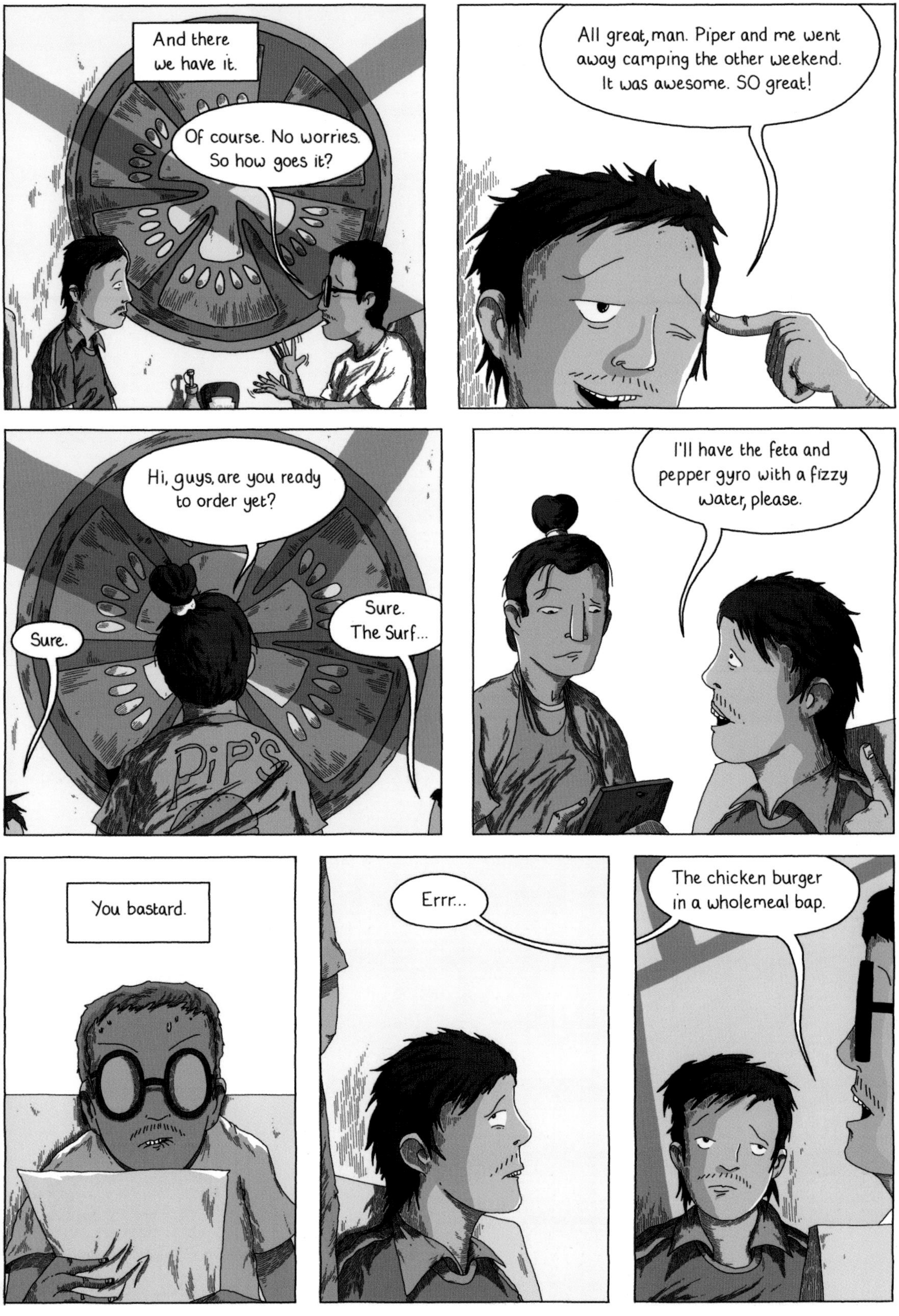
And there we have it.
Of course. No worries. So how goes it?
All great, man. Piper and me went away camping the other weekend. It was awesome. SO great!
Hi, guys, are you ready to order yet?
Sure.
Sure. The Surf...
PiP'S
I'll have the feta and pepper gyro with a fizzy water, please.
You bastard.
Errr...
The chicken burger in a wholemeal bap.

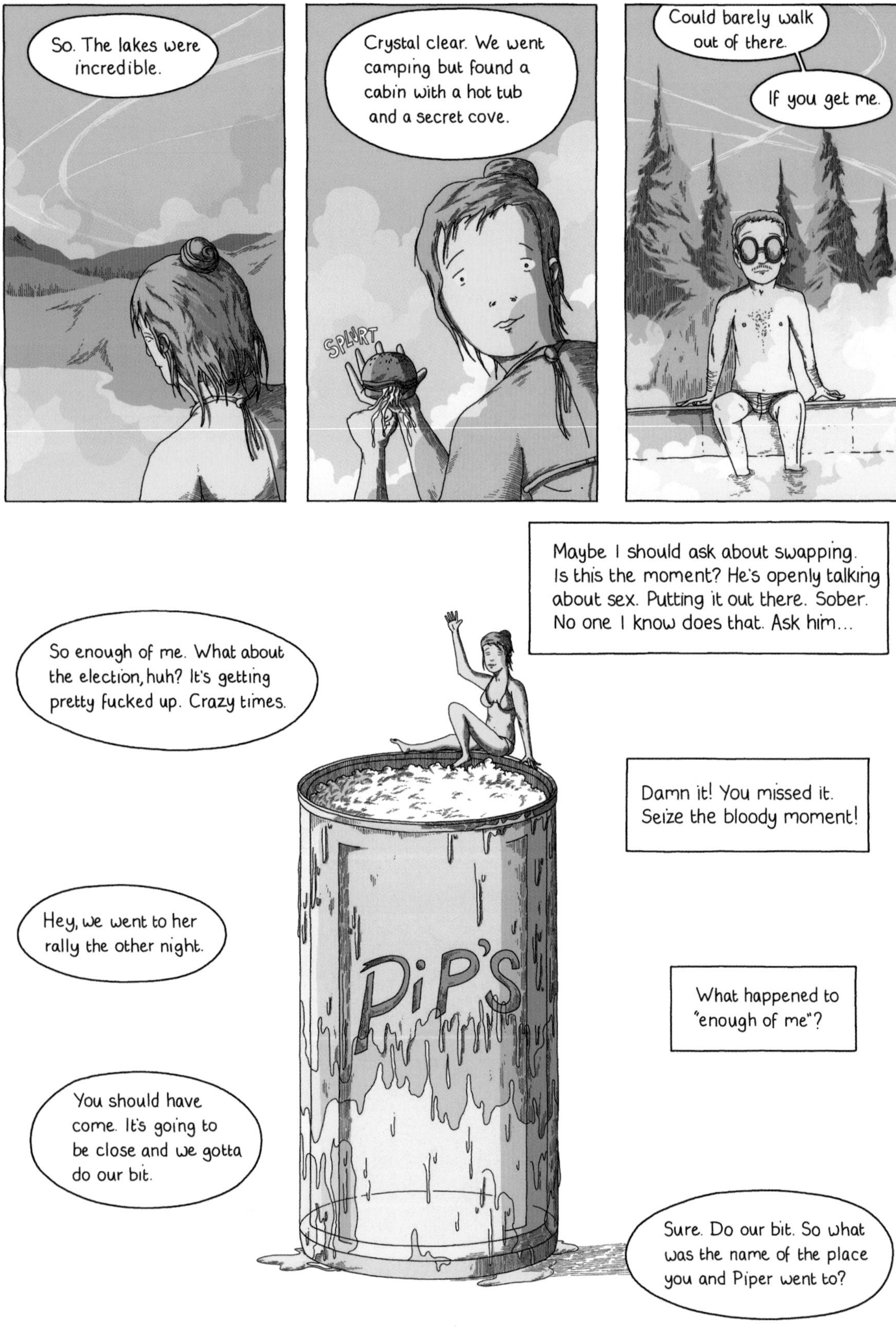
So. The lakes were incredible.
Crystal clear. We went camping but found a cabin with a hot tub and a secret cove.
SPLURT
Could barely walk out of there.
If you get me.
Maybe I should ask about swapping. Is this the moment? He's openly talking about sex. Putting it out there. Sober. No one I know does that. Ask him...
So enough of me. What about the election, huh? It's getting pretty fucked up. Crazy times.
Damn it! You missed it. Seize the bloody moment!
Hey, we went to her rally the other night.
PiP'S
What happened to "enough of me"?
You should have come. It's going to be close and we gotta do our bit.
Sure. Do our bit. So what was the name of the place you and Piper went to?

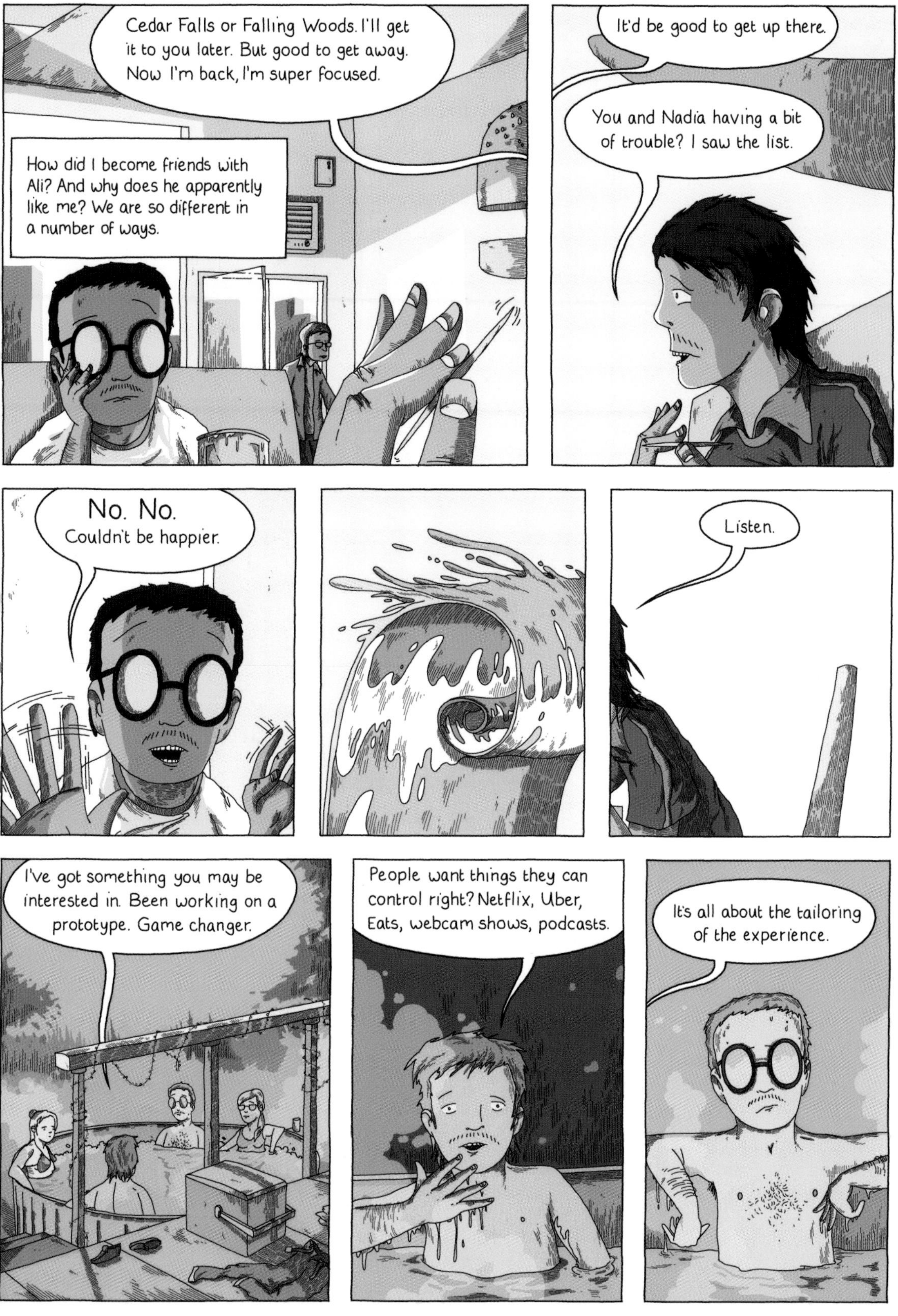
Cedar Falls or Falling Woods. I'll get it to you later. But good to get away. Now I'm back, I'm super focused.
How did I become friends with Ali? And why does he apparently like me? We are so different in a number of ways.
It'd be good to get up there.
You and Nadia having a bit of trouble? I saw the list.
No. No. Couldn't be happier.
Listen.
I've got something you may be interested in. Been working on a prototype. Game changer.
People want things they can control right? Netflix, Uber, Eats, webcam shows, podcasts.
It's all about the tailoring of the experience.

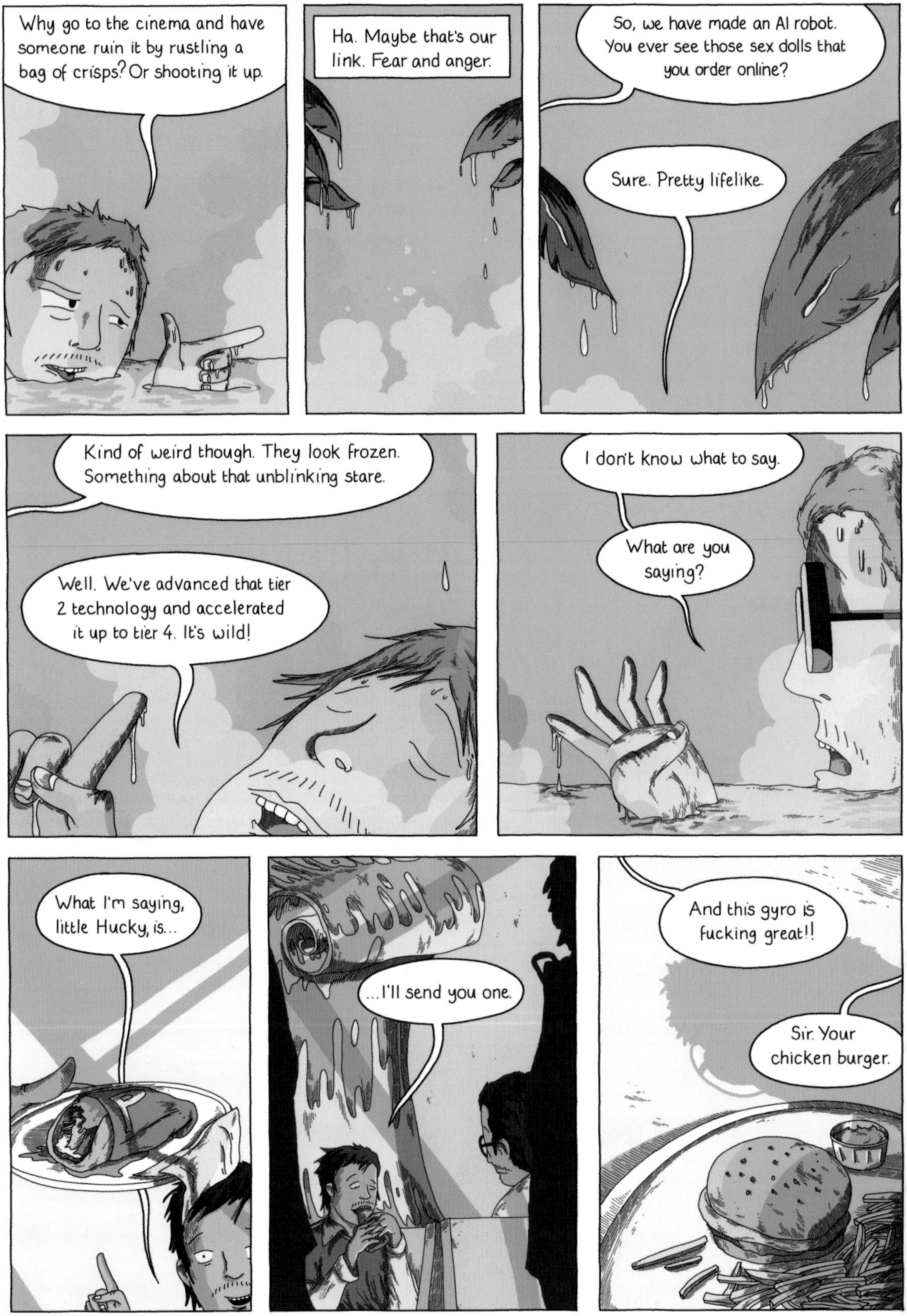
Why go to the cinema and have someone ruin it by rustling a bag of crisps? Or shooting it up.
Ha. Maybe that's our link. Fear and anger.
So, we have made an AI robot. You ever see those sex dolls that you order online?
Sure. Pretty lifelike.
Kind of weird though. They look frozen. Something about that unblinking stare.
Well. We've advanced that tier 2 technology and accelerated it up to tier 4. It's wild!
I don't know what to say.
What are you saying?
What I'm saying, little Hucky, is...
...I'll send you one.
And this gyro is fucking great!!
Sir. Your chicken burger.

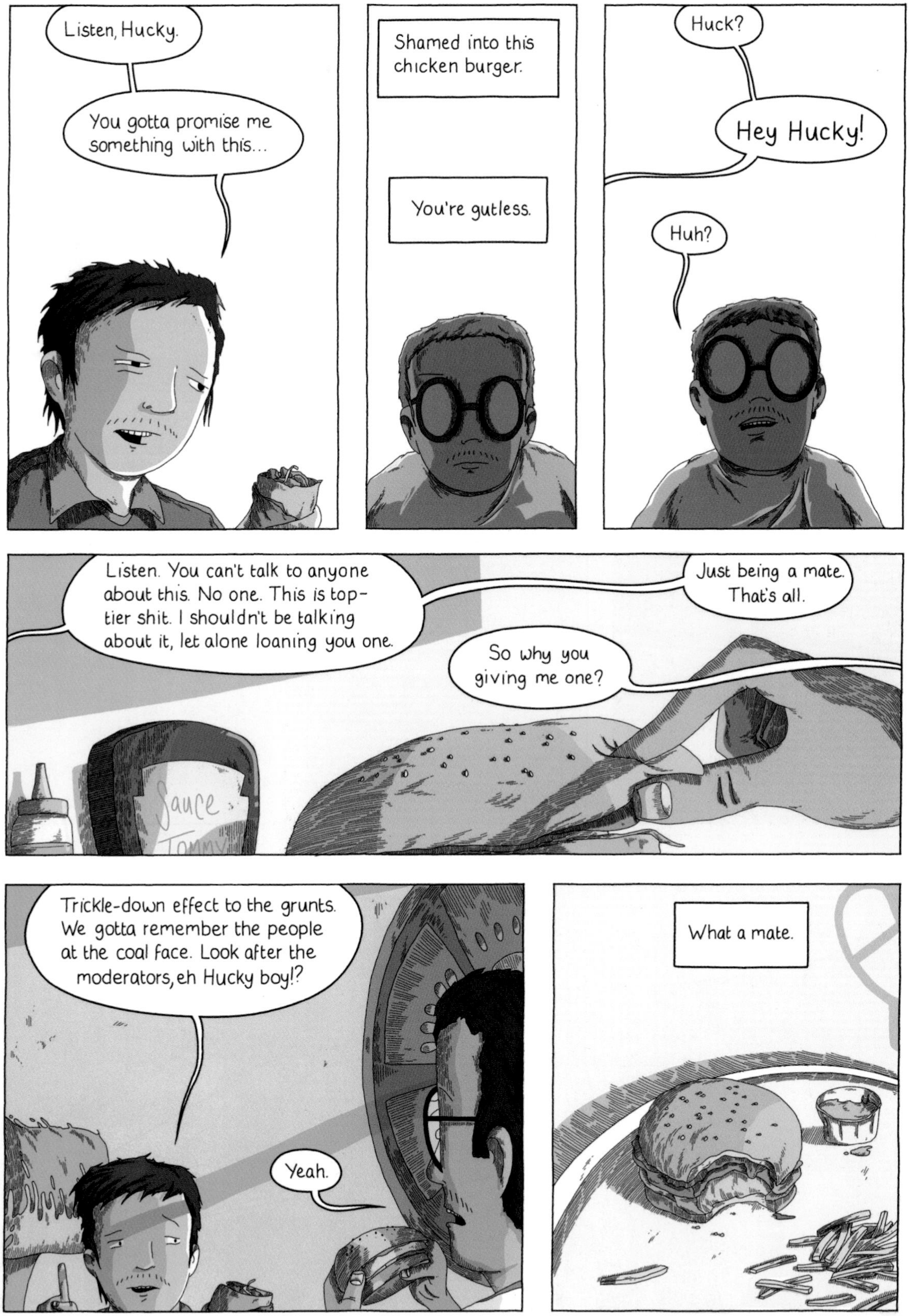
Listen, Hucky.
You gotta promise me something with this...
Shamed into this chicken burger.
You're gutless.
Huck?
Hey Hucky!
Huh?
Listen. You can't talk to anyone about this. No one. This is top-tier shit. I shouldn't be talking about it, let alone loaning you one.
Just being a mate. That's all.
So why you giving me one?
Sauce
Tommy
Trickle-down effect to the grunts. We gotta remember the people at the coal face. Look after the moderators, eh Hucky boy!?
Yeah.
What a mate.

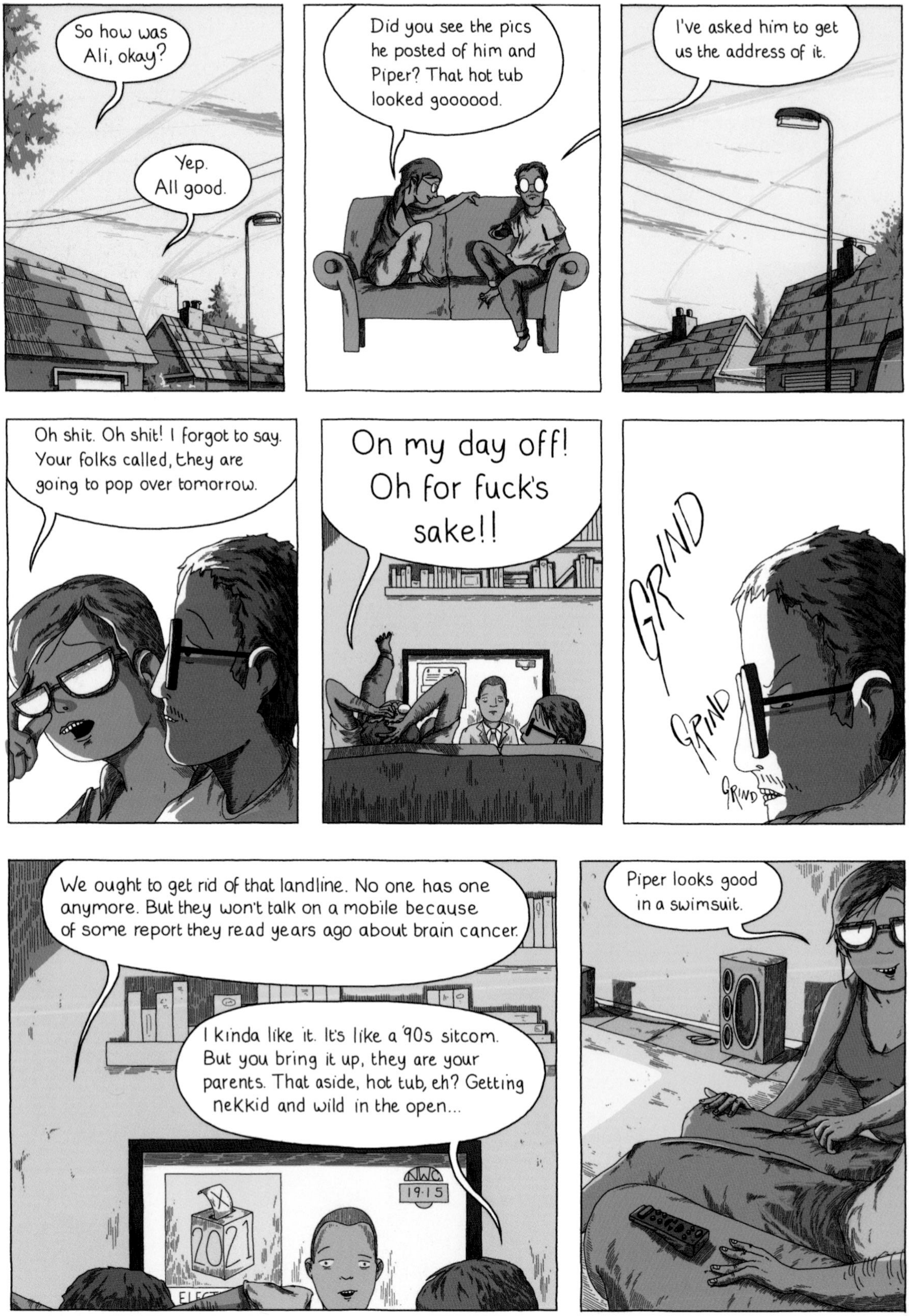
So how was Ali, okay?
Yep. All good.
Did you see the pics he posted of him and Piper? That hot tub looked goooood.
I've asked him to get us the address of it.
Oh shit. Oh shit! I forgot to say. Your folks called, they are going to pop over tomorrow.
On my day off! Oh for fuck's sake!!
GRIND
GRIND
GRIND
We ought to get rid of that landline. No one has one anymore. But they won't talk on a mobile because of some report they read years ago about brain cancer.
I kinda like it. It's like a '90s sitcom. But you bring it up, they are your parents. That aside, hot tub, eh? Getting nekkid and wild in the open...
NWC
19·15
2021
Piper looks good in a swimsuit.

I want you to watch me walk across that hot tub towards Ali and Piper pulling my swimsuit...

POP POP

...down over my breasts. My nipples are really hard and then Ali unties Piper's top...

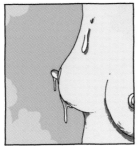
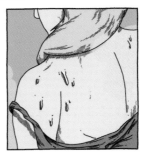

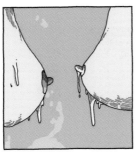

ATARI

Sorry. I'm in a bad mood at the moment.

I want to see that list on Friday, lover boy! I've nearly finished mine.

FLAP FLAP

Welcome
To The
FWB
Arena

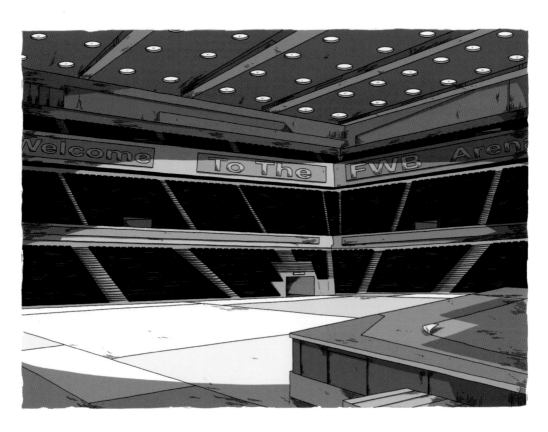

12 days to election.

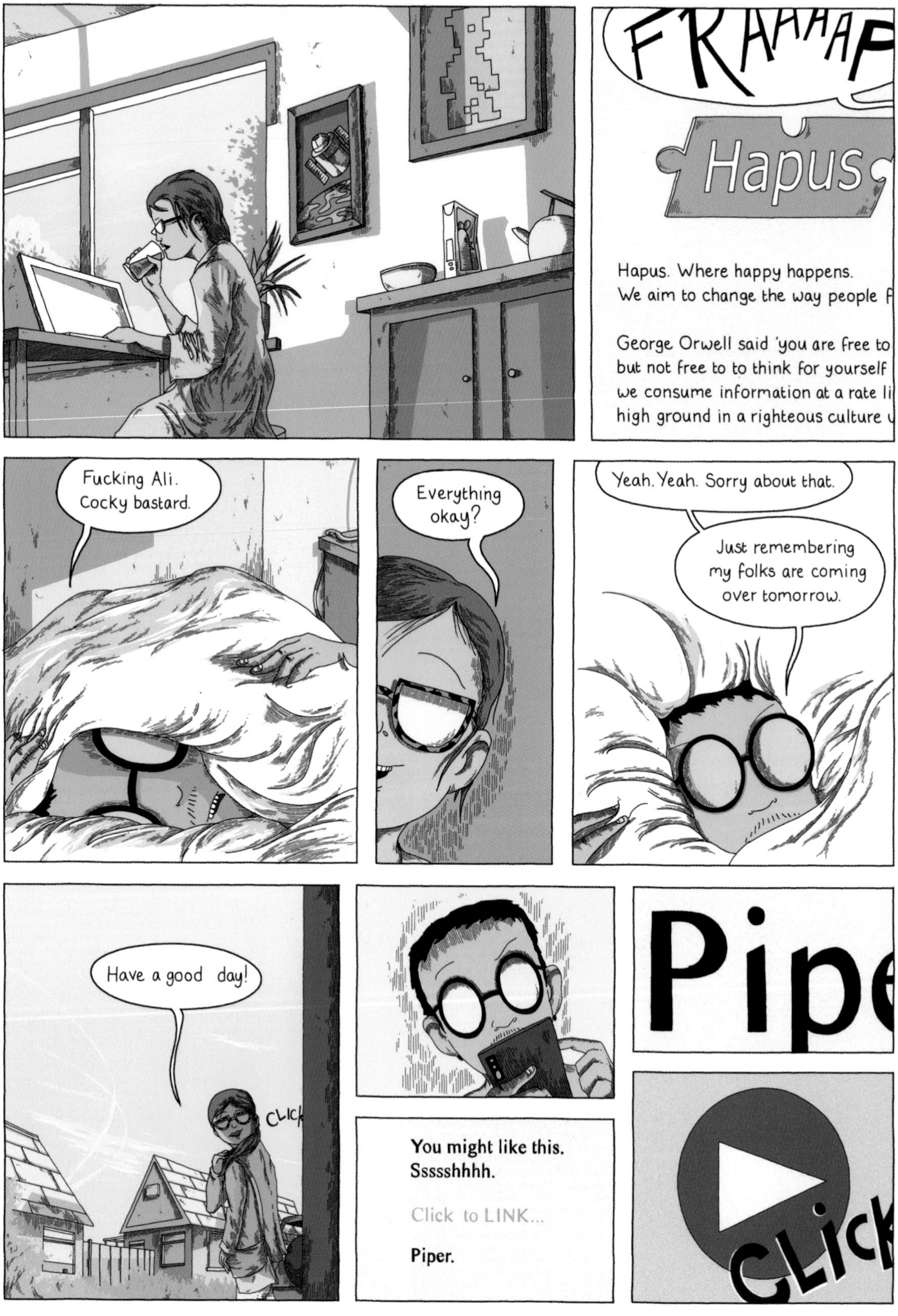
FRAAAAP
Hapus
Hapus. Where happy happens.
We aim to change the way people f
George Orwell said 'you are free to
but not free to to think for yourself
we consume information at a rate li
high ground in a righteous culture
Fucking Ali. Cocky bastard.
Everything okay?
Yeah. Yeah. Sorry about that.
Just remembering my folks are coming over tomorrow.
Have a good day!
CLICK
Pipe
You might like this.
Ssssshhhh.
Click to LINK...
Piper.
CLICK

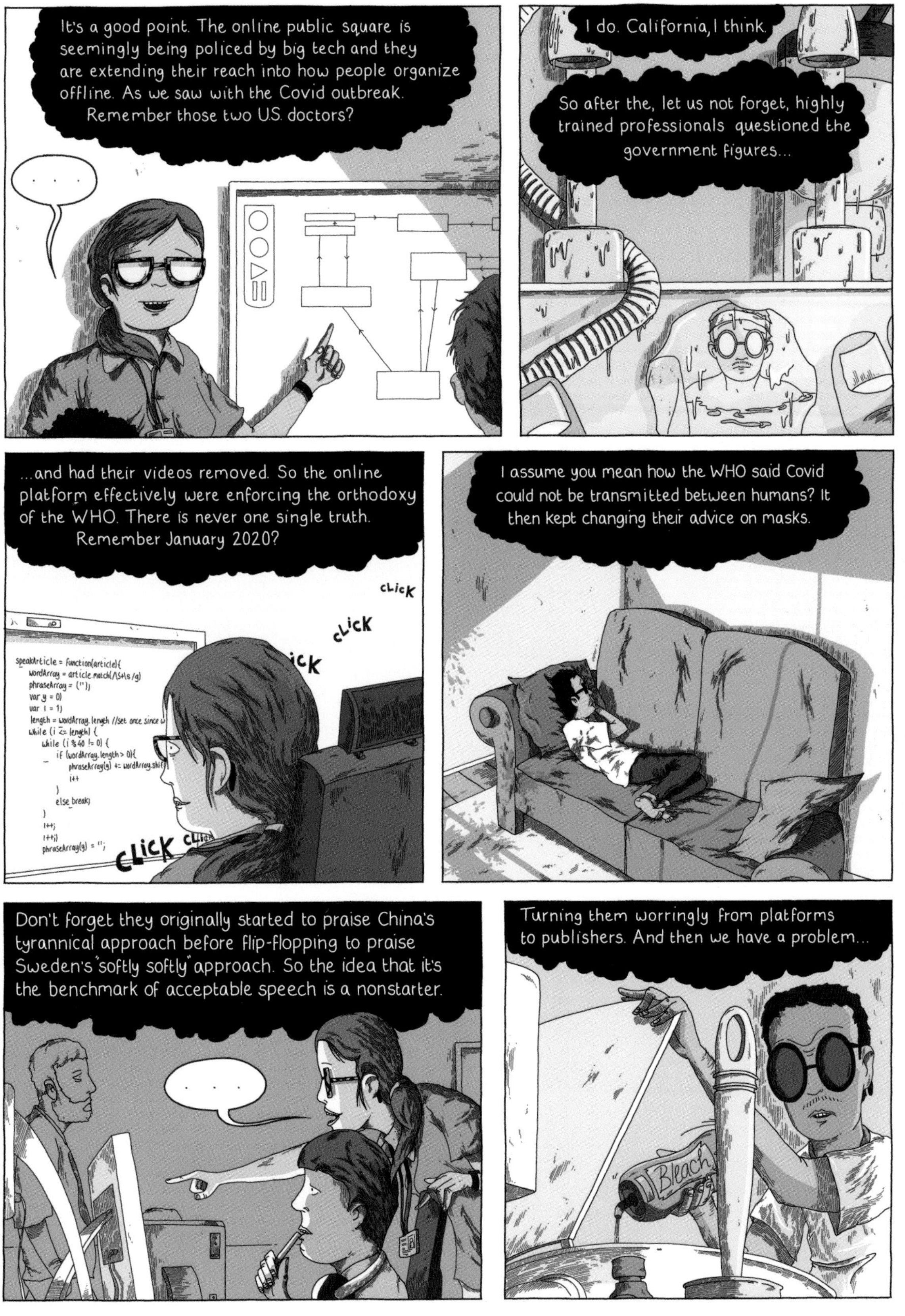
It's a good point. The online public square is seemingly being policed by big tech and they are extending their reach into how people organize offline. As we saw with the Covid outbreak. Remember those two U.S. doctors?
. . .
I do. California, I think.
So after the, let us not forget, highly trained professionals questioned the government figures...
...and had their videos removed. So the online platform effectively were enforcing the orthodoxy of the WHO. There is never one single truth. Remember January 2020?
CLICK
CLICK
CLICK
CLICK
I assume you mean how the WHO said Covid could not be transmitted between humans? It then kept changing their advice on masks.
Don't forget they originally started to praise China's tyrannical approach before flip-flopping to praise Sweden's "softly softly" approach. So the idea that it's the benchmark of acceptable speech is a nonstarter.
. . .
Turning them worringly from platforms to publishers. And then we have a problem...
Bleach

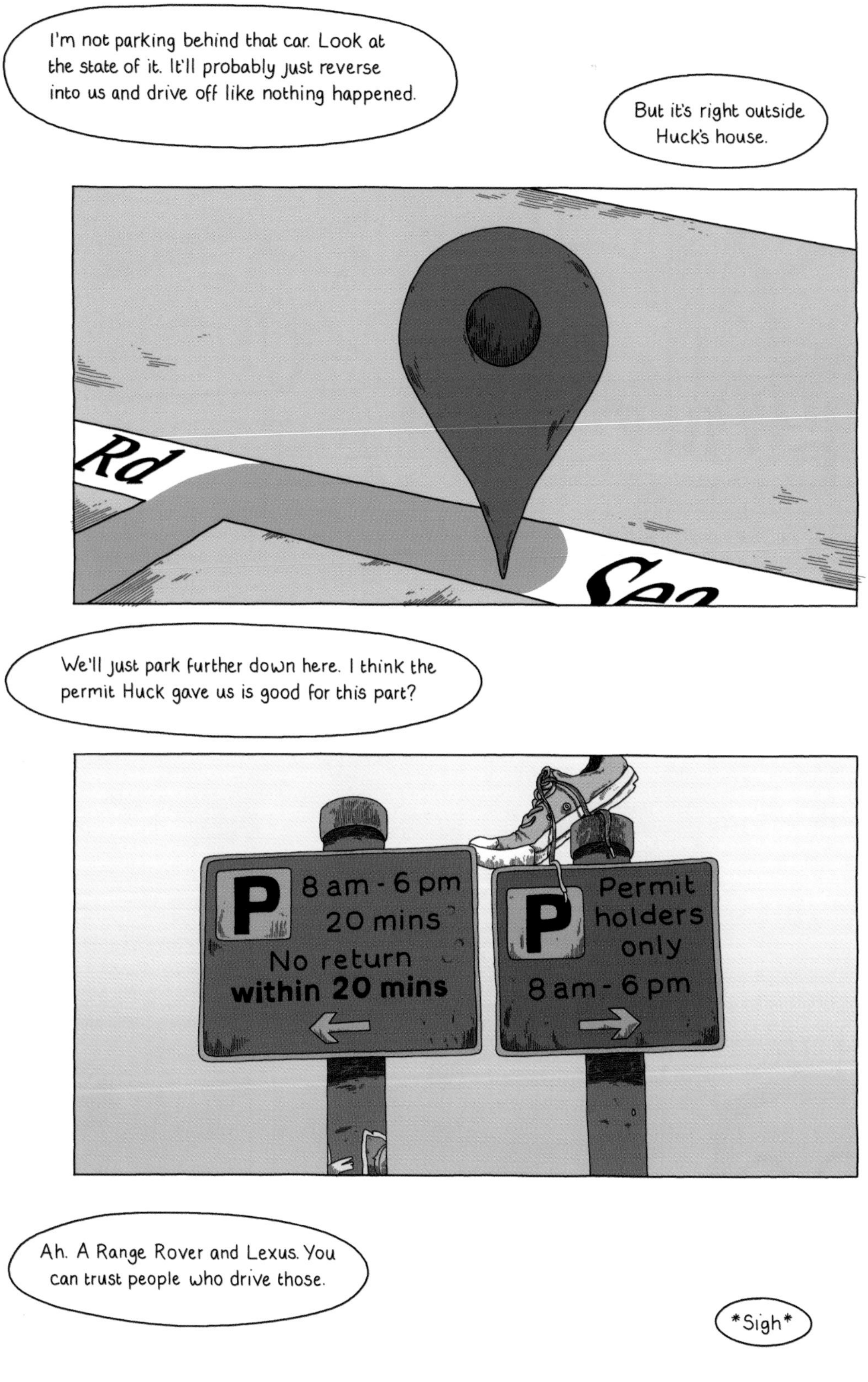
I'm not parking behind that car. Look at the state of it. It'll probably just reverse into us and drive off like nothing happened.
But it's right outside Huck's house.
Rd
We'll just park further down here. I think the permit Huck gave us is good for this part?
P 8 am - 6 pm 20 mins No return within 20 mins
P Permit holders only 8 am - 6 pm
Ah. A Range Rover and Lexus. You can trust people who drive those.
Sigh

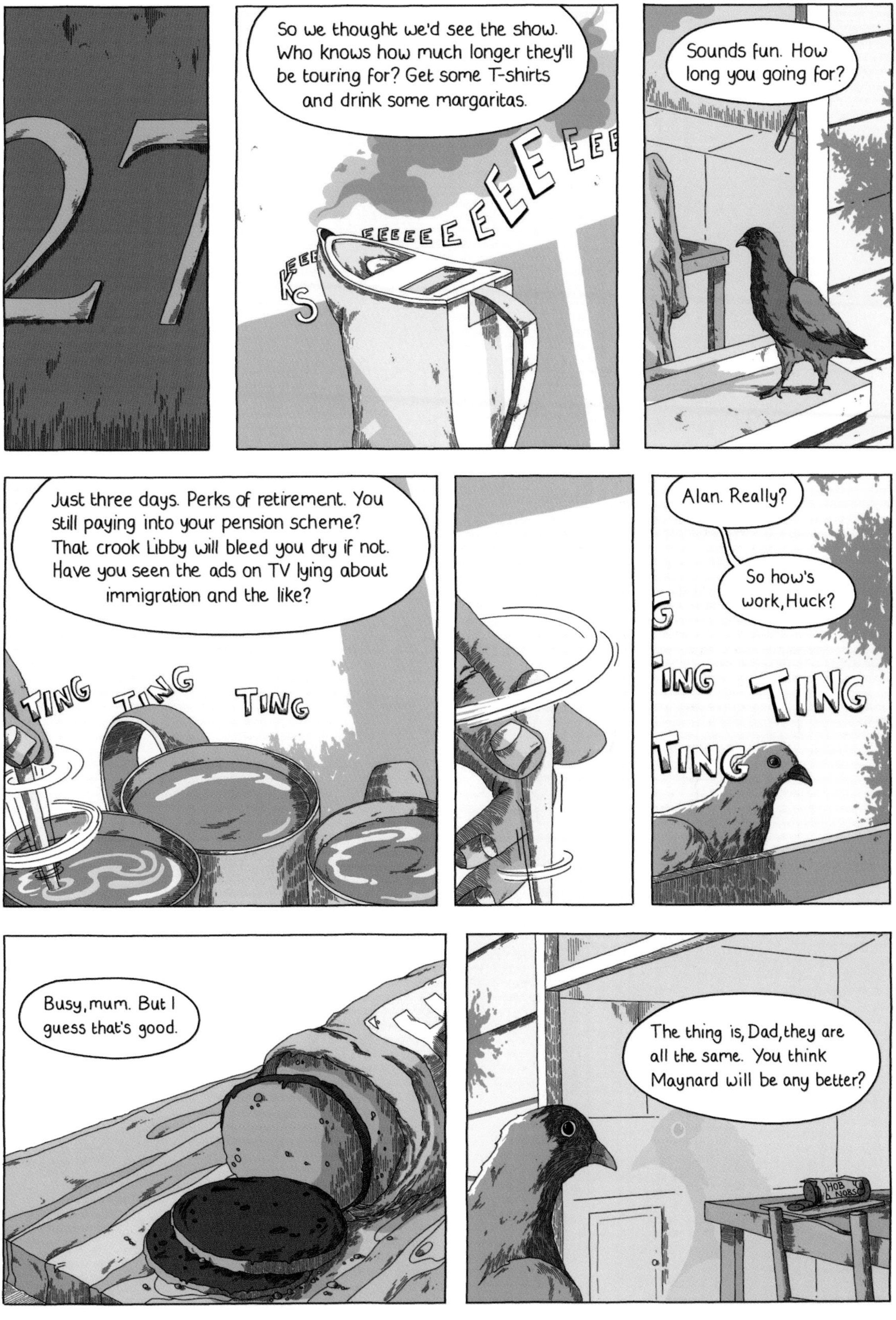
27
So we thought we'd see the show. Who knows how much longer they'll be touring for? Get some T-shirts and drink some margaritas.
EEEEEEEEEEEEEEEEE
KS
Sounds fun. How long you going for?
Just three days. Perks of retirement. You still paying into your pension scheme? That crook Libby will bleed you dry if not. Have you seen the ads on TV lying about immigration and the like?
TING TING TING
Alan. Really?
So how's work, Huck?
TING TING TING
Busy, mum. But I guess that's good.
The thing is, Dad, they are all the same. You think Maynard will be any better?
HOB NOBS

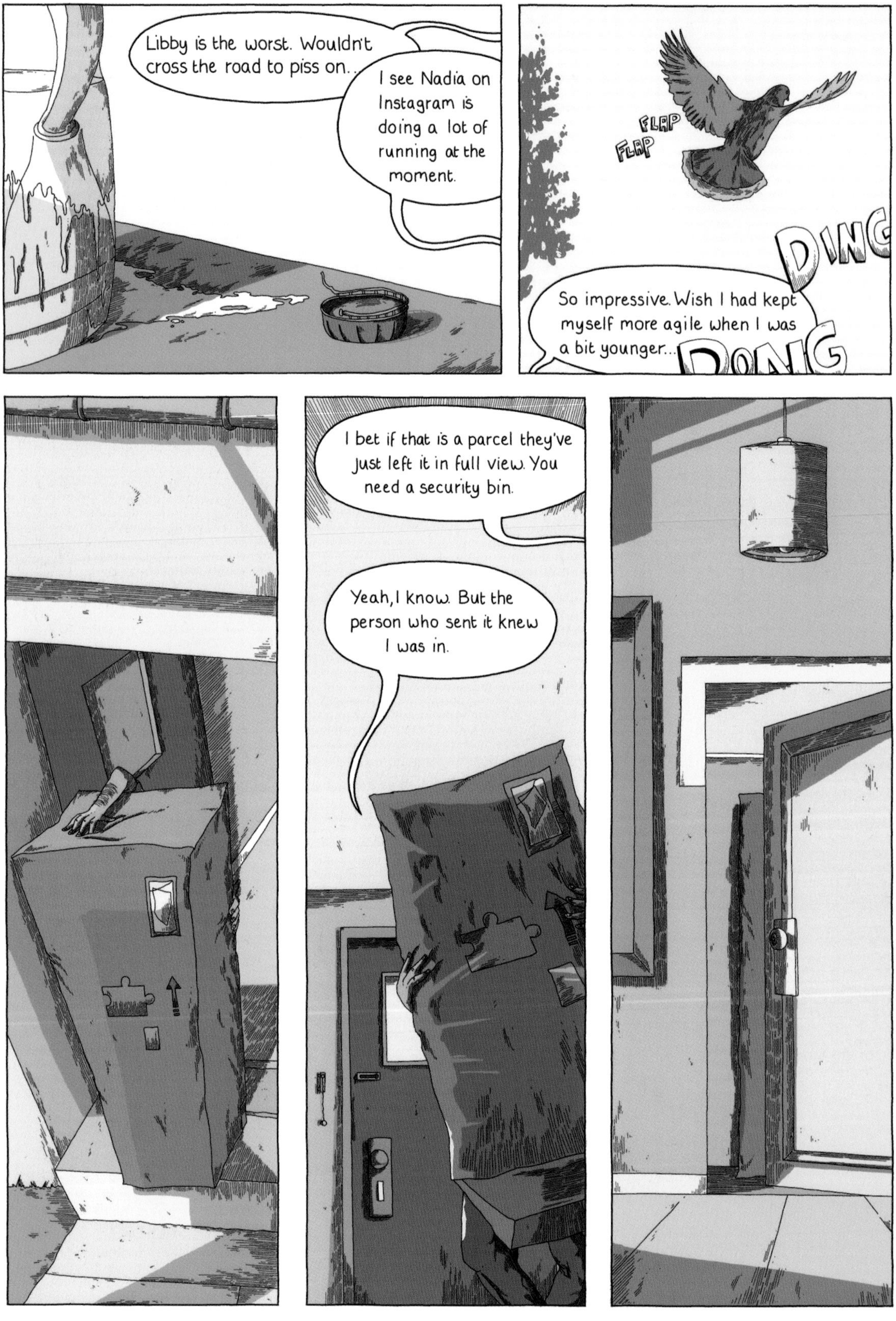
Libby is the worst. Wouldn't cross the road to piss on..
I see Nadia on Instagram is doing a lot of running at the moment.
FLAP FLAP
DING
So impressive. Wish I had kept myself more agile when I was a bit younger...
DONG
I bet if that is a parcel they've just left it in full view. You need a security bin.
Yeah, I know. But the person who sent it knew I was in.

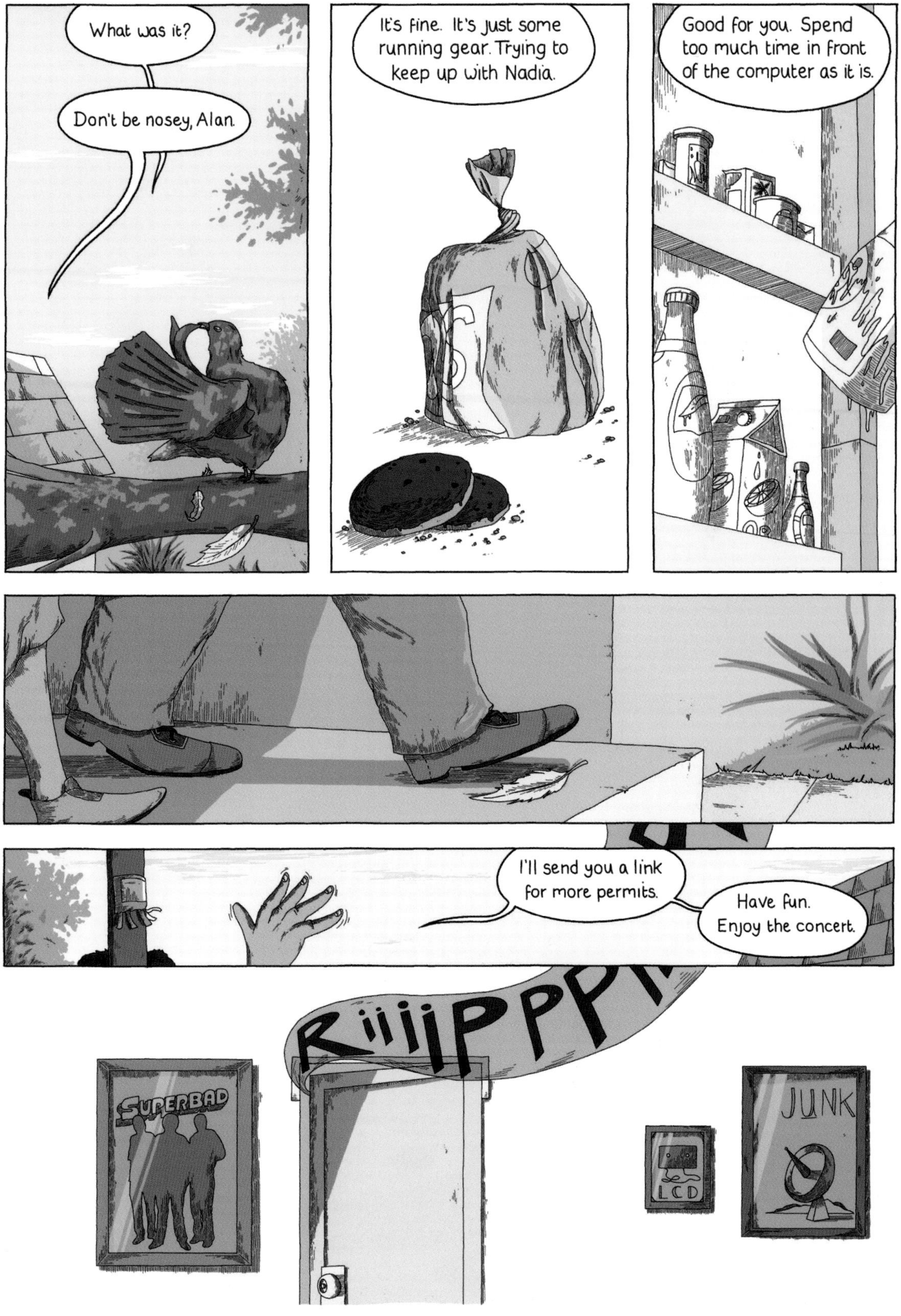
What was it?
Don't be nosey, Alan.
It's fine. It's just some running gear. Trying to keep up with Nadia.
Good for you. Spend too much time in front of the computer as it is.
I'll send you a link for more permits.
Have fun. Enjoy the concert.
RiiiiPPPP
SUPERBAD
LCD
JUNK

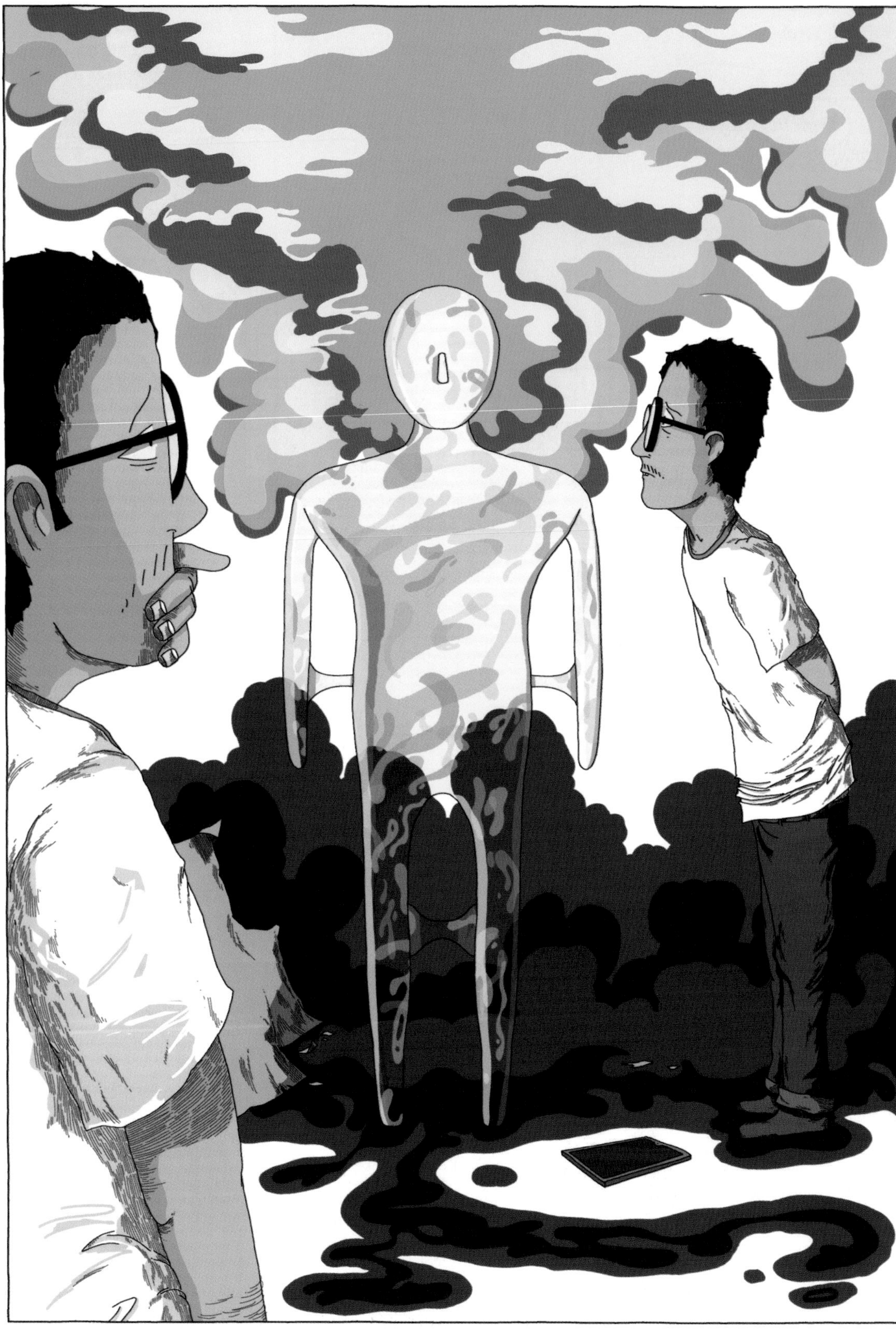

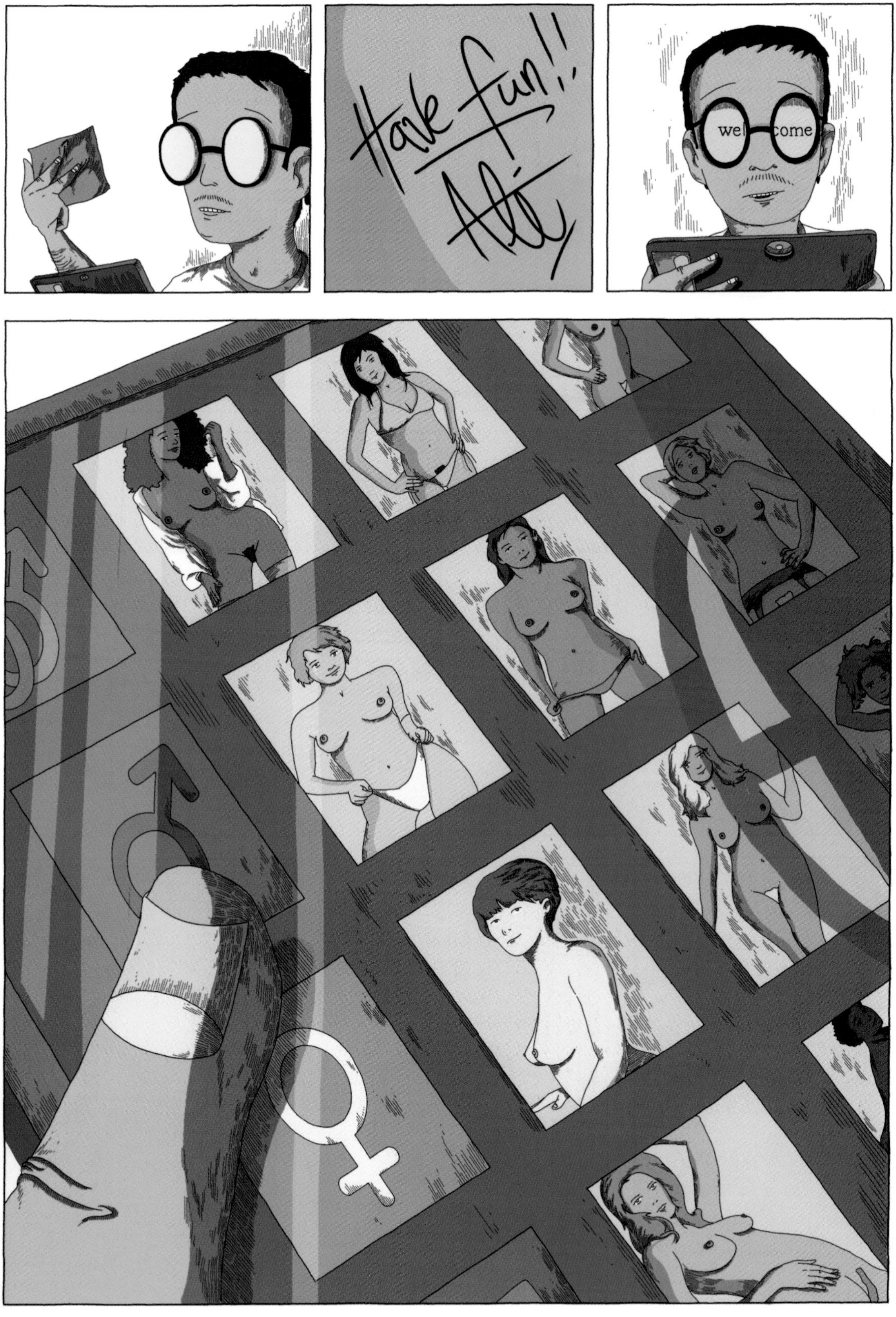
Have fun!!
Ali
welcome

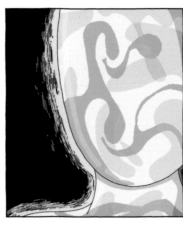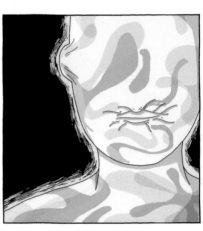

BEEEEP

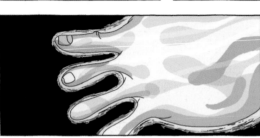

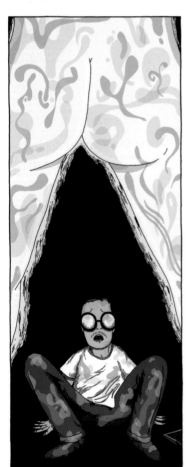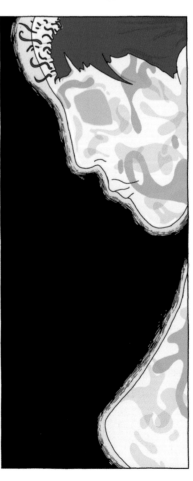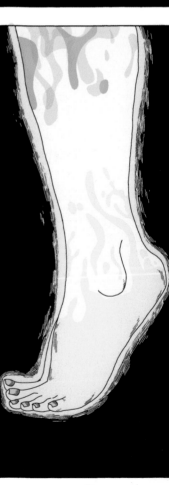

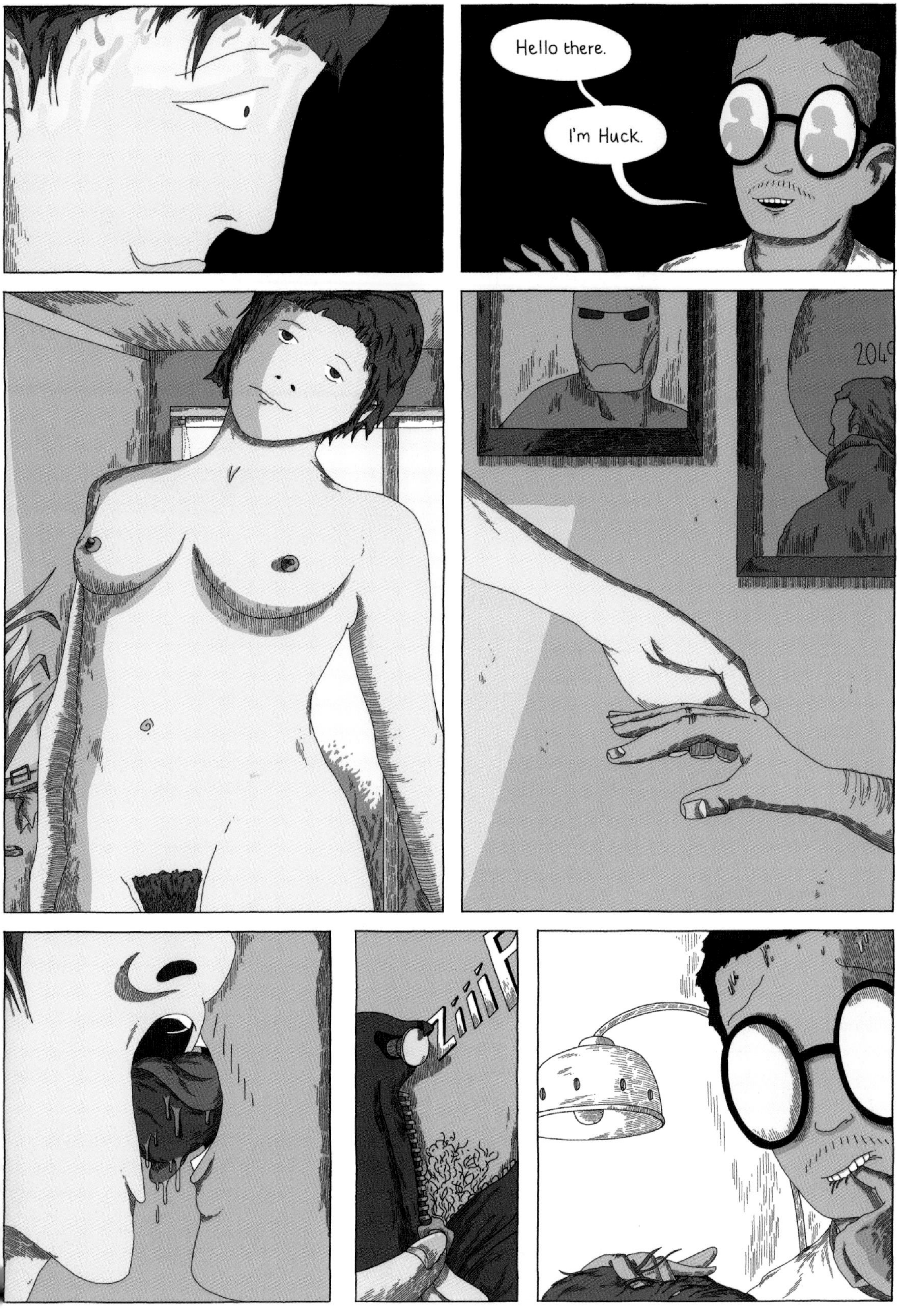
Hello there.
I'm Huck.
ziiiP

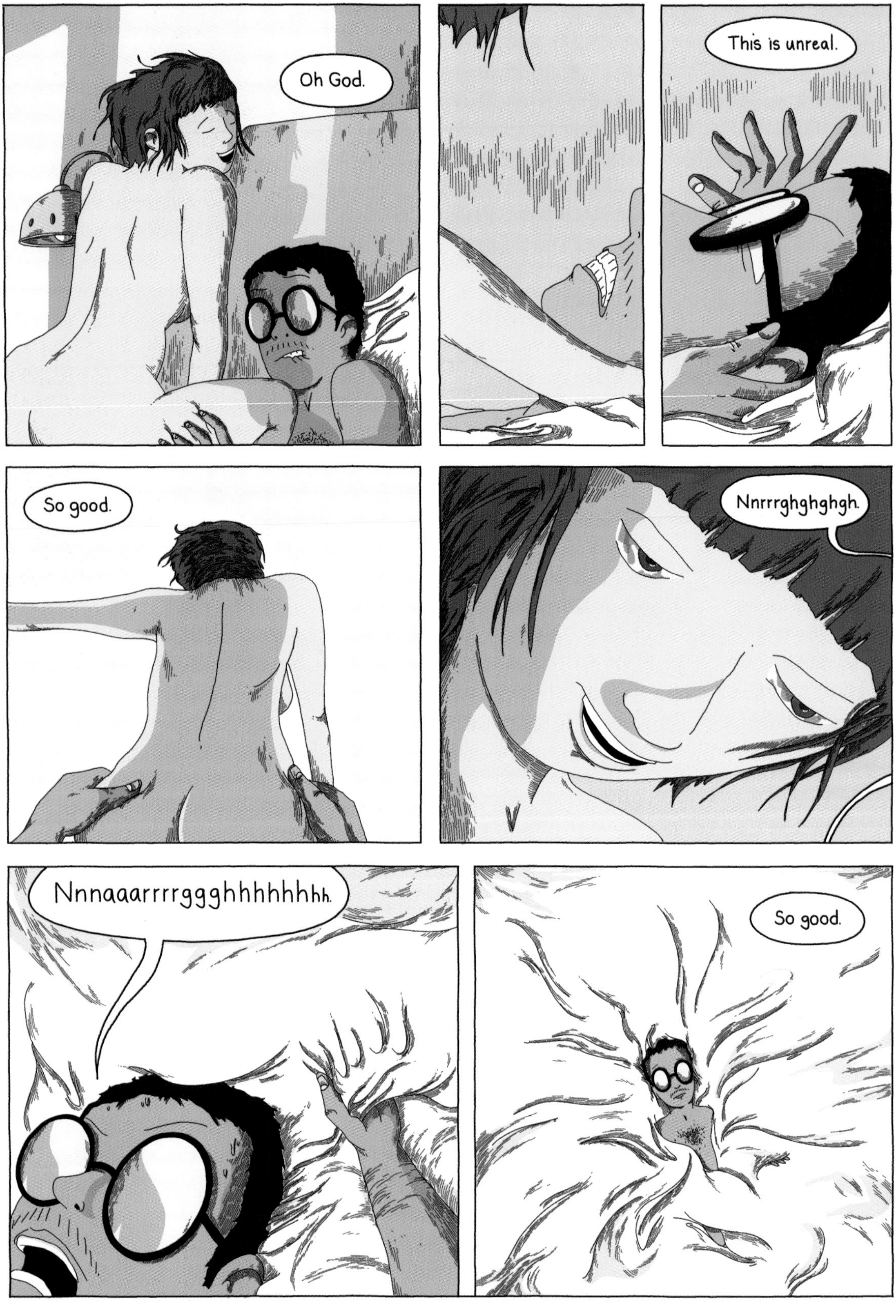
Oh God.
This is unreal.
So good.
Nnrrrghghghgh.
Nnnaaarrrrggghhhhhhhh.
So good.

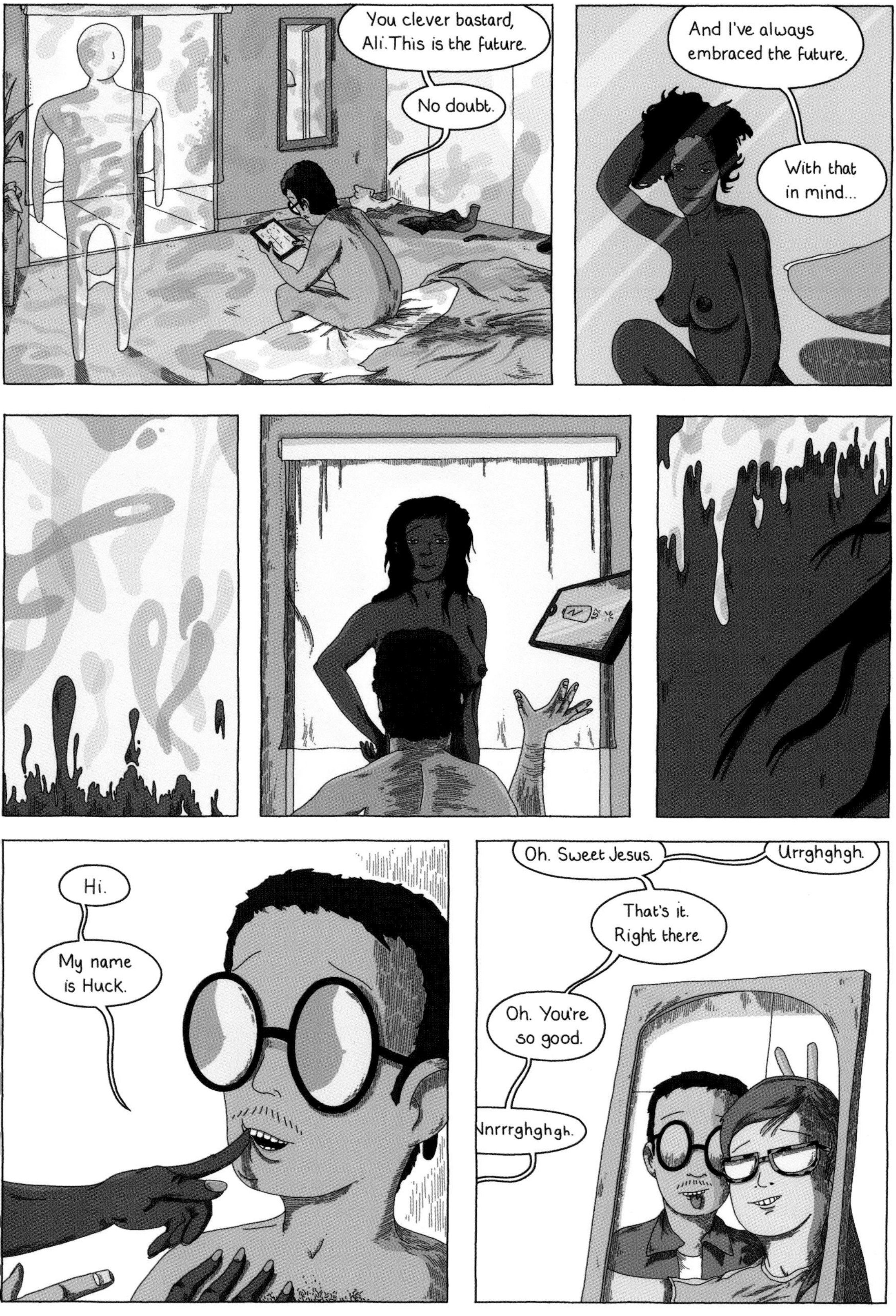
You clever bastard, Ali. This is the future.
No doubt.
And I've always embraced the future.
With that in mind...
Hi.
My name is Huck.
Oh. Sweet Jesus.
Urrghghgh.
That's it. Right there.
Oh. You're so good.
Nnrrrghghgh.

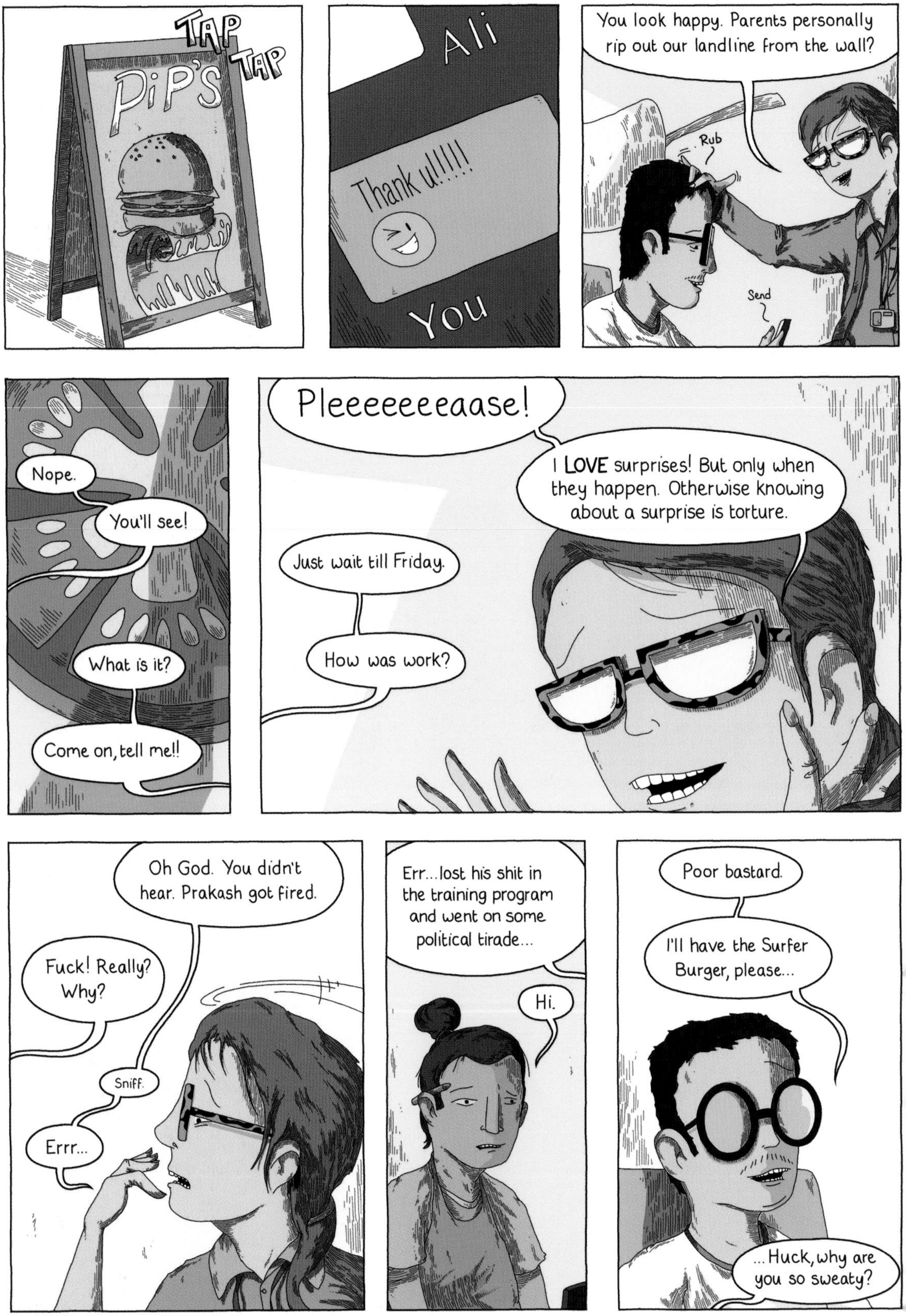
TAP TAP
PiP'S
Ali
Thank u!!!!!
You
You look happy. Parents personally rip out our landline from the wall?
Rub
Send
Nope.
You'll see!
What is it?
Come on, tell me!!
Pleeeeeeeaase!
I LOVE surprises! But only when they happen. Otherwise knowing about a surprise is torture.
Just wait till Friday.
How was work?
Oh God. You didn't hear. Prakash got fired.
Fuck! Really? Why?
Sniff.
Errr...
Err...lost his shit in the training program and went on some political tirade...
Hi.
Poor bastard.
I'll have the Surfer Burger, please...
...Huck, why are you so sweaty?

Welcome
To The
FWB
Arena

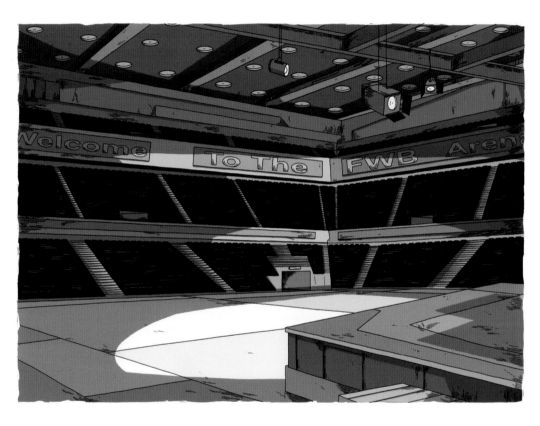

11 days to election.

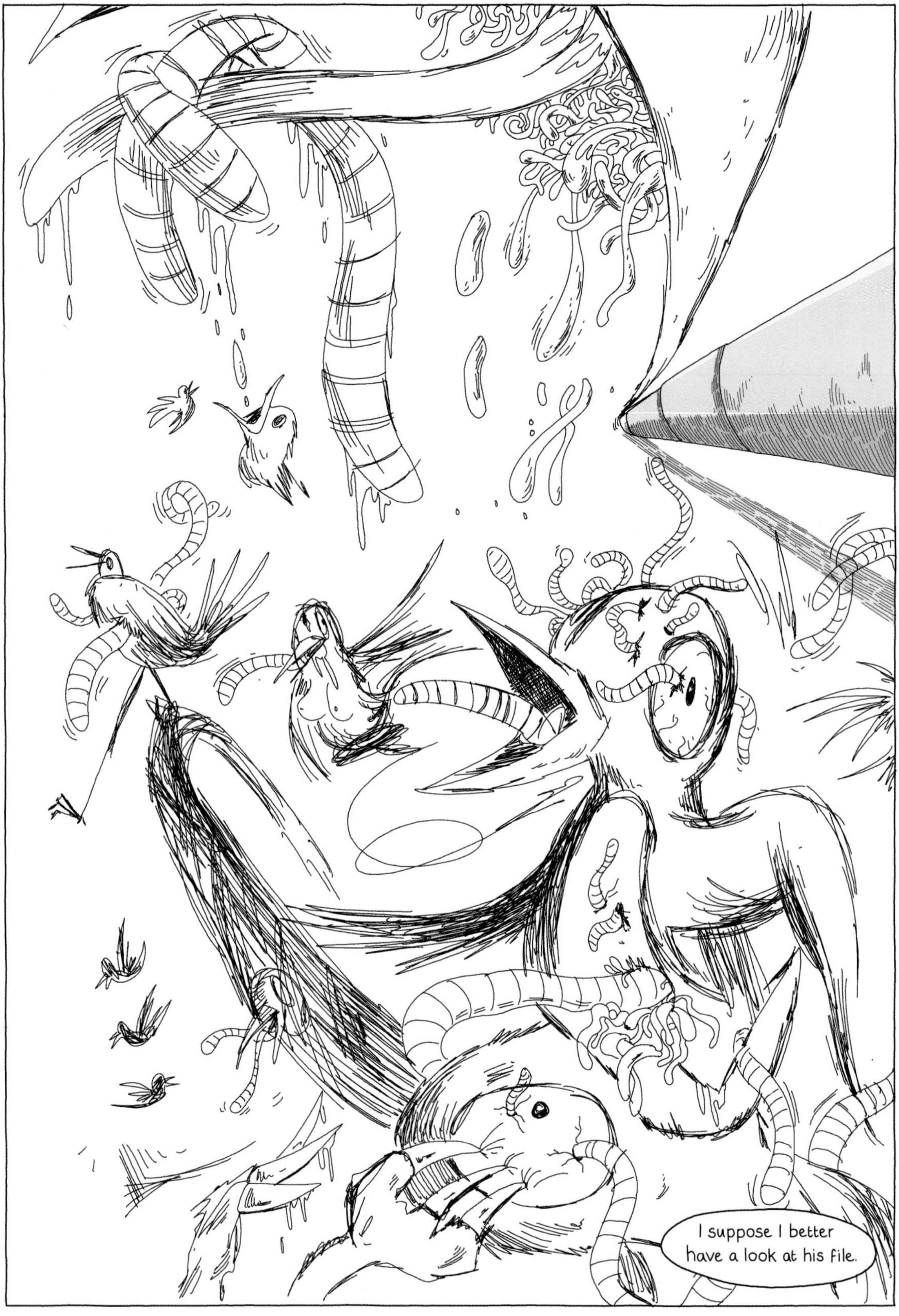
I suppose I better have a look at his file.

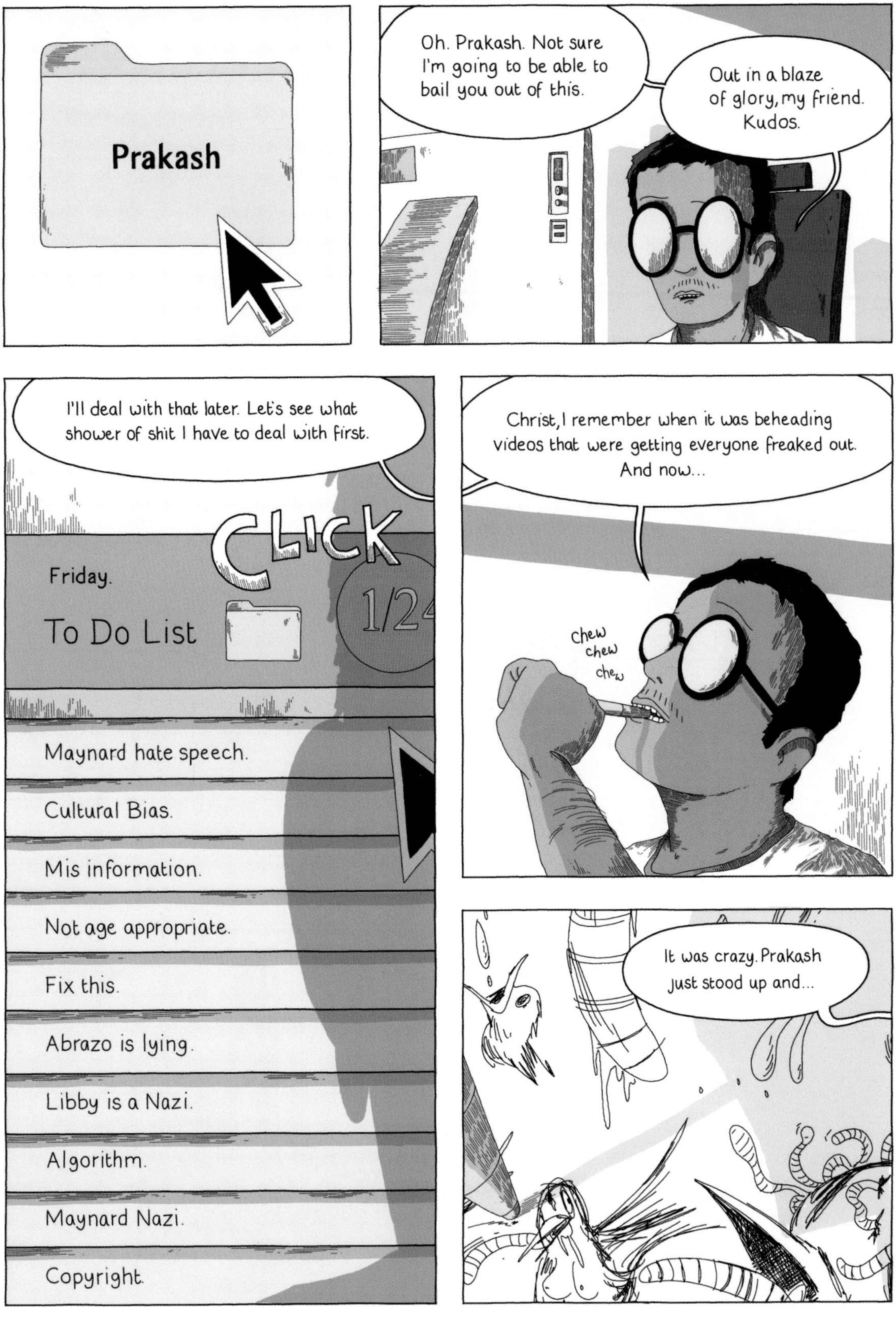

Prakash
Oh. Prakash. Not sure I'm going to be able to bail you out of this.
Out in a blaze of glory, my friend. Kudos.
I'll deal with that later. Let's see what shower of shit I have to deal with first.
CLICK
Friday.
To Do List
1/24
Maynard hate speech.
Cultural Bias.
Mis information.
Not age appropriate.
Fix this.
Abrazo is lying.
Libby is a Nazi.
Algorithm.
Maynard Nazi.
Copyright.
Christ, I remember when it was beheading videos that were getting everyone freaked out. And now...
chew chew chew
It was crazy. Prakash just stood up and...

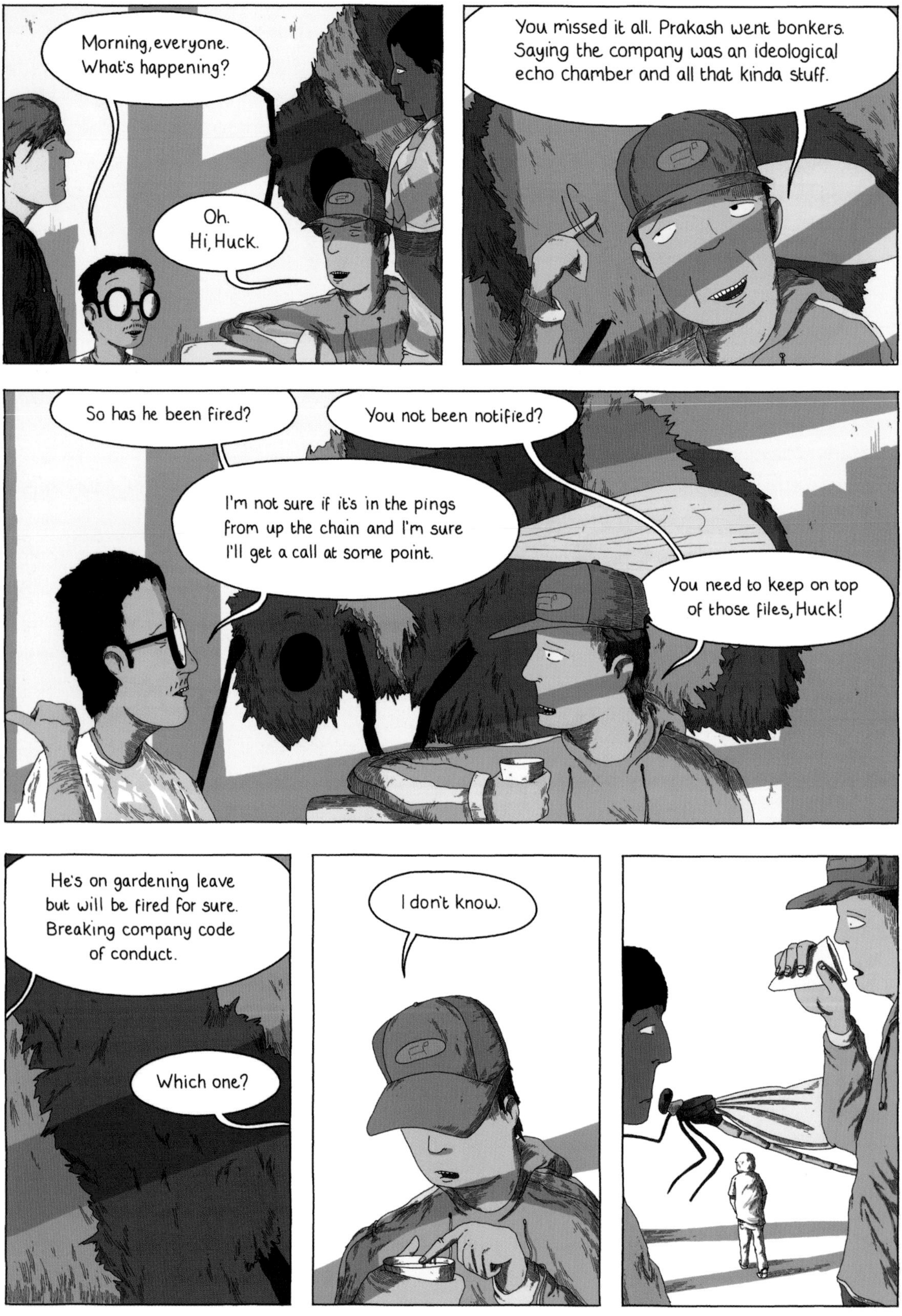
Morning, everyone. What's happening?
Oh. Hi, Huck.
You missed it all. Prakash went bonkers. Saying the company was an ideological echo chamber and all that kinda stuff.
So has he been fired?
You not been notified?
I'm not sure if it's in the pings from up the chain and I'm sure I'll get a call at some point.
You need to keep on top of those files, Huck!
He's on gardening leave but will be fired for sure. Breaking company code of conduct.
Which one?
I don't know.

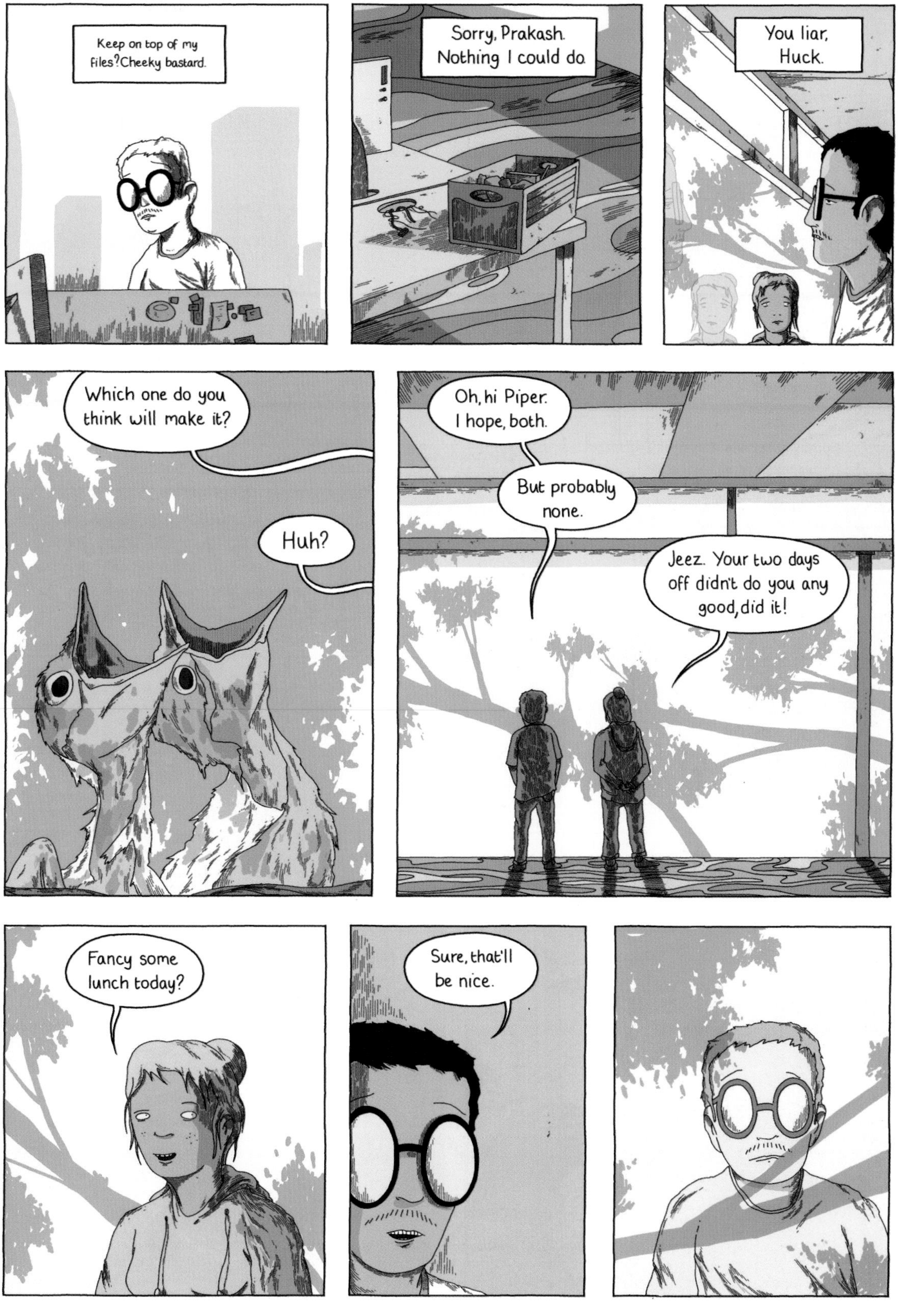

Keep on top of my files? Cheeky bastard.
Sorry, Prakash. Nothing I could do.
You liar, Huck.
Which one do you think will make it?
Huh?
Oh, hi Piper. I hope, both.
But probably none.
Jeez. Your two days off didn't do you any good, did it!
Fancy some lunch today?
Sure, that'll be nice.

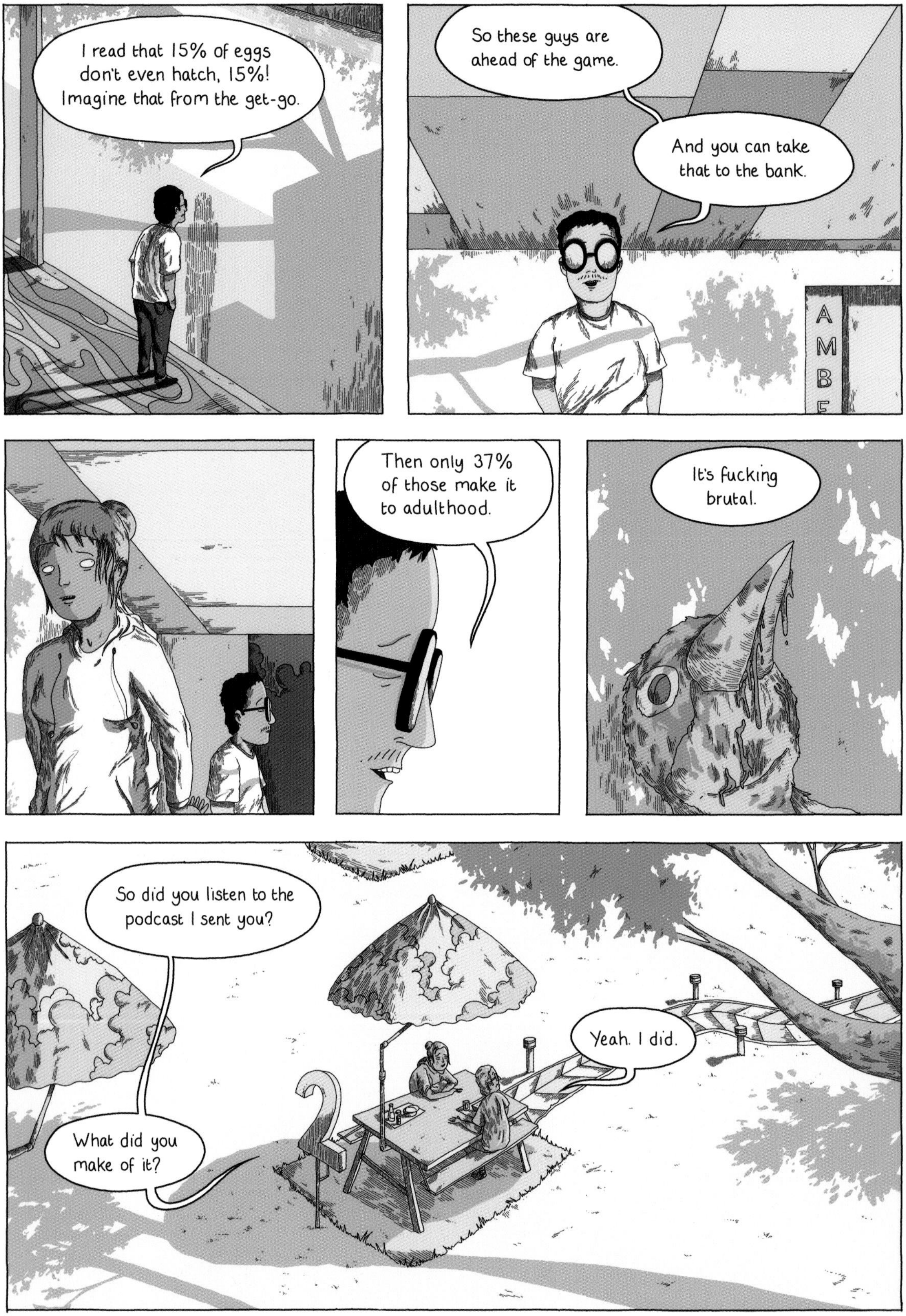
I read that 15% of eggs don't even hatch, 15%! Imagine that from the get-go.
So these guys are ahead of the game.
And you can take that to the bank.
AMB
Then only 37% of those make it to adulthood.
It's fucking brutal.
So did you listen to the podcast I sent you?
Yeah. I did.
What did you make of it?

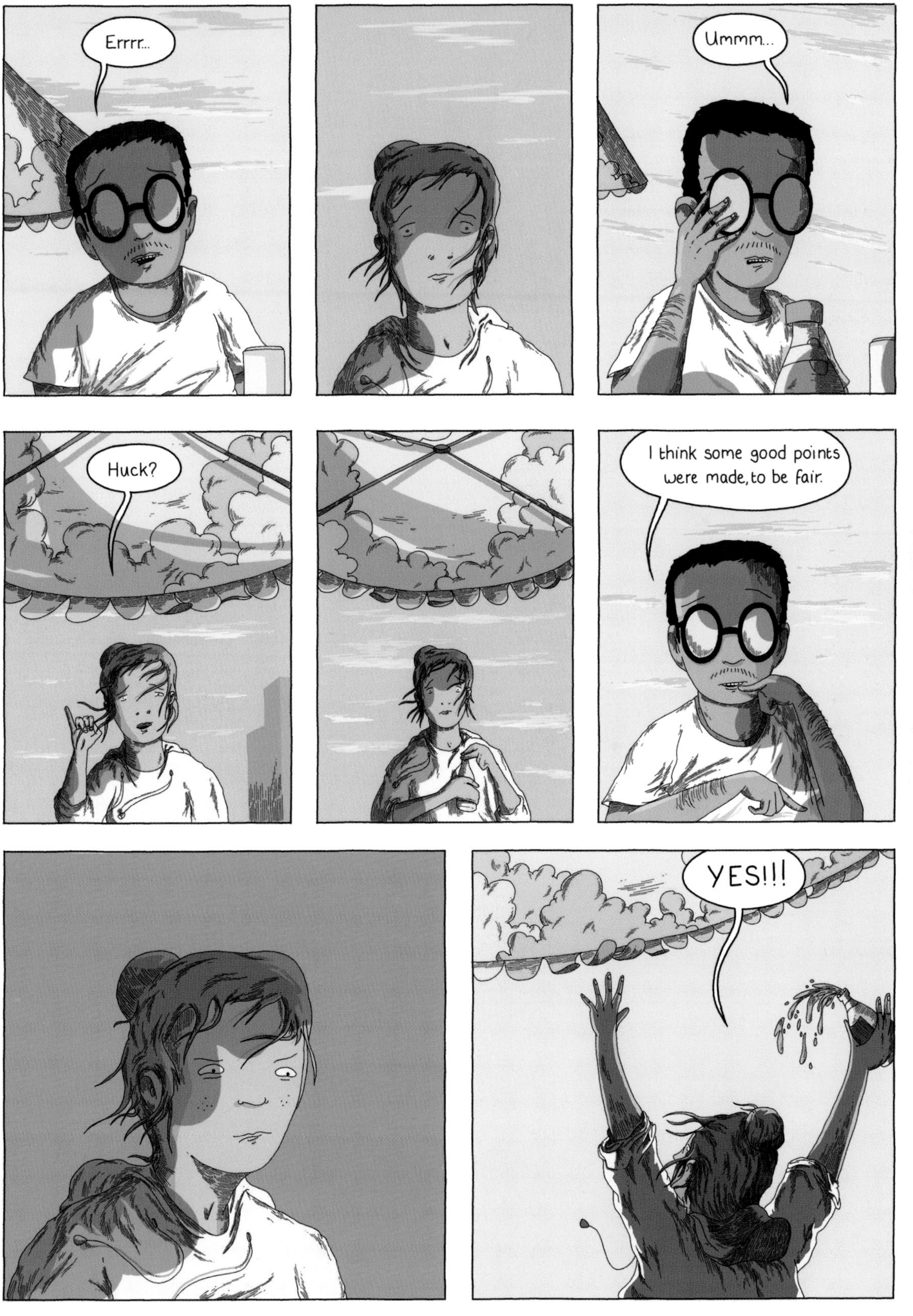
Errrr...
Ummm...
Huck?
I think some good points were made, to be fair.
YES!!!

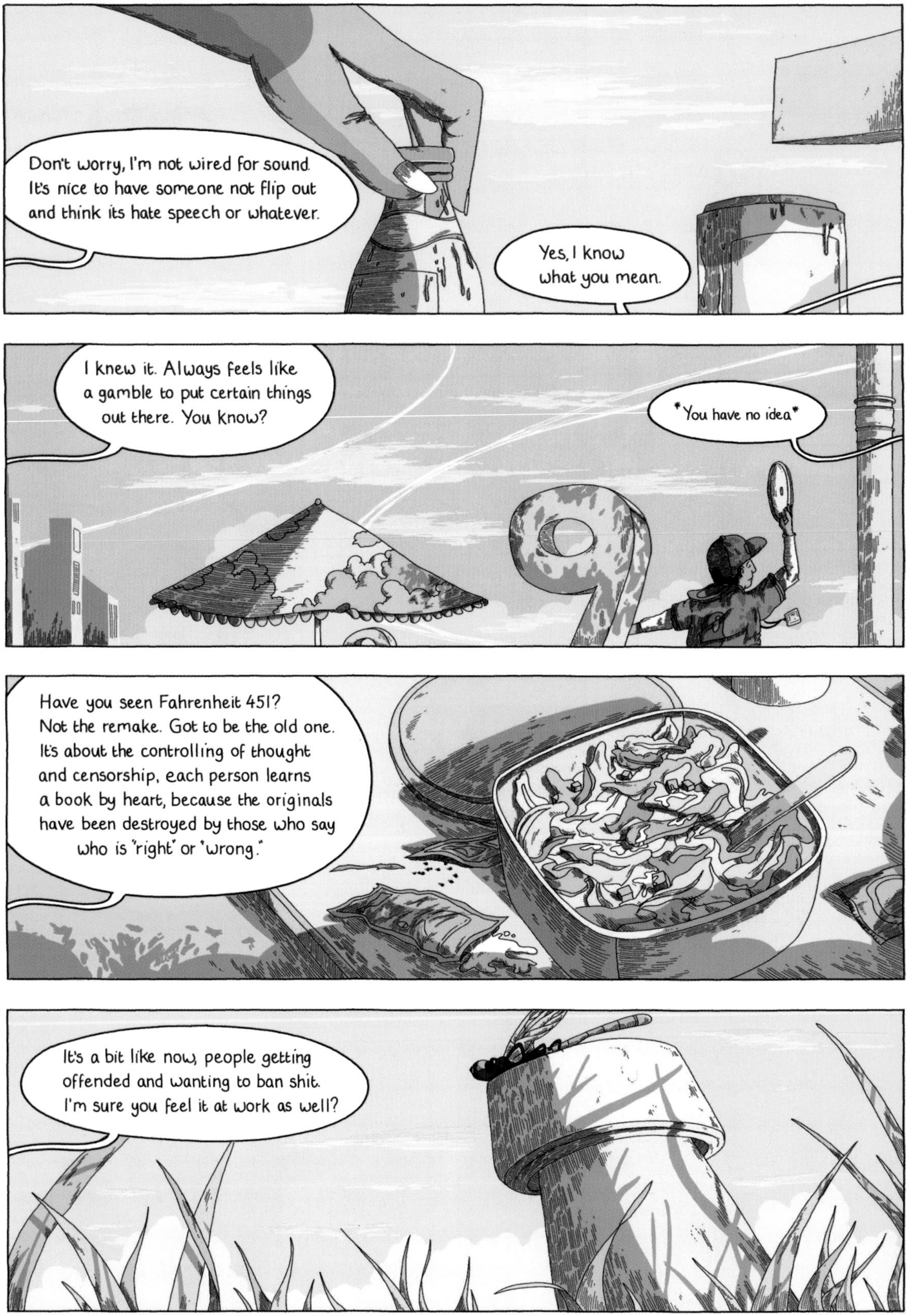
Don't worry, I'm not wired for sound. It's nice to have someone not flip out and think its hate speech or whatever.
Yes, I know what you mean.
I knew it. Always feels like a gamble to put certain things out there. You know?
You have no idea
Have you seen Fahrenheit 451? Not the remake. Got to be the old one. It's about the controlling of thought and censorship, each person learns a book by heart, because the originals have been destroyed by those who say who is "right" or "wrong."
It's a bit like now, people getting offended and wanting to ban shit. I'm sure you feel it at work as well?

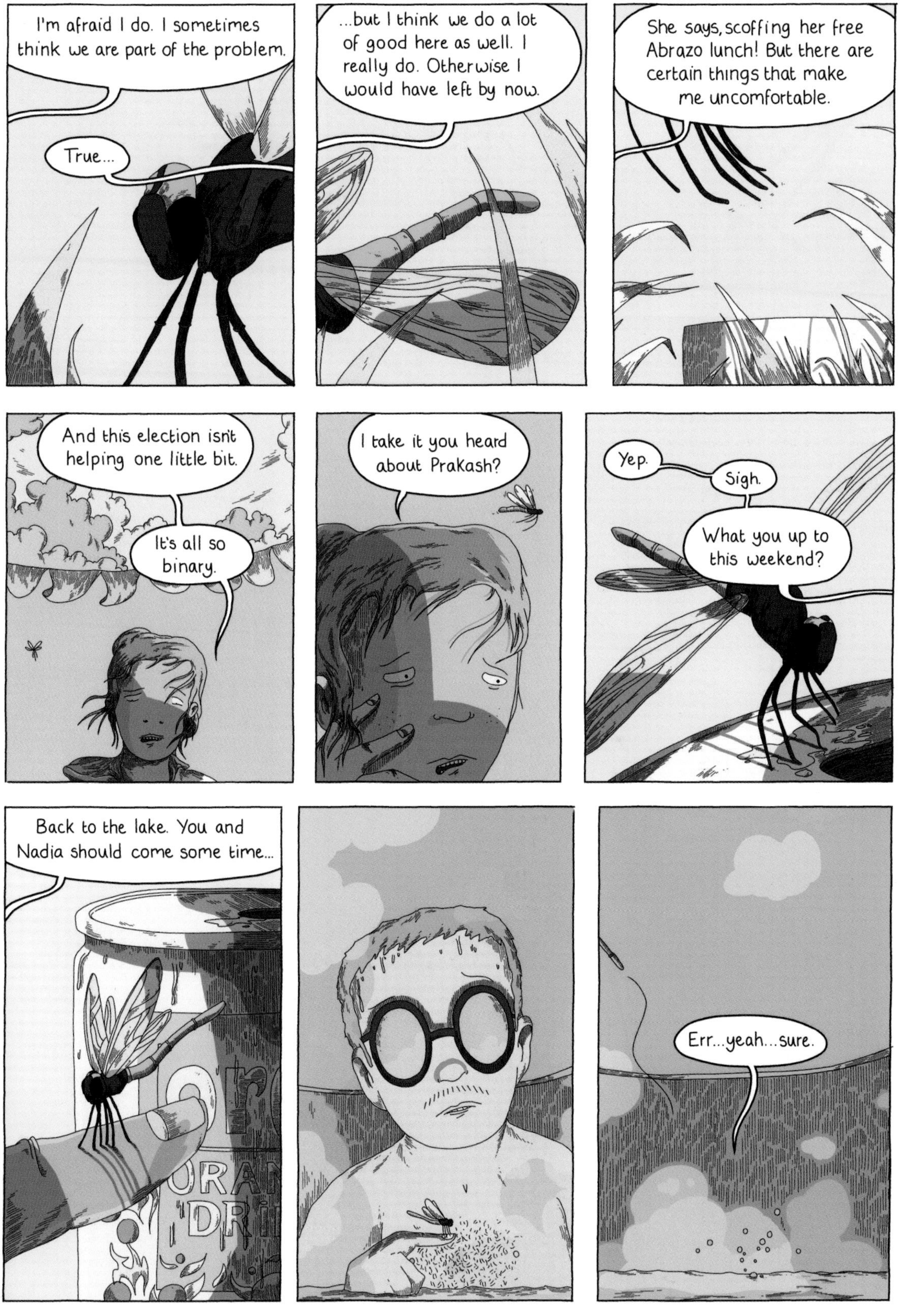
I'm afraid I do. I sometimes think we are part of the problem.
True...
...but I think we do a lot of good here as well. I really do. Otherwise I would have left by now.
She says, scoffing her free Abrazo lunch! But there are certain things that make me uncomfortable.
And this election isn't helping one little bit.
It's all so binary.
I take it you heard about Prakash?
Yep.
Sigh.
What you up to this weekend?
Back to the lake. You and Nadia should come some time...
Err...yeah...sure.

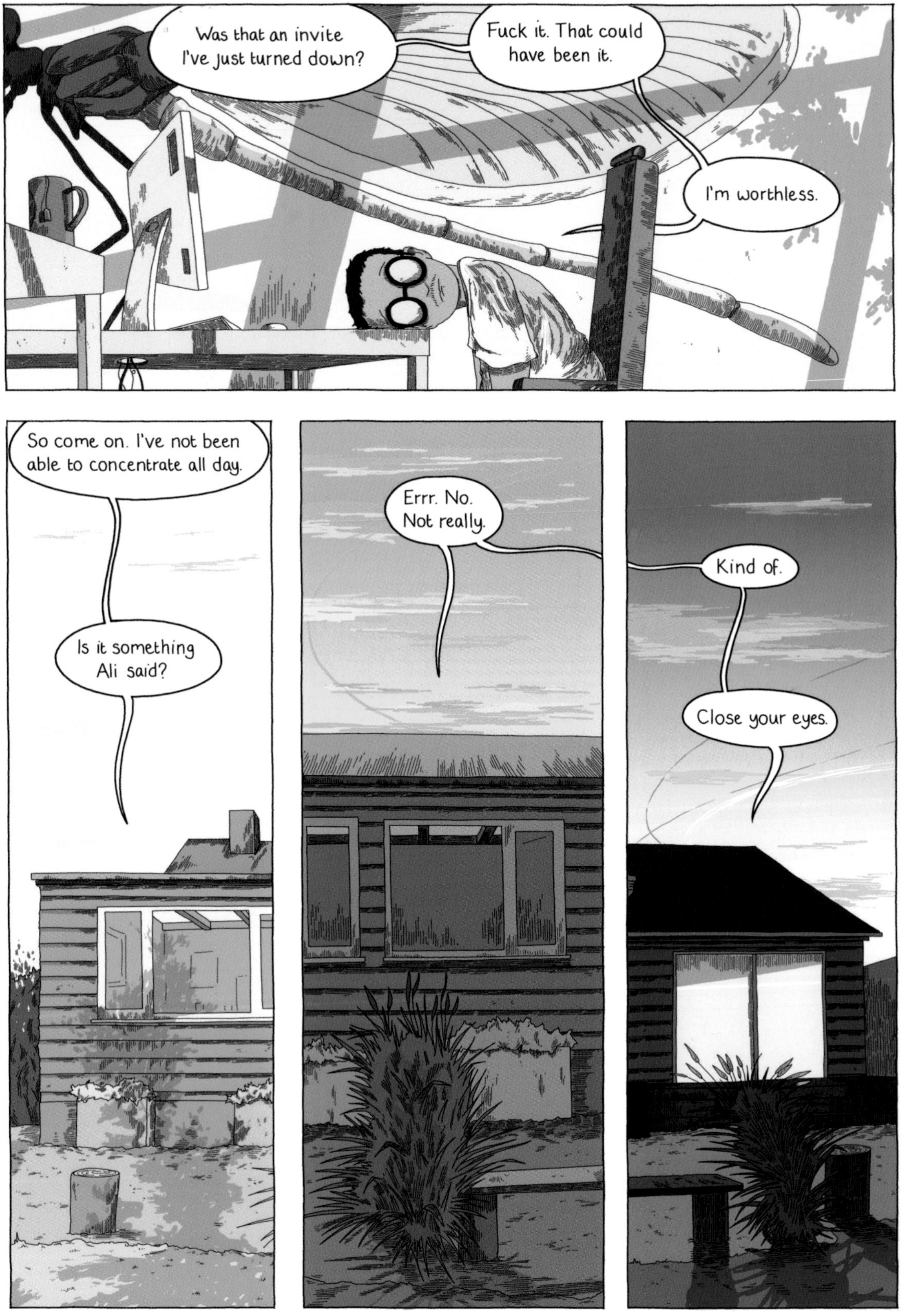
Was that an invite
I've just turned down?
Fuck it. That could
have been it.
I'm worthless.
So come on. I've not been
able to concentrate all day.
Is it something
Ali said?
Errr. No.
Not really.
Kind of.
Close your eyes.

AQUAMAN
What.
The.
Fuck.

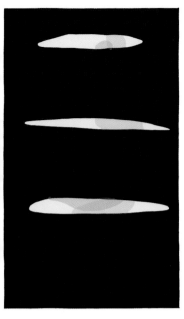

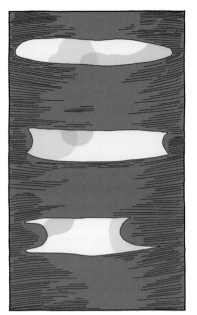

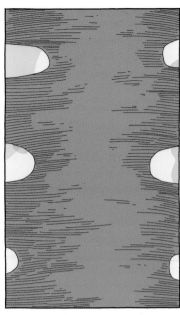

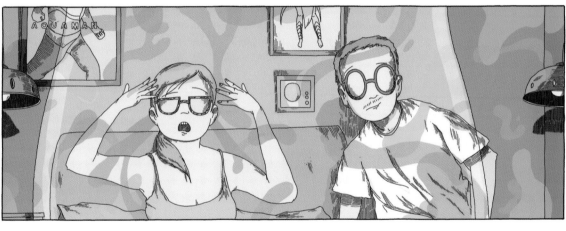

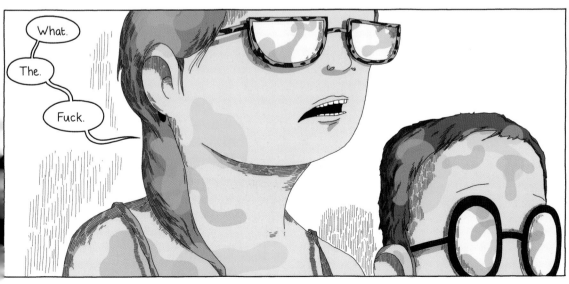

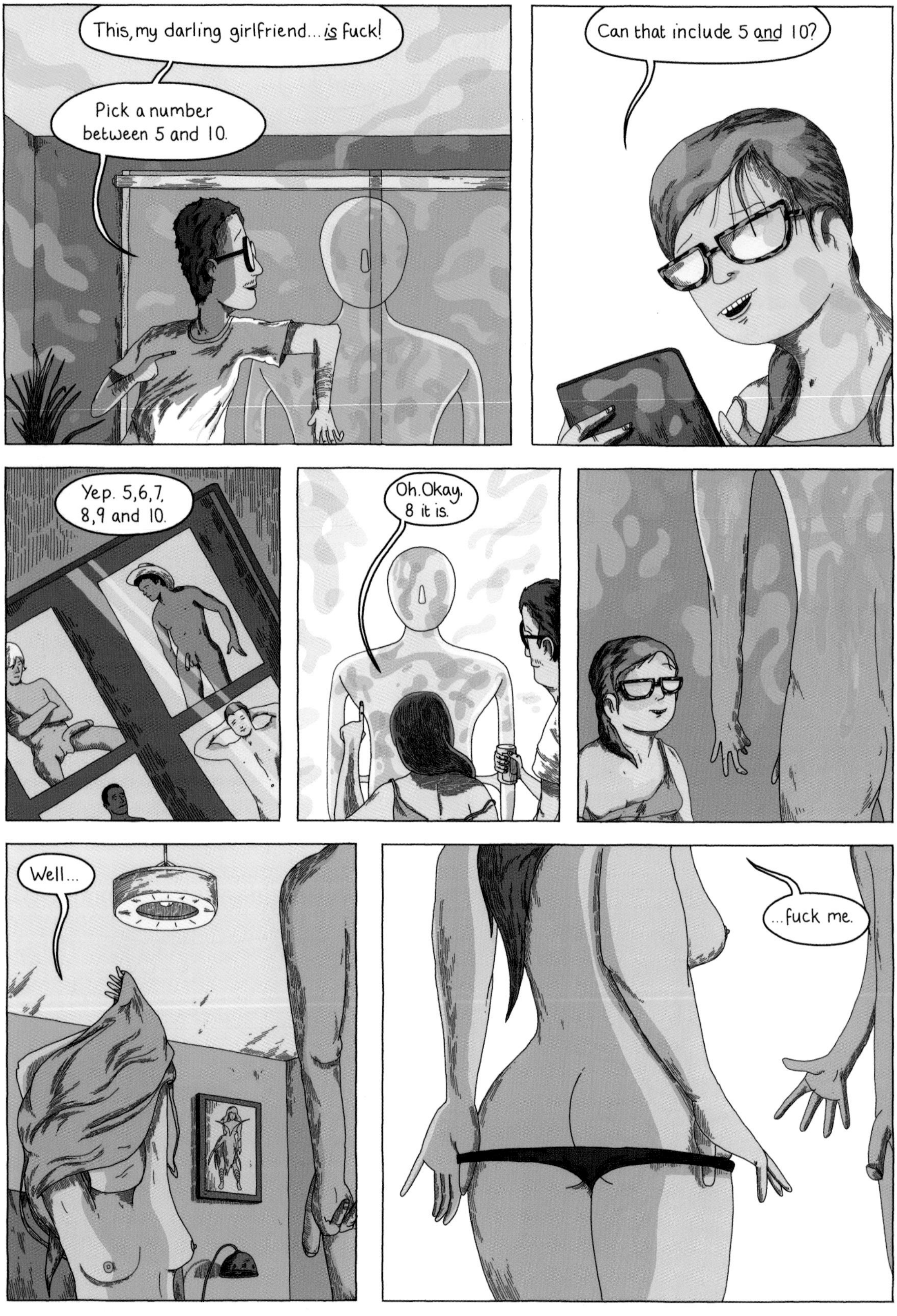
This, my darling girlfriend... *is* fuck!
Pick a number between 5 and 10.
Can that include 5 and 10?
Yep. 5,6,7, 8,9 and 10.
Oh. Okay, 8 it is.
Well...
...fuck me.

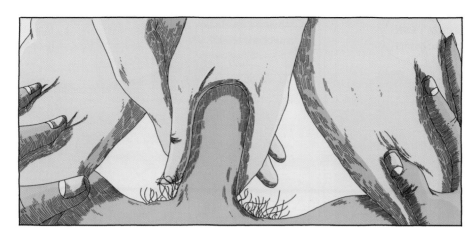

5

9

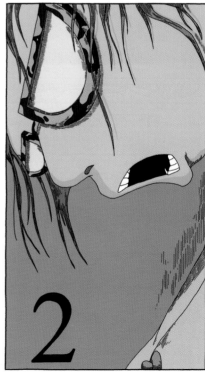

2

Put that tablet down in there, you. You've been fiddling with it for ages.

Uh-huh.

There's something about this portal config that just doesn't seem right...

TAP TAP TAP TAP TAP TAP TAP TAP TAP TAP TAP

It's more like a facade to something.

AP TAP

r)((s=t, c(
+B)-))u=[], t
){return
ate:fund
se().

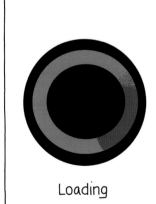

Loading

Bingo!

Search...

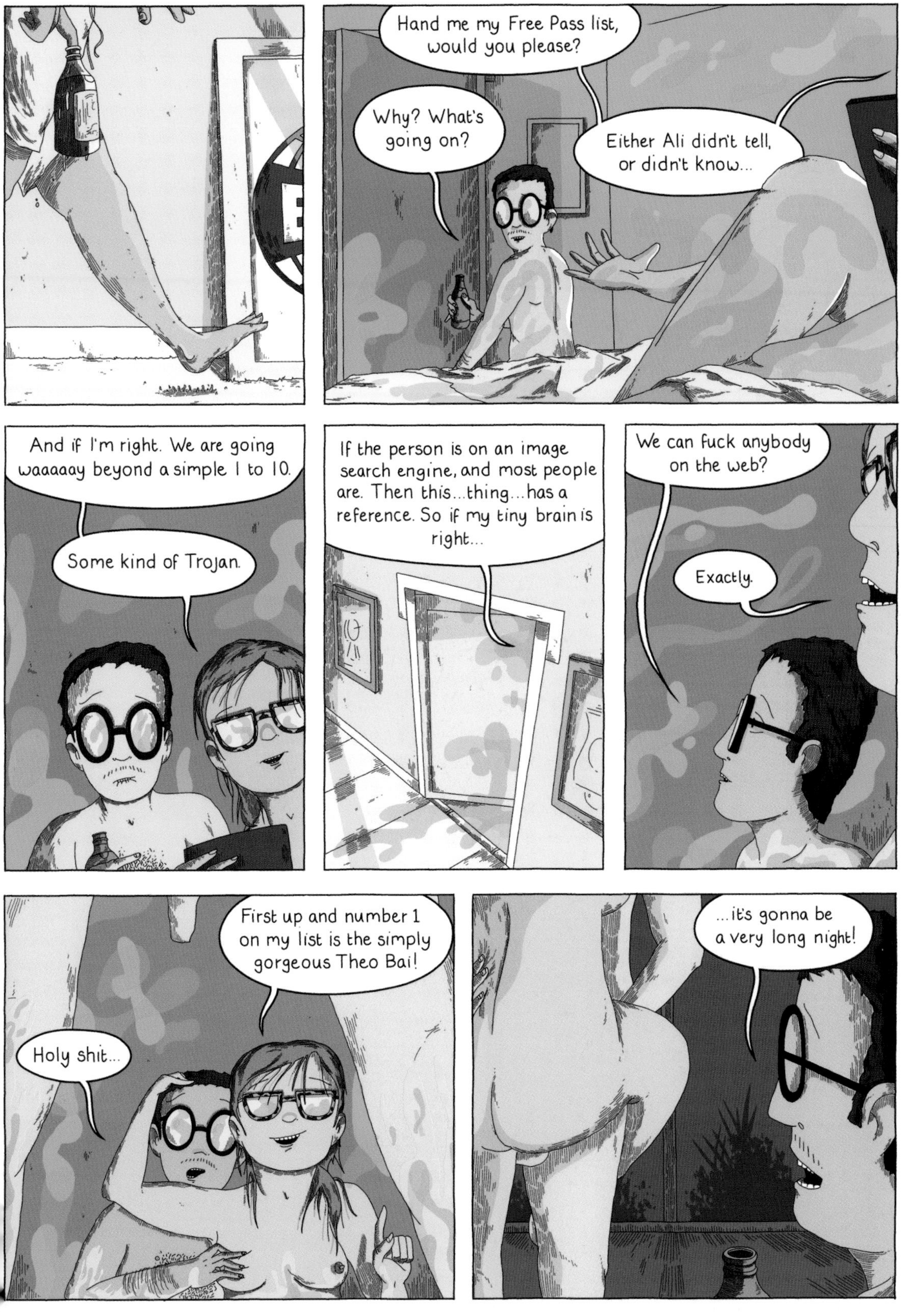
Hand me my Free Pass list, would you please?
Why? What's going on?
Either Ali didn't tell, or didn't know...
And if I'm right. We are going waaaaay beyond a simple 1 to 10.
Some kind of Trojan.
If the person is on an image search engine, and most people are. Then this...thing...has a reference. So if my tiny brain is right...
We can fuck anybody on the web?
Exactly.
First up and number 1 on my list is the simply gorgeous Theo Bai!
Holy shit...
...it's gonna be a very long night!

Welcome
To The
FWB
Aren

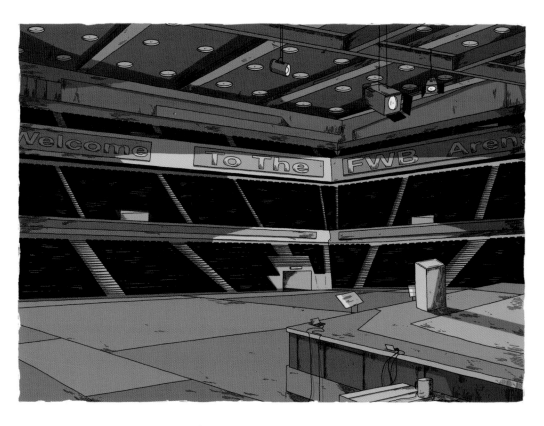

10 days to election.

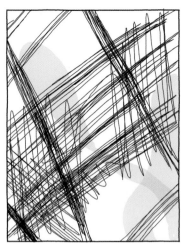

That. Was. Insane.

NADIA
Theo Bai.
Ash Polizzi
Mark Six
Em M
UCKS
PASS
st

We destroyed those lists. It was a celeb fuck fest in here last night.

Yep. I think it's time we cranked up the laptop, hit IMDB and get us some new names.

Are we bad doing this...I mean...just a little bit?

Maybe a tiny bit. But that's what makes it sooooo good.

And Ali didn't mention this? The tech is insane as it is, but with this dark feature...it's like improving God. Or something.

He didn't. I like to think he doesn't know. Above his pay grade...

TAP TAP TAP TAP TAP TAP TAP TAP TAP TAP

Shit's about to get freaky, my man.

I Q
I
IMD

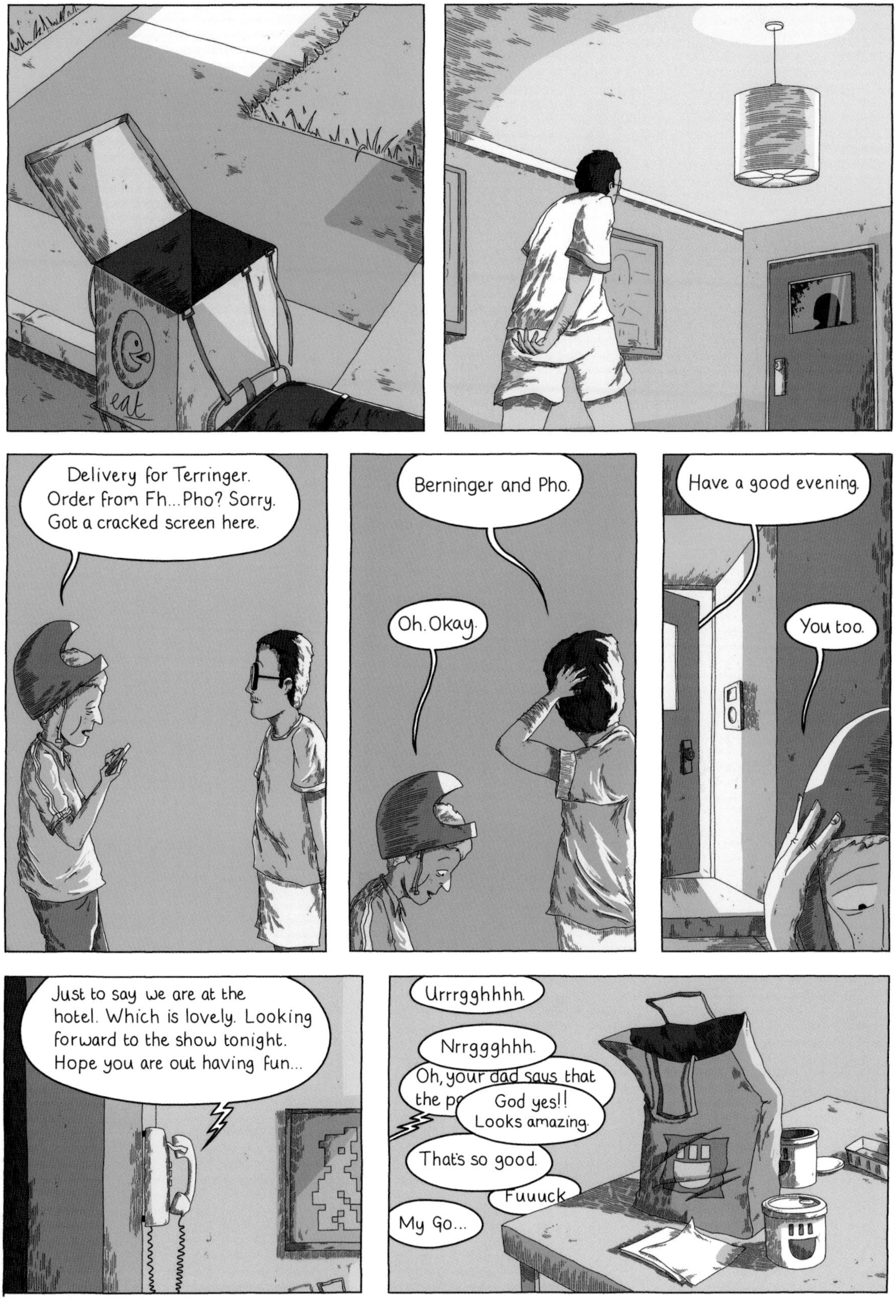

eat
Delivery for Terringer. Order from Fh...Pho? Sorry. Got a cracked screen here.
Berninger and Pho.
Oh. Okay.
Have a good evening.
You too.
Just to say we are at the hotel. Which is lovely. Looking forward to the show tonight. Hope you are out having fun...
Urrrgghhhh.
Nrrggghhh.
Oh, your dad says that the p
God yes!! Looks amazing.
That's so good.
Fuuuck
My Go...

Welcome
To The
FWB
Arena

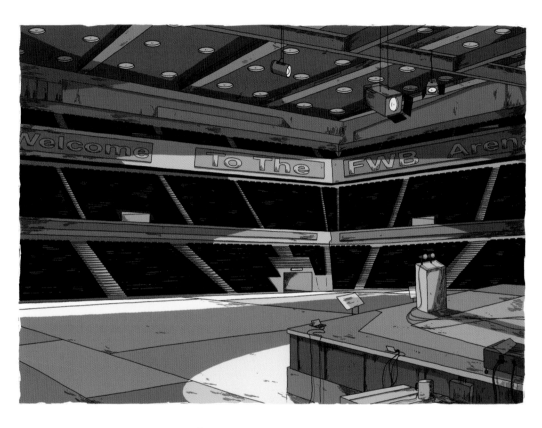

9 days to election.

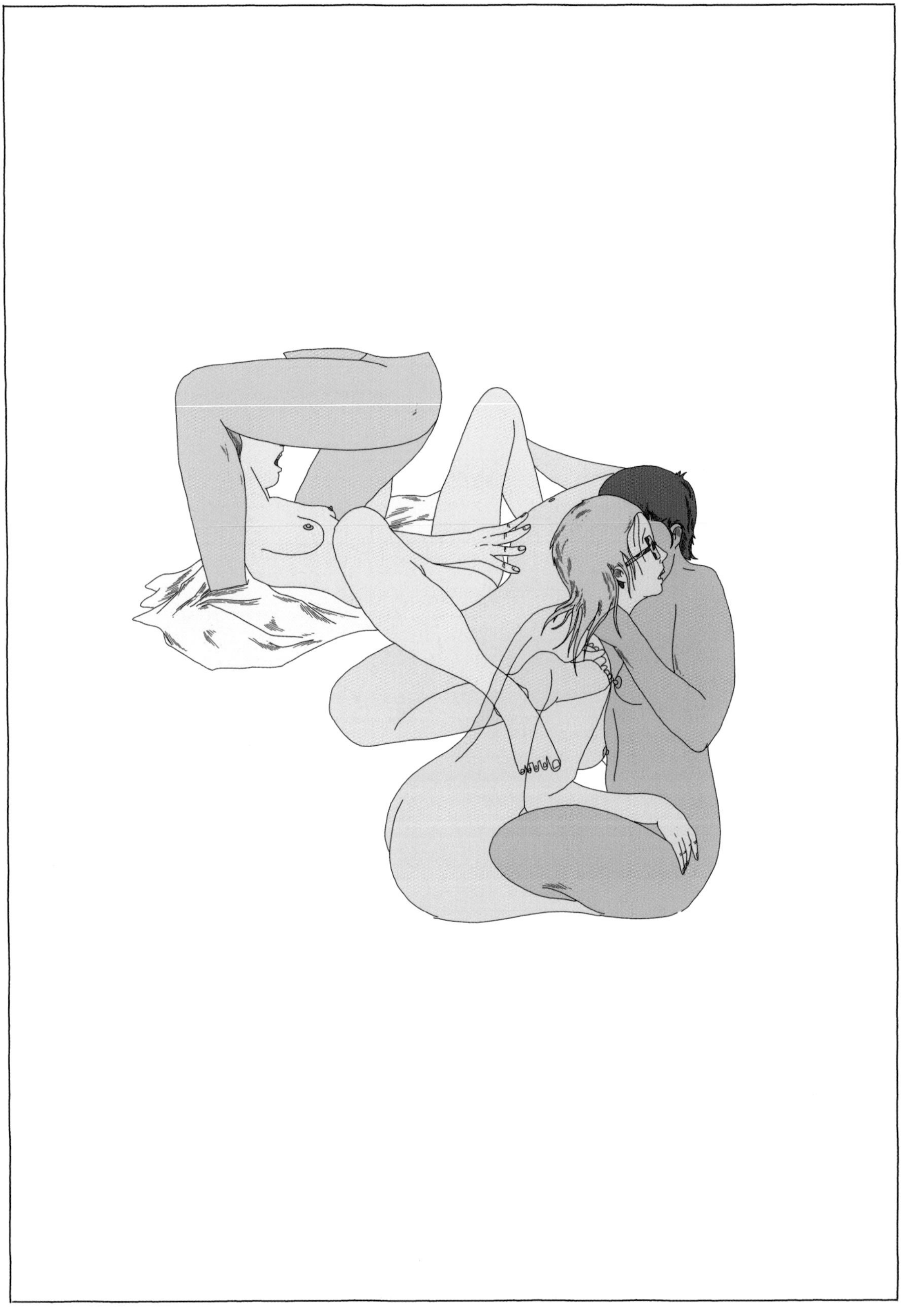

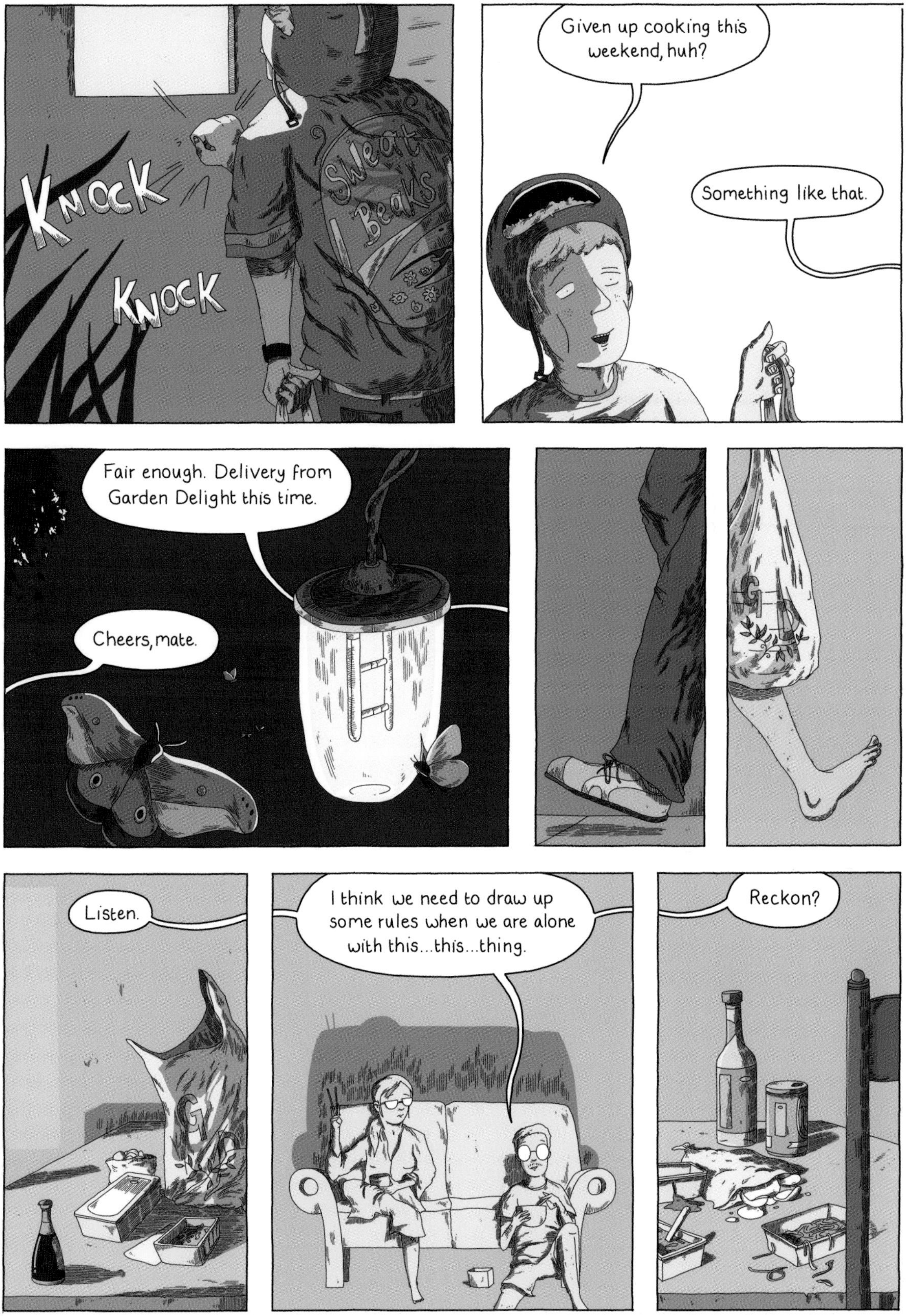
KNOCK
KNOCK
Given up cooking this weekend, huh?
Something like that.
Fair enough. Delivery from Garden Delight this time.
Cheers, mate.
Listen.
I think we need to draw up some rules when we are alone with this...this...thing.
Reckon?

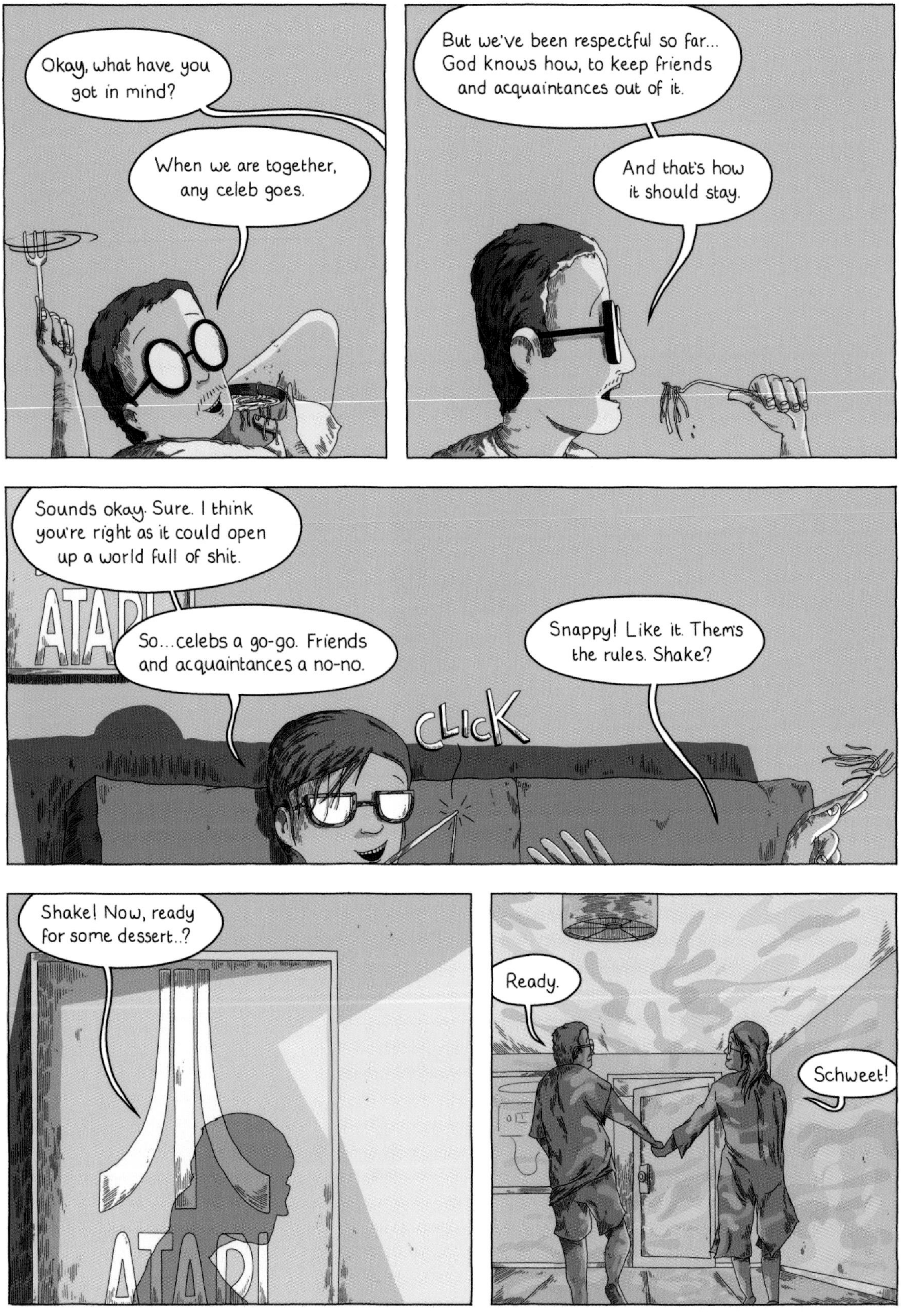
Okay, what have you got in mind?
When we are together, any celeb goes.
But we've been respectful so far... God knows how, to keep friends and acquaintances out of it.
And that's how it should stay.
Sounds okay. Sure. I think you're right as it could open up a world full of shit.
ATARI
So...celebs a go-go. Friends and acquaintances a no-no.
CLICK
Snappy! Like it. Them's the rules. Shake?
Shake! Now, ready for some dessert..?
ATARI
Ready.
Schweet!

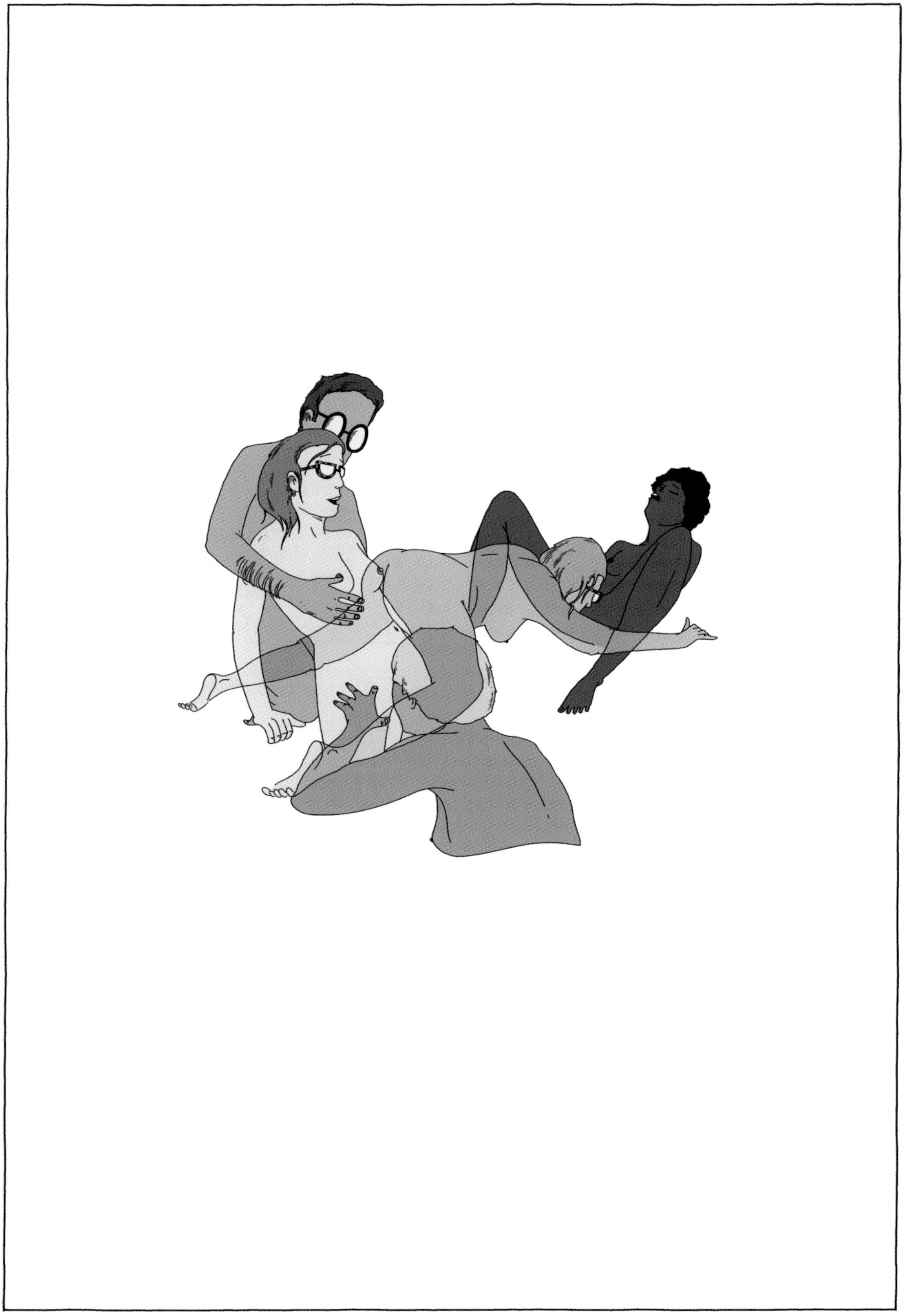

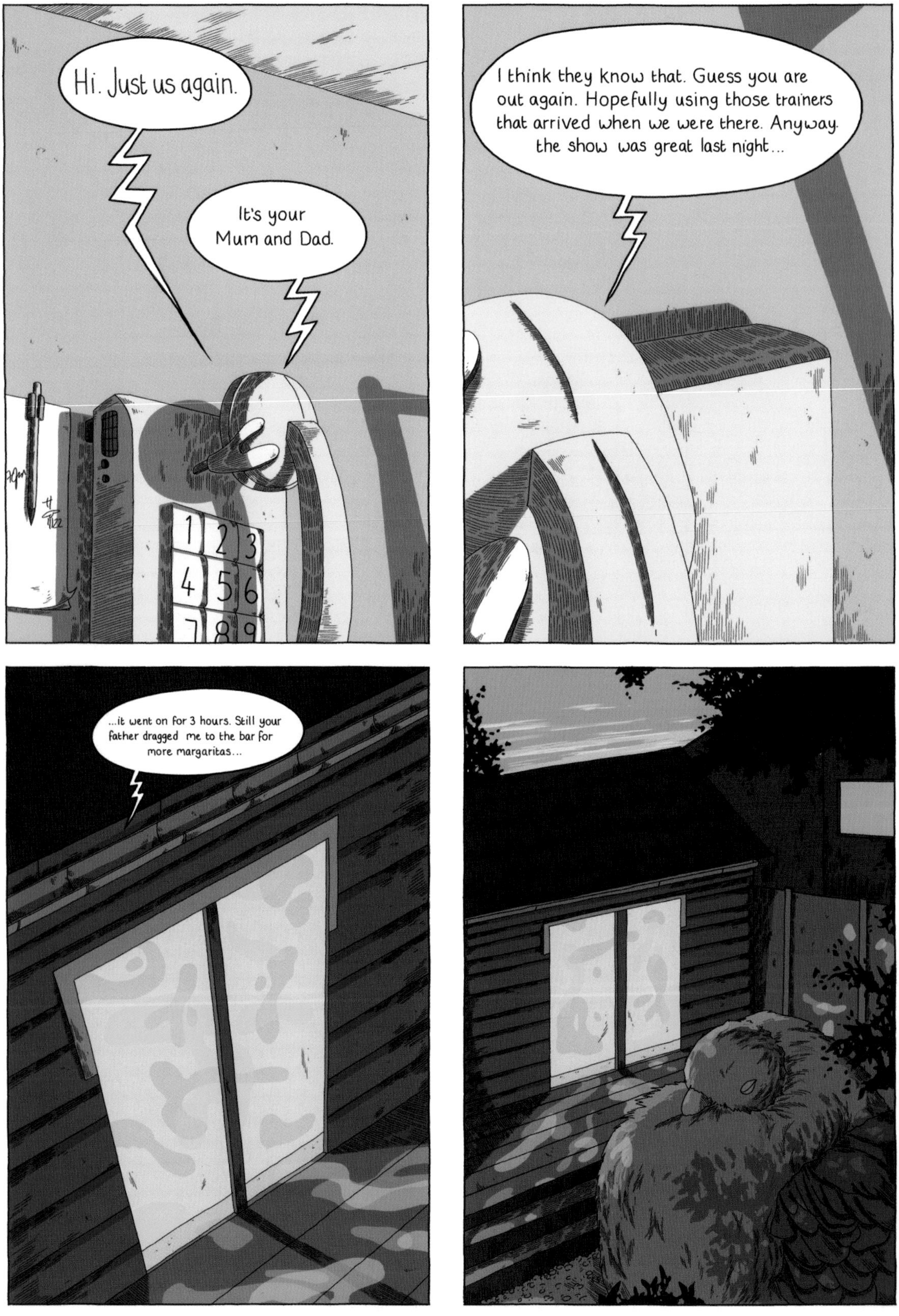

Hi. Just us again.
It's your Mum and Dad.
I think they know that. Guess you are out again. Hopefully using those trainers that arrived when we were there. Anyway, the show was great last night...
...it went on for 3 hours. Still your father dragged me to the bar for more margaritas...

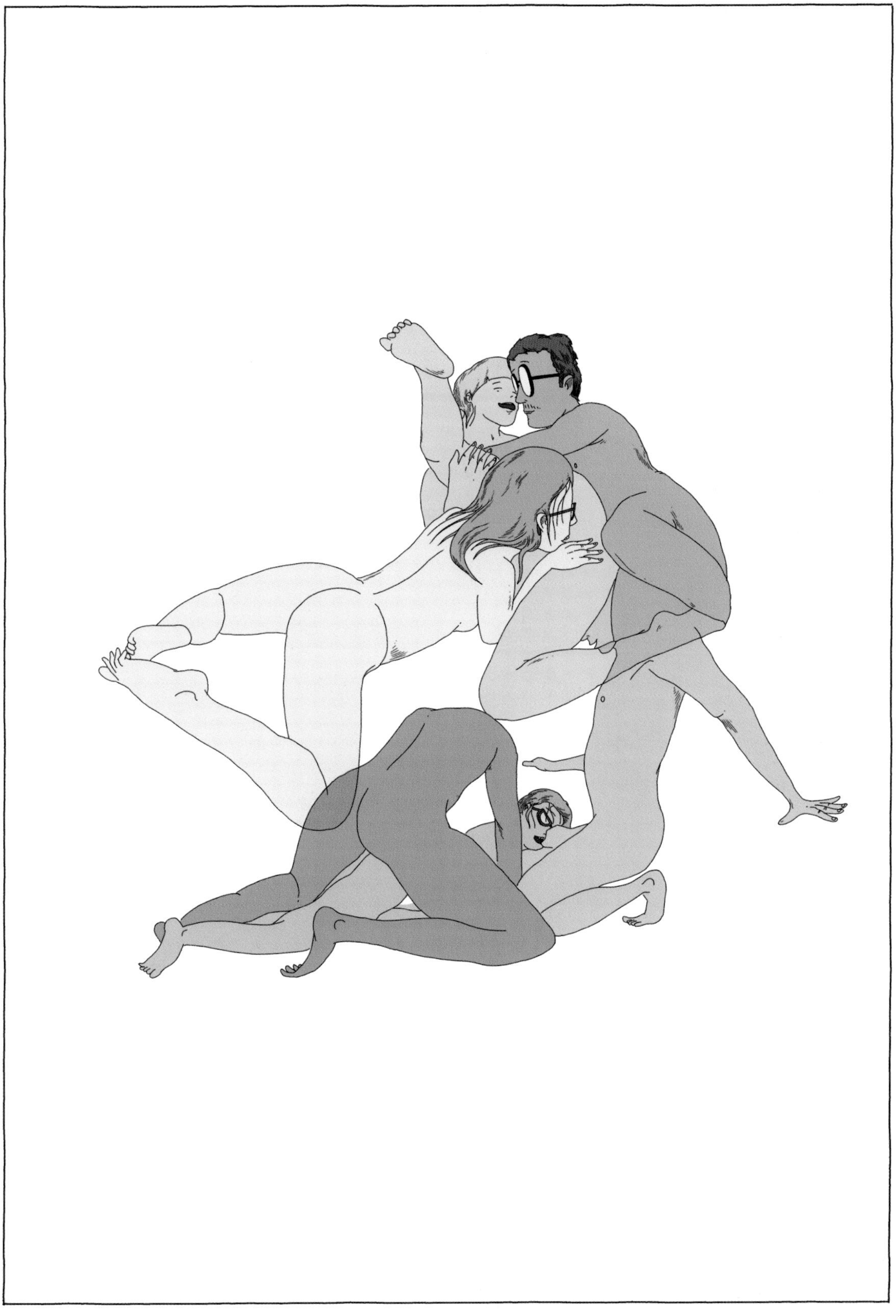

Welcome
To The
FWB
Arena

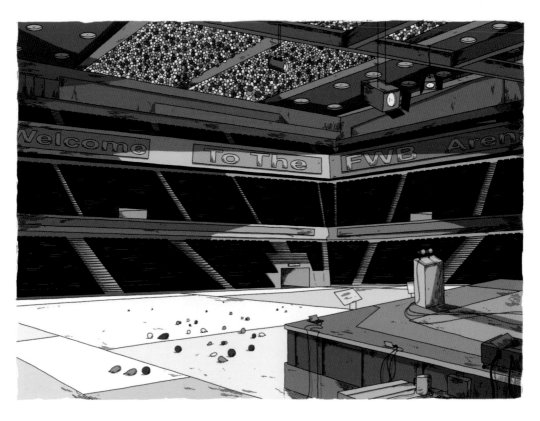

8 days to election.

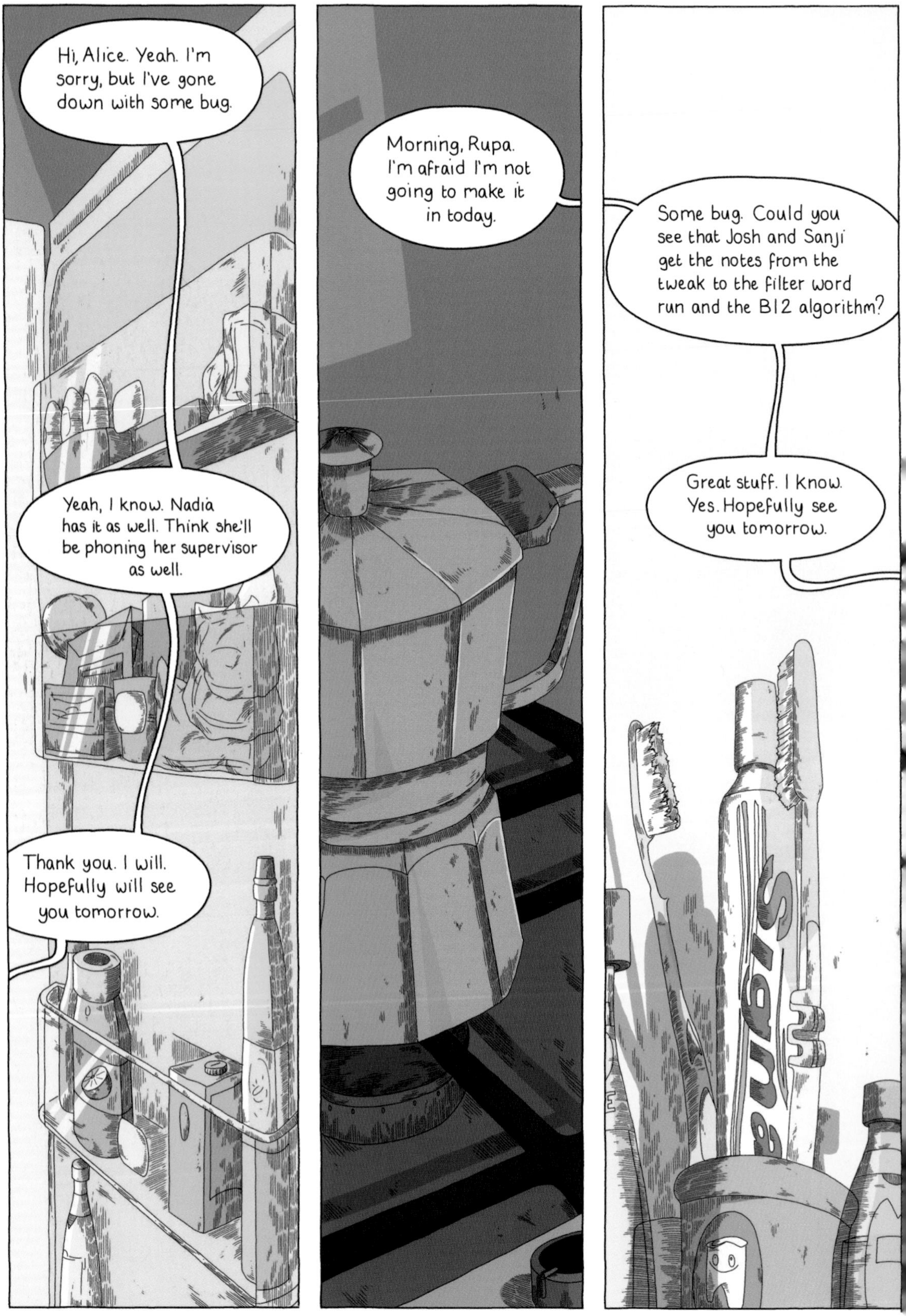
Hi, Alice. Yeah. I'm sorry, but I've gone down with some bug.
Yeah, I know. Nadia has it as well. Think she'll be phoning her supervisor as well.
Thank you. I will. Hopefully will see you tomorrow.
Morning, Rupa. I'm afraid I'm not going to make it in today.
Some bug. Could you see that Josh and Sanji get the notes from the tweak to the filter word run and the B12 algorithm?
Great stuff. I know. Yes. Hopefully see you tomorrow.

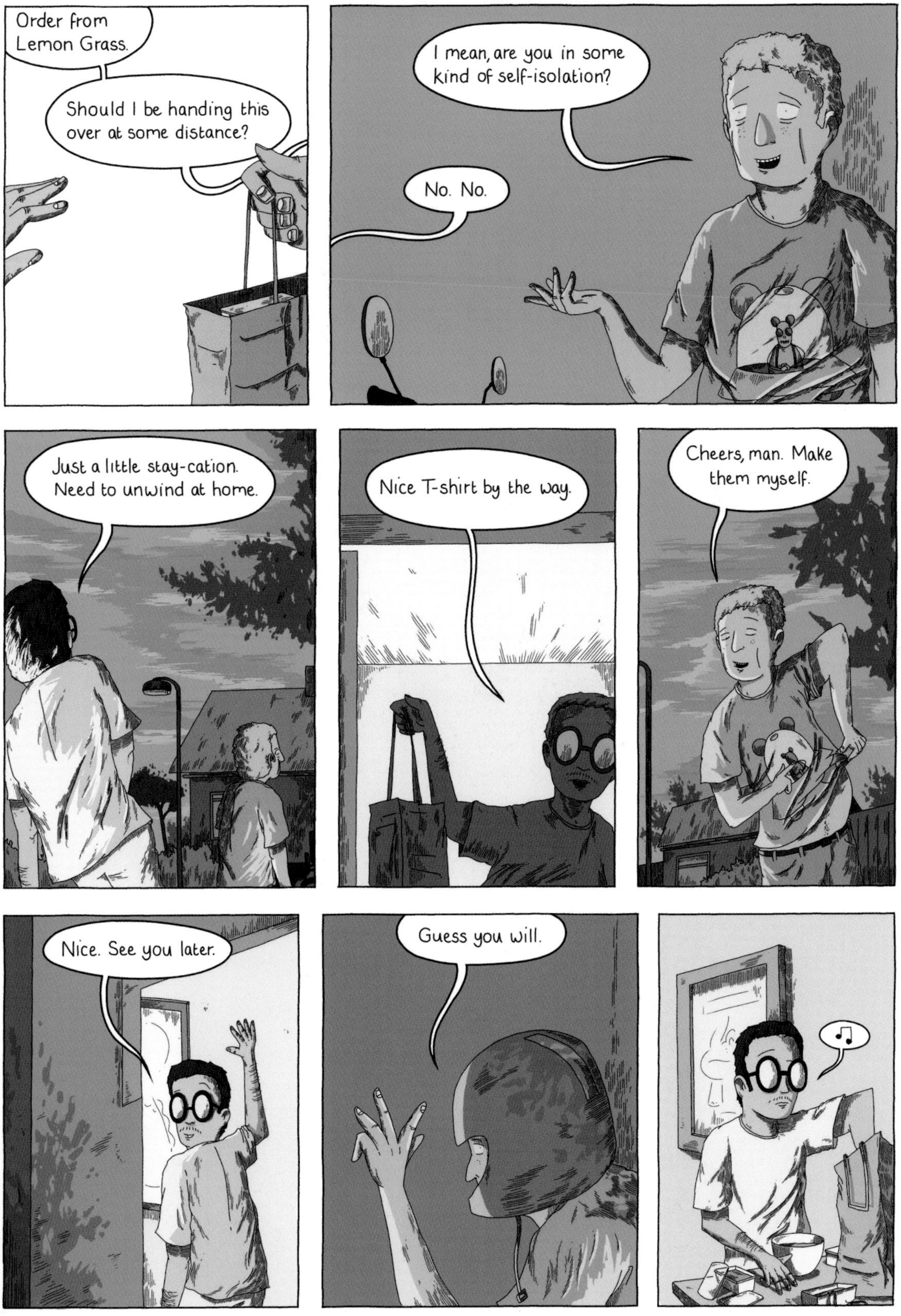
Order from Lemon Grass.
Should I be handing this over at some distance?
I mean, are you in some kind of self-isolation?
No. No.
Just a little stay-cation. Need to unwind at home.
Nice T-shirt by the way.
Cheers, man. Make them myself.
Nice. See you later.
Guess you will.
♫

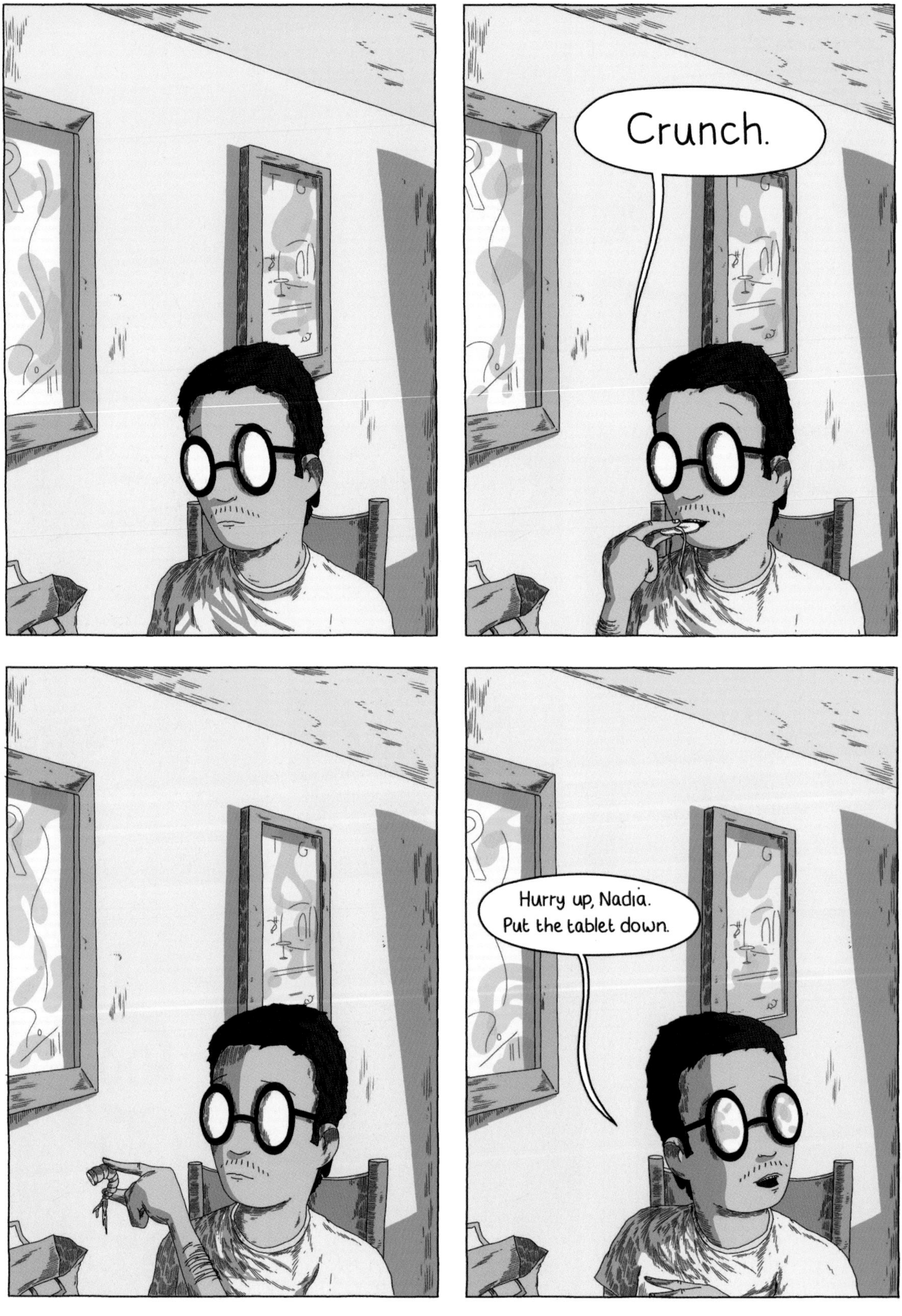
Crunch.
Hurry up, Nadia.
Put the tablet down.

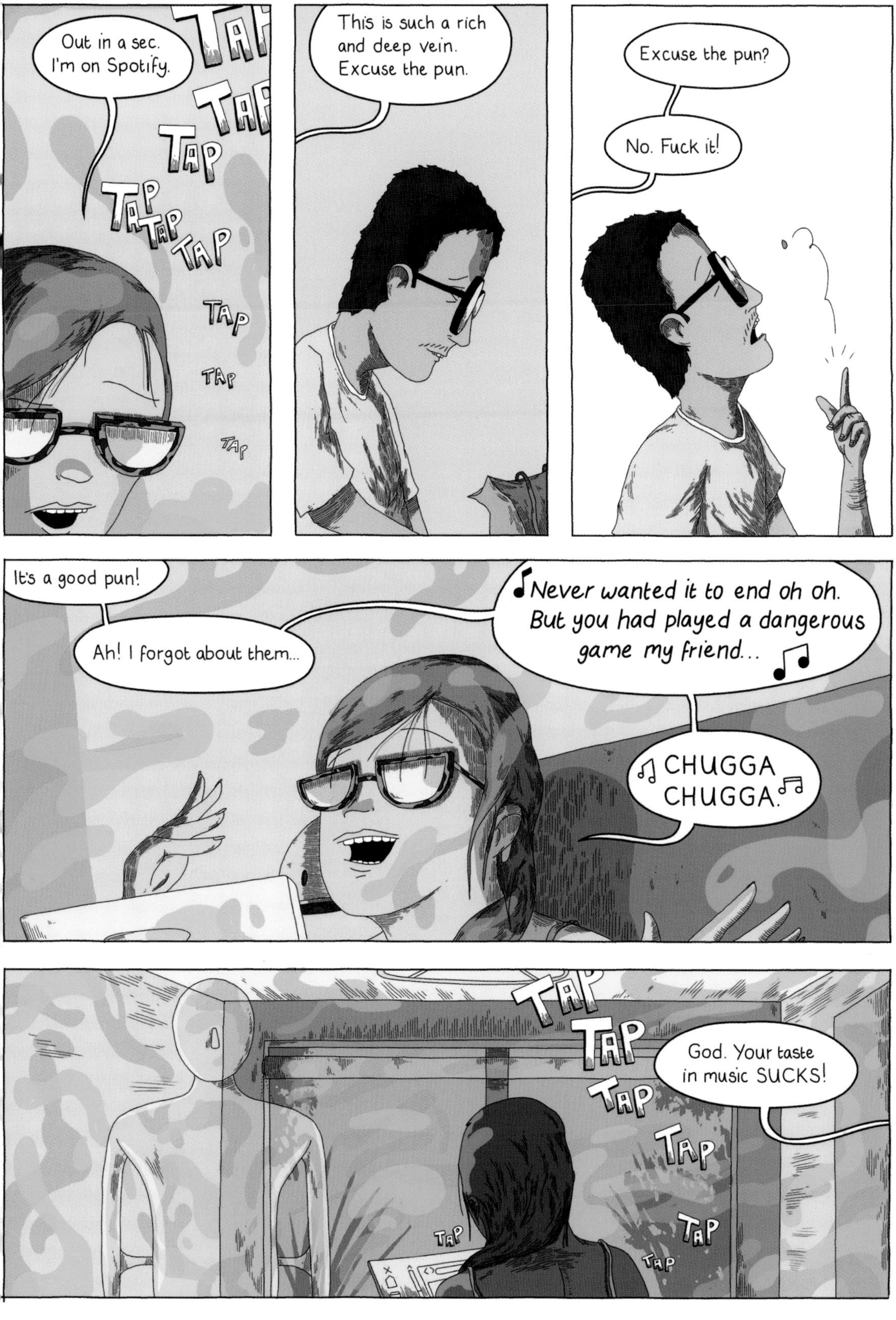
Out in a sec. I'm on Spotify.
TAP TAP TAP TAP TAP TAP TAP TAP TAP
This is such a rich and deep vein. Excuse the pun.
Excuse the pun?
No. Fuck it!
It's a good pun!
Ah! I forgot about them...
Never wanted it to end oh oh. But you had played a dangerous game my friend...
CHUGGA CHUGGA.
TAP TAP TAP TAP TAP TAP TAP
God. Your taste in music SUCKS!

Welcome To The FWB Arena

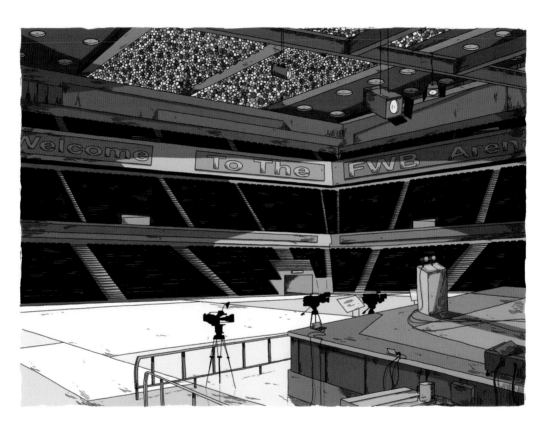

7 days to election.

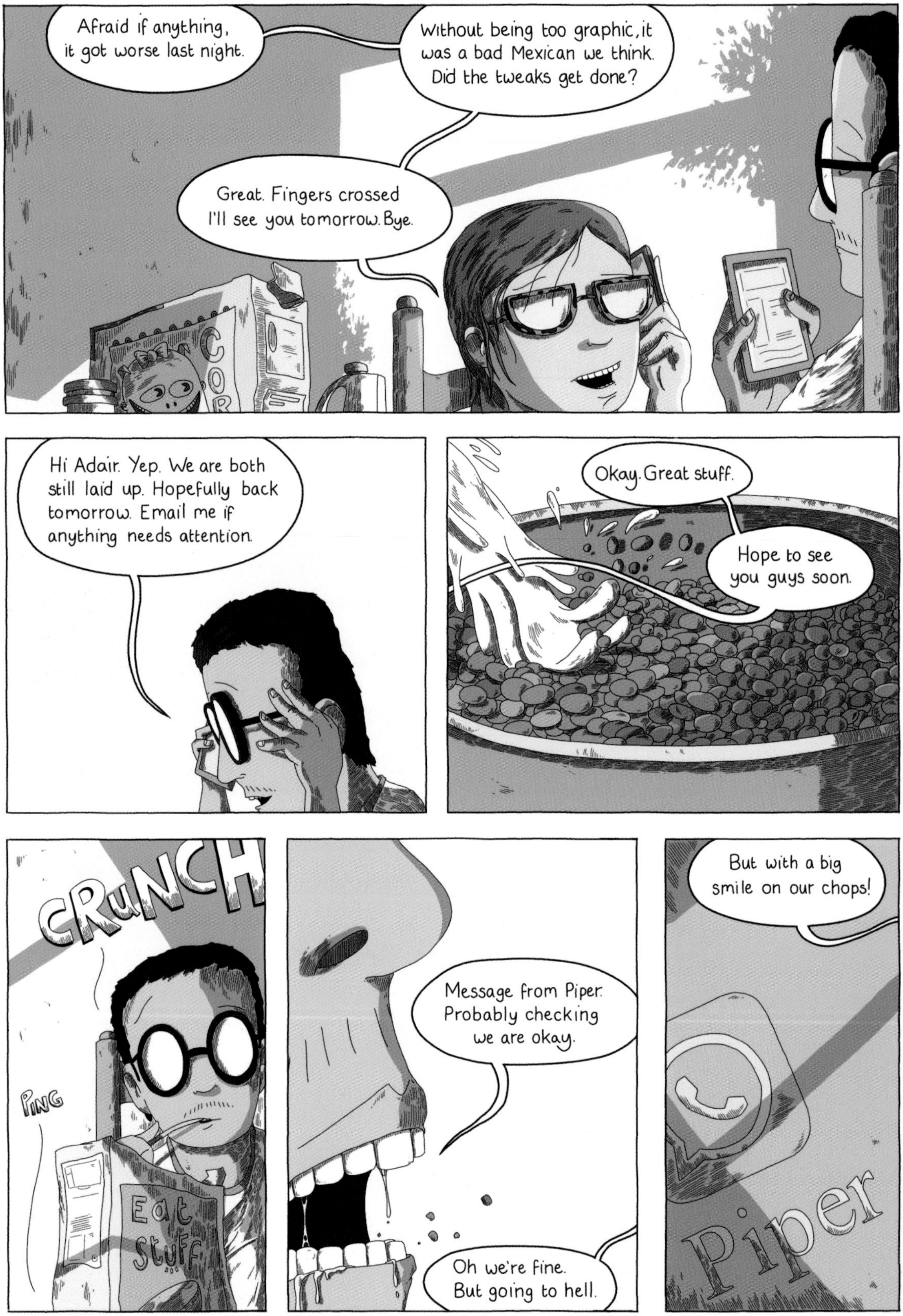
Afraid if anything, it got worse last night.
Without being too graphic, it was a bad Mexican we think. Did the tweaks get done?
Great. Fingers crossed I'll see you tomorrow. Bye.
Hi Adair. Yep. We are both still laid up. Hopefully back tomorrow. Email me if anything needs attention.
Okay. Great stuff.
Hope to see you guys soon.
CRUNCH
PING
Eat stuff
Message from Piper. Probably checking we are okay.
Oh we're fine. But going to hell.
But with a big smile on our chops!
Piper

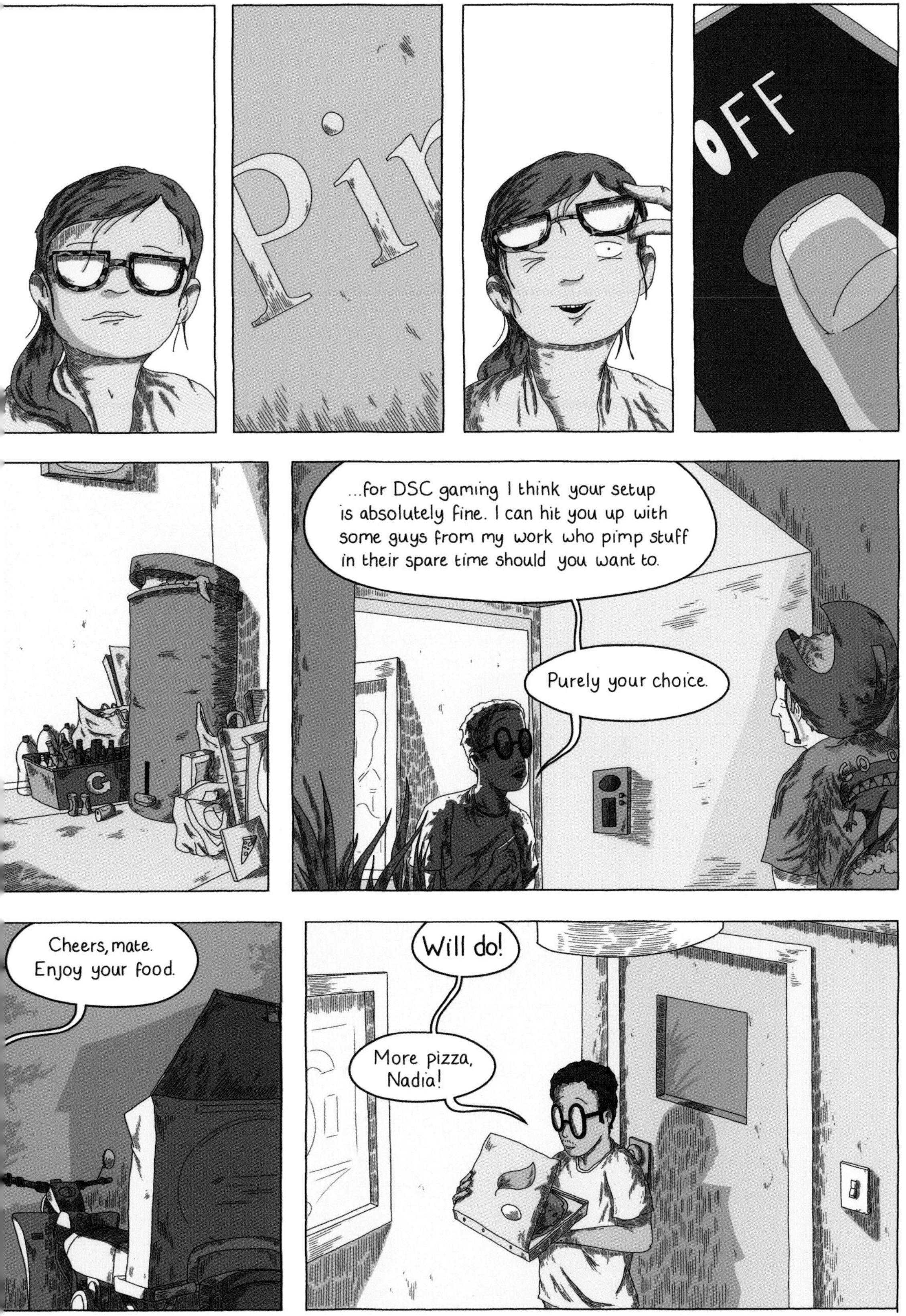
Pi
OFF
...for DSC gaming I think your setup is absolutely fine. I can hit you up with some guys from my work who pimp stuff in their spare time should you want to.
Purely your choice.
Cheers, mate. Enjoy your food.
Will do!
More pizza, Nadia!

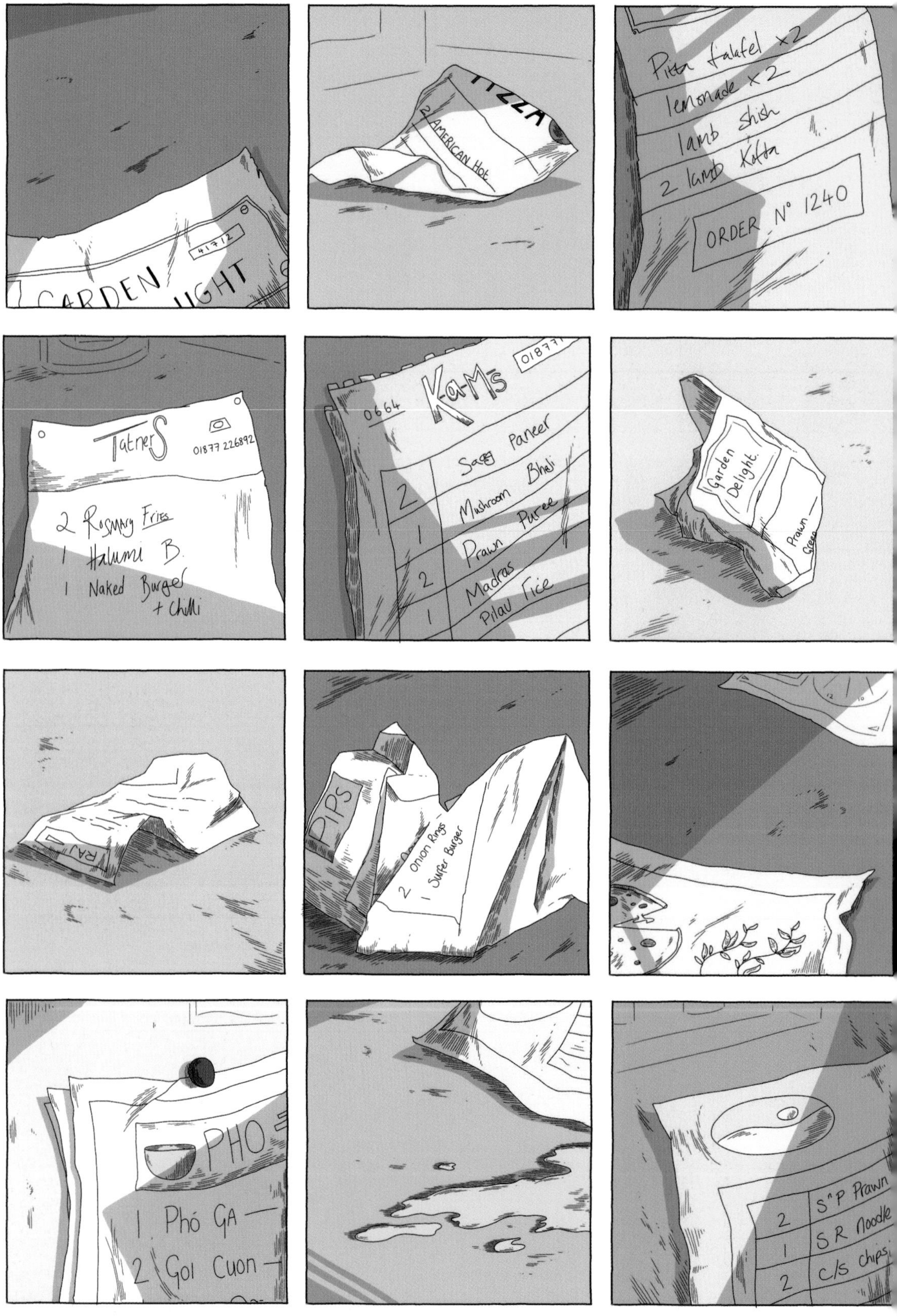

41712
GARDEN
IGHT
2 AMERICAN Hot
Pitta falafel x2
lemonade x2
lamb shish
2 lamb Kofta
ORDER N° 1240
Tatners
01877 226892
2 Rosmary Fries
1 Halumi B.
1 Naked Burger + Chilli
0664
Ka-M's
01877
2 Sagg Paneer
Mushroom Bhaji
1 Prawn Puree
2 Madras
1 Pilau rice
Garden Delight.
Prawn
Green
RAJ
DIPS
2 Onion Rings
1 Surfer Burger
PHO
1 Phó GA
2 Goi Cuon
2 S&P Prawn
1 S R Noodle
2 C/S Chips

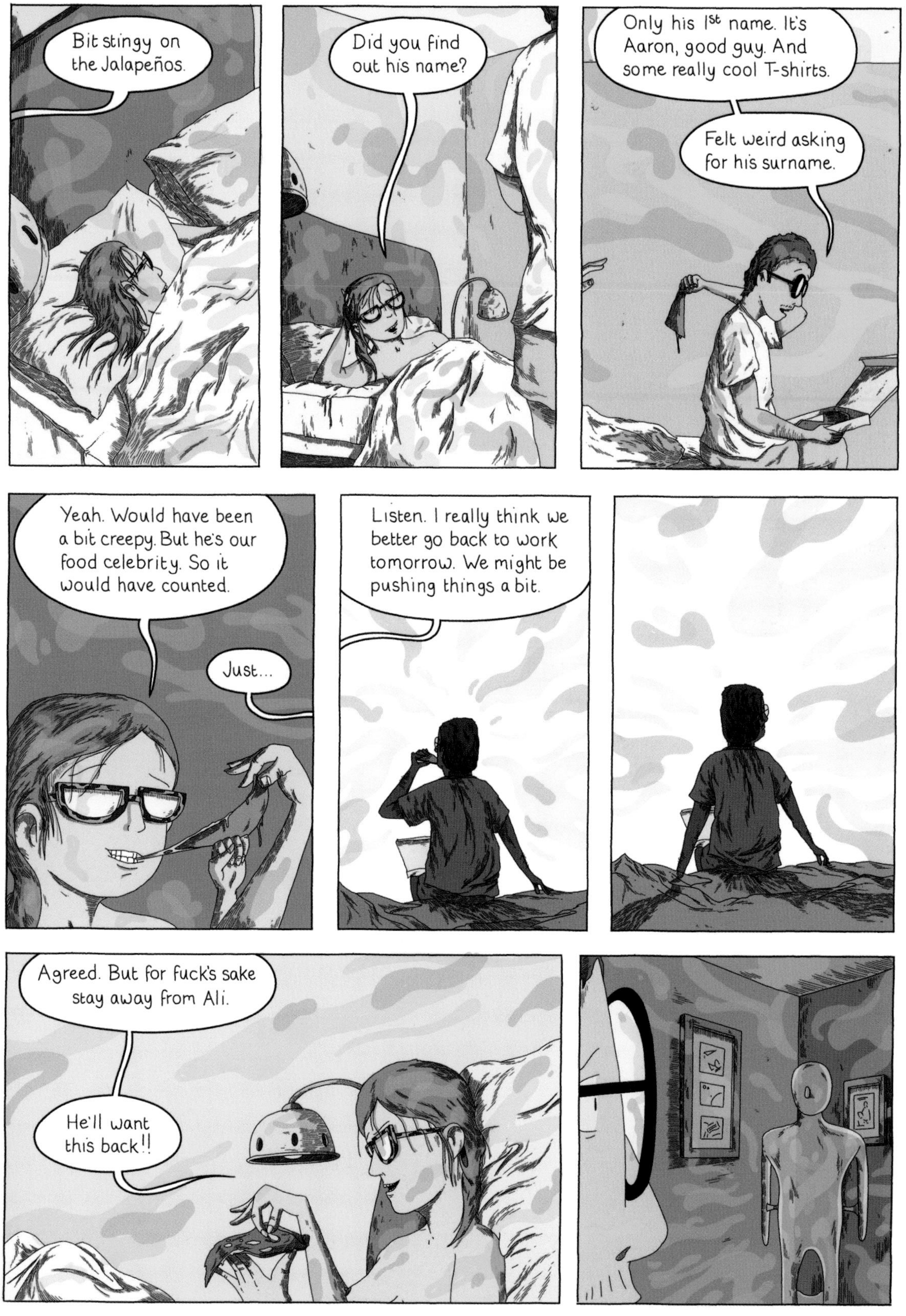
Bit stingy on the Jalapeños.
Did you find out his name?
Only his 1st name. It's Aaron, good guy. And some really cool T-shirts.
Felt weird asking for his surname.
Yeah. Would have been a bit creepy. But he's our food celebrity. So it would have counted.
Just...
Listen. I really think we better go back to work tomorrow. We might be pushing things a bit.
Agreed. But for fuck's sake stay away from Ali.
He'll want this back!!

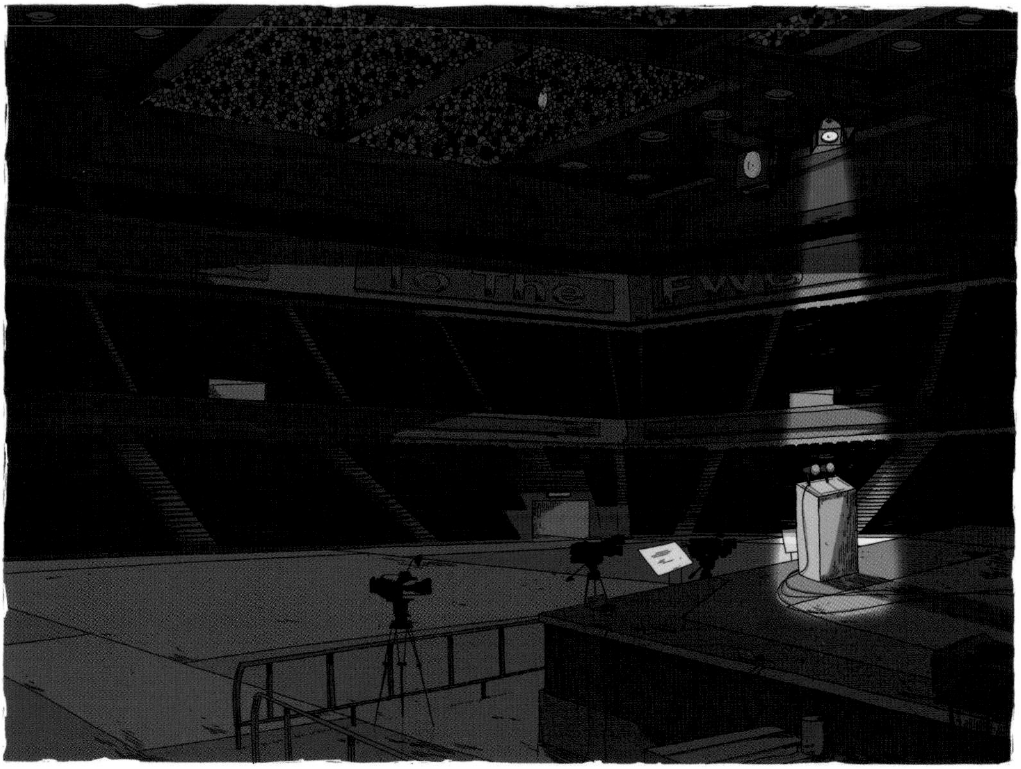
To The

6 days to election.

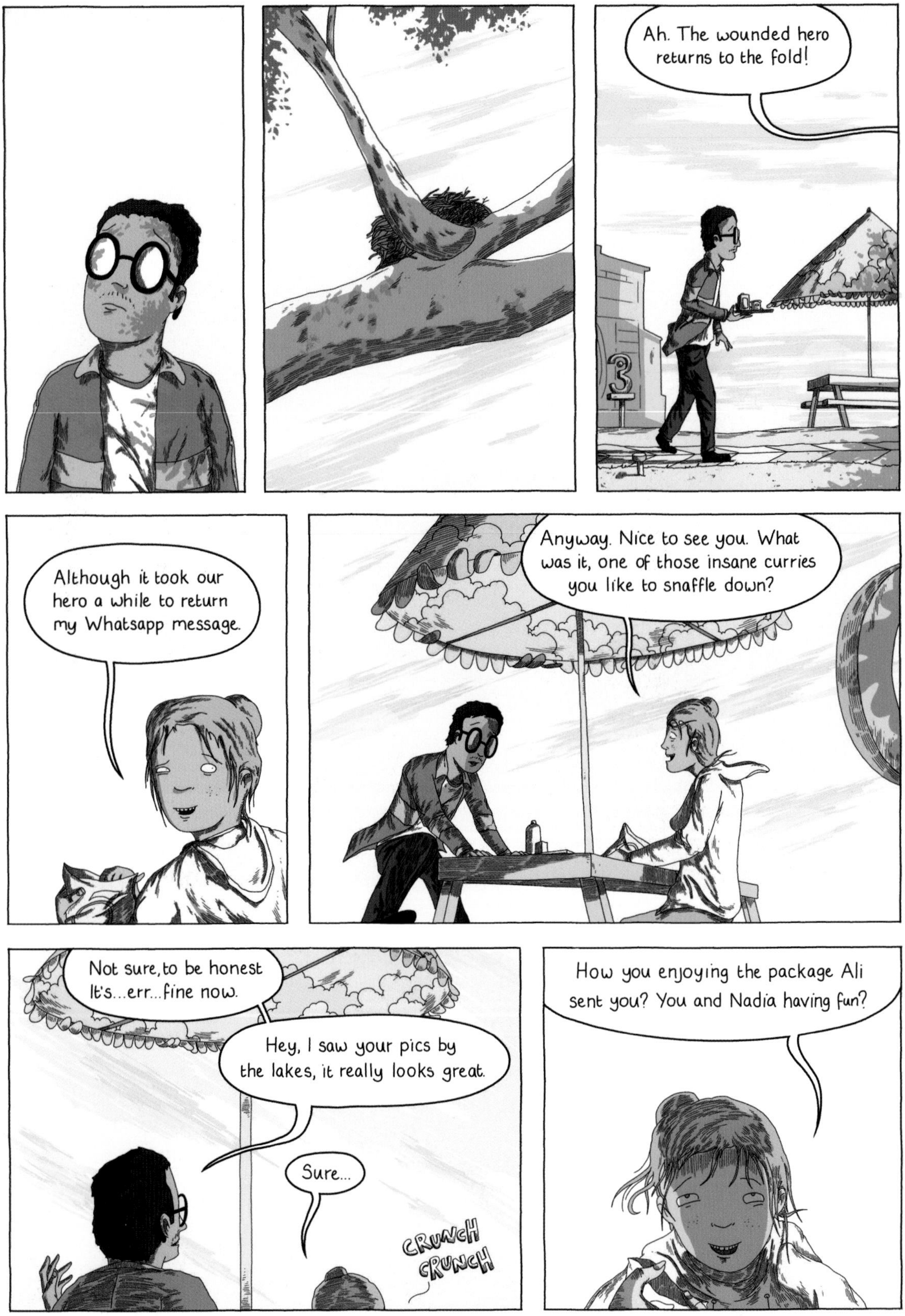
Ah. The wounded hero returns to the fold!
Although it took our hero a while to return my Whatsapp message.
Anyway. Nice to see you. What was it, one of those insane curries you like to snaffle down?
Not sure, to be honest It's...err...fine now.
Hey, I saw your pics by the lakes, it really looks great.
Sure...
CRUNCH CRUNCH
How you enjoying the package Ali sent you? You and Nadia having fun?

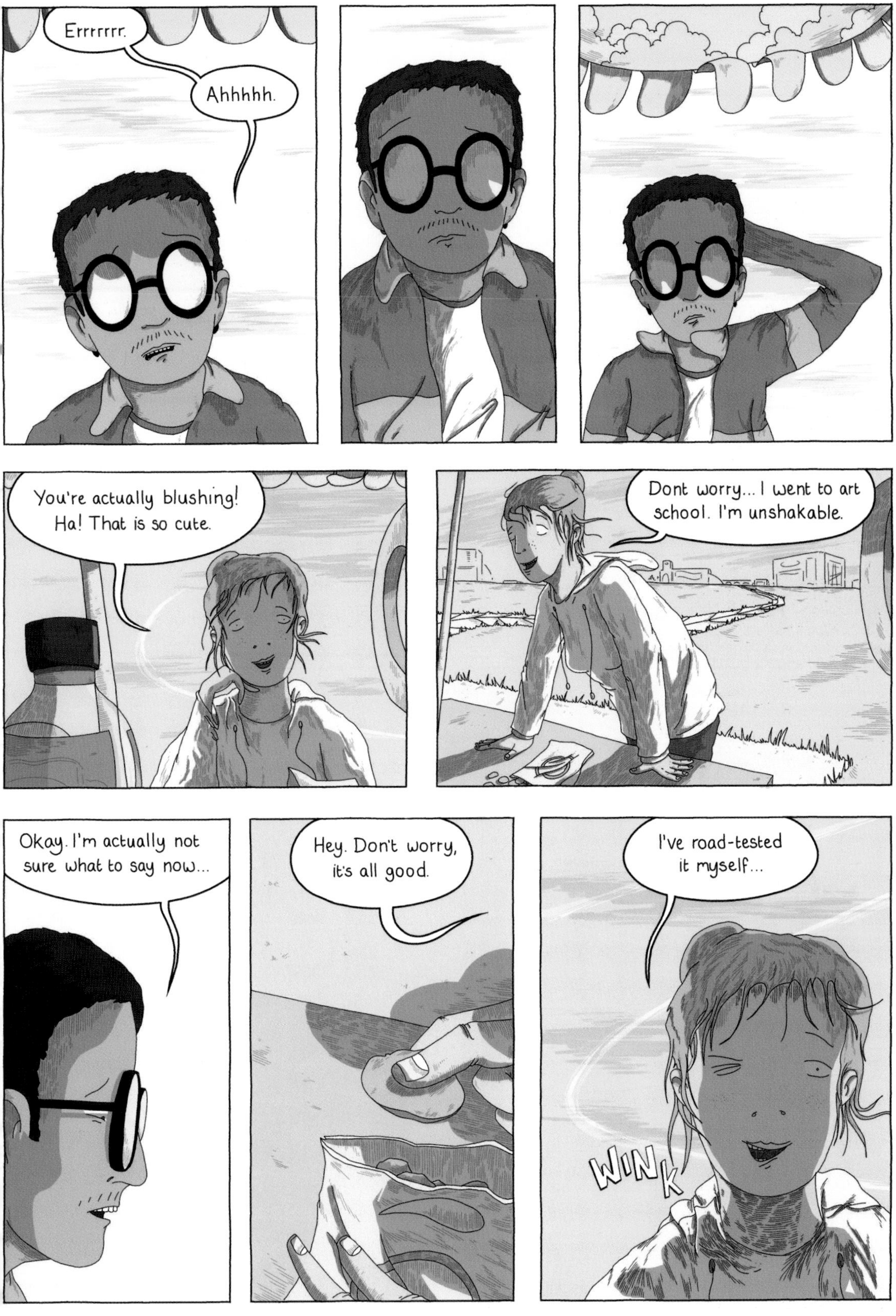
Errrrrrr.
Ahhhhh.
You're actually blushing! Ha! That is so cute.
Dont worry... I went to art school. I'm unshakable.
Okay. I'm actually not sure what to say now...
Hey. Don't worry, it's all good.
I've road-tested it myself...
WINK

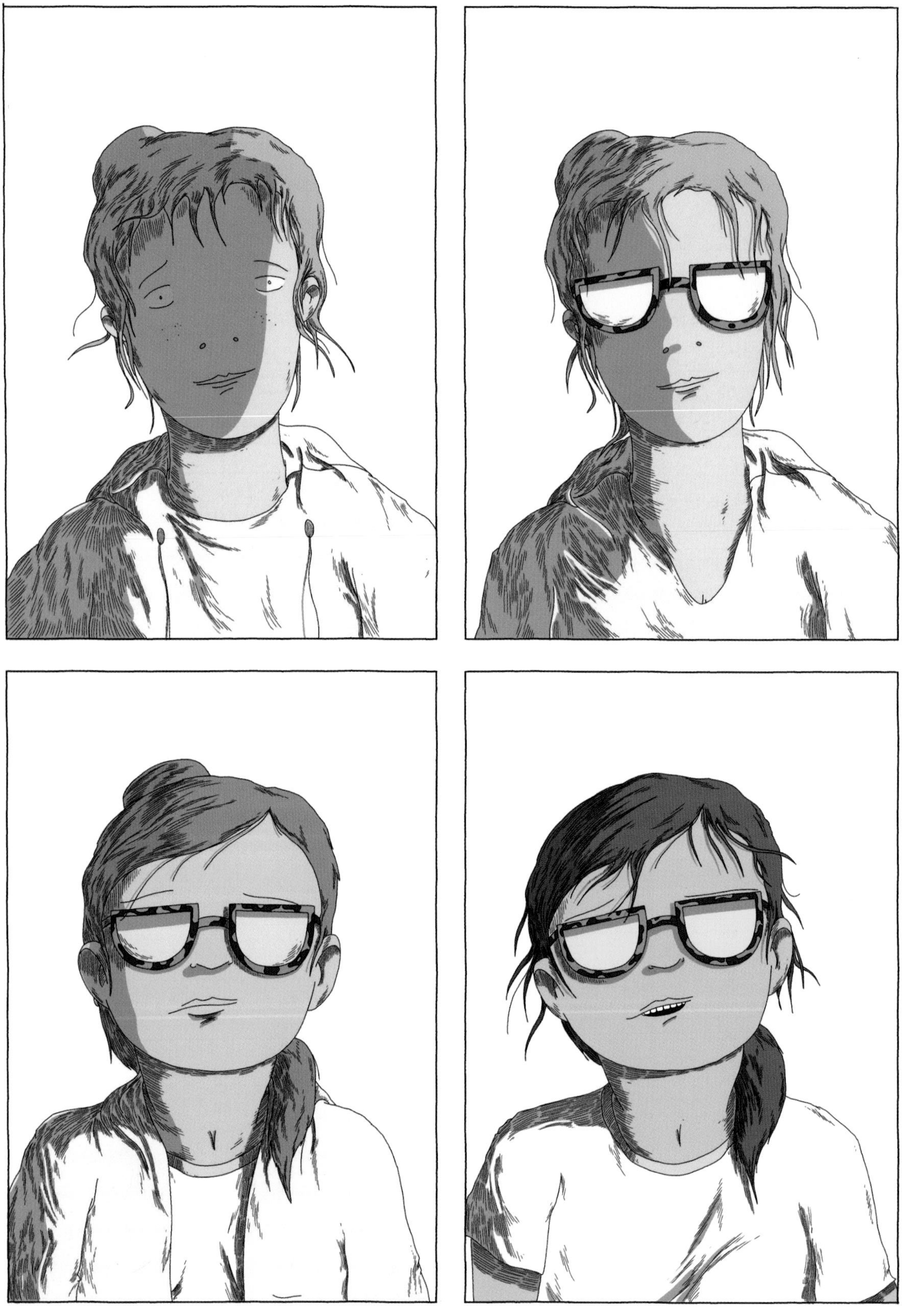

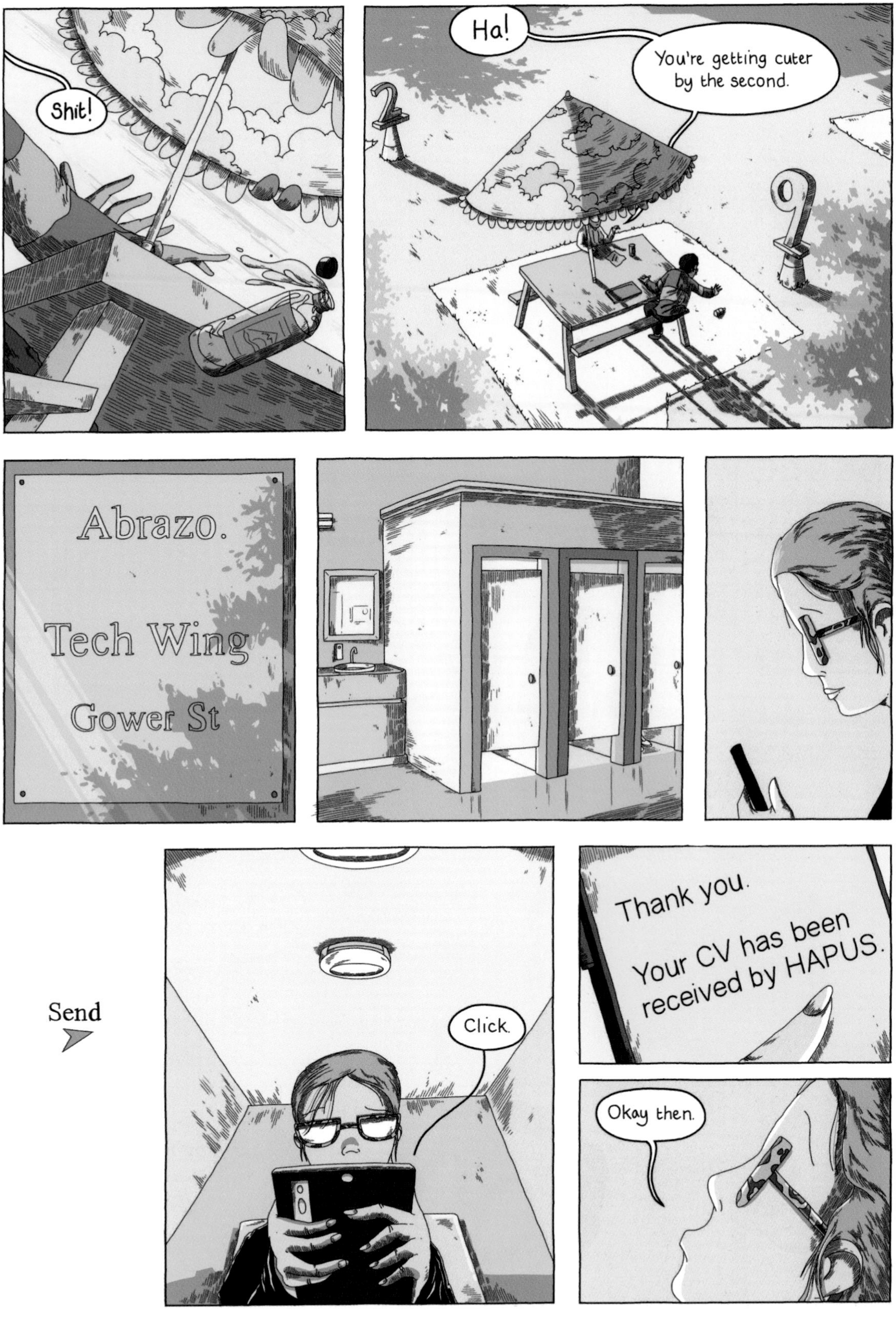
Shit!
Ha!
You're getting cuter by the second.
2
9
Abrazo.
Tech Wing
Gower St
Send
Click.
Thank you.
Your CV has been received by HAPUS.
Okay then.

You...

home...

...Nadia?

Oh. Shit.

Google — Images

Piper

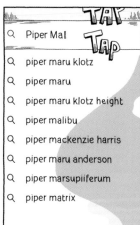

TAP TAP

Q Piper Mall
Q piper maru klotz
Q piper maru
Q piper maru klotz height
Q piper malibu
Q piper mackenzie harris
Q piper maru anderson
Q piper marsupiiferum
Q piper matrix

I can't. I mean, I want to. But it's not fair. I promised.

Hello?

Huck?

Heh.

I'm in here!

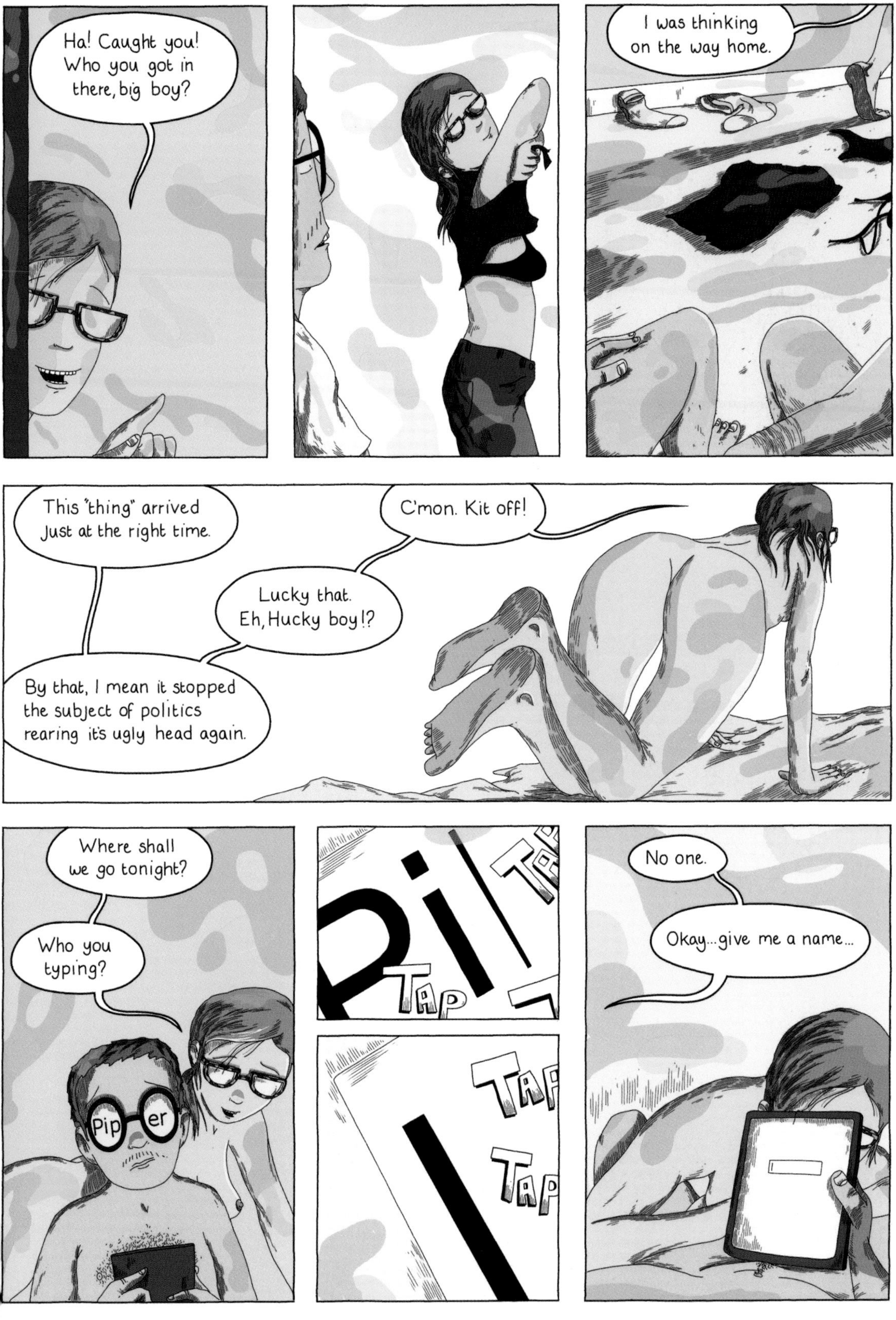
Ha! Caught you! Who you got in there, big boy?
I was thinking on the way home.
This "thing" arrived Just at the right time.
By that, I mean it stopped the subject of politics rearing it's ugly head again.
Lucky that. Eh, Hucky boy!?
C'mon. Kit off!
Where shall we go tonight?
Who you typing?
Pip er
Pi
TAP
TAP
TAP
TAP
No one.
Okay...give me a name...

Welcome
To The
FWB
Arena

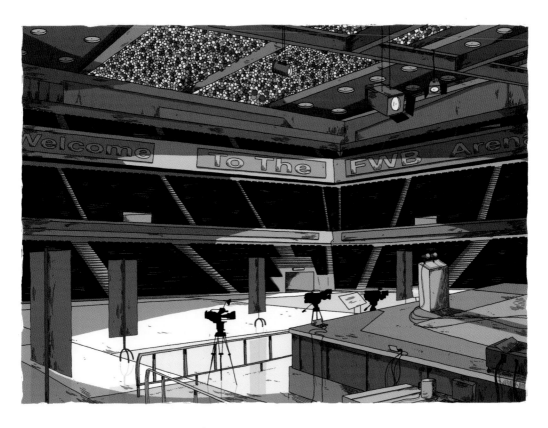

5 days to election.

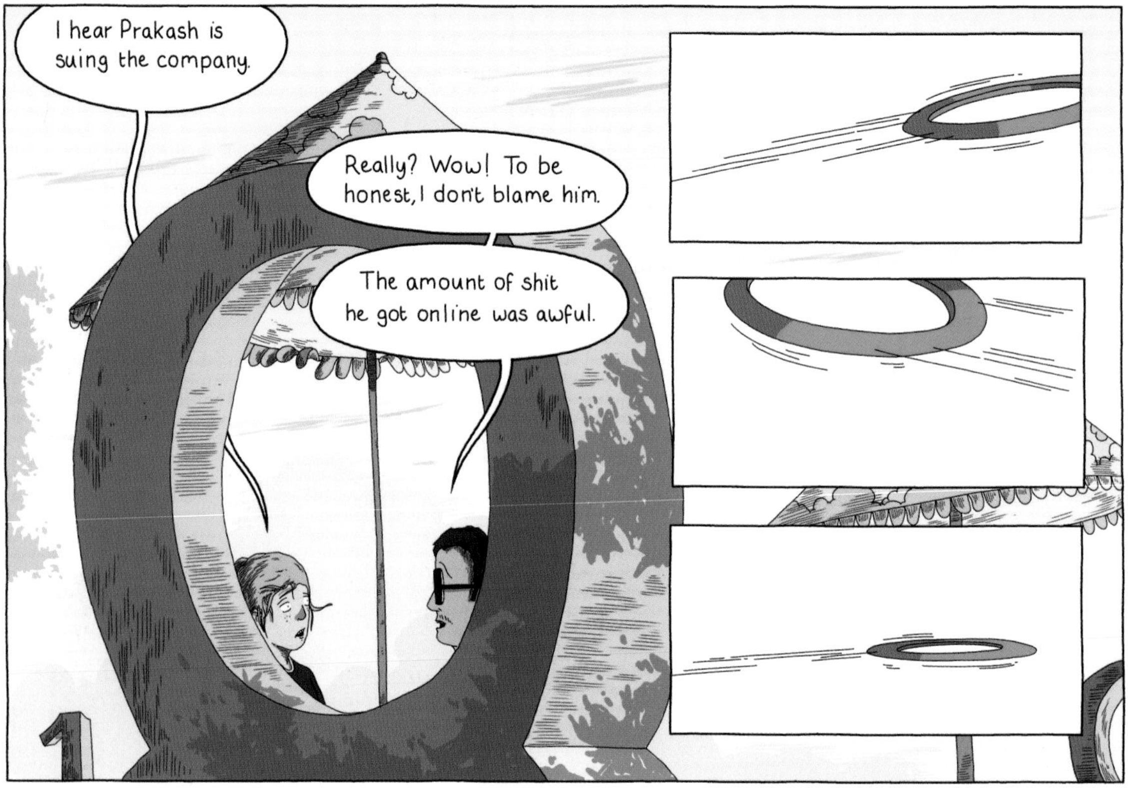
I hear Prakash is suing the company.
Really? Wow! To be honest, I don't blame him.
The amount of shit he got online was awful.

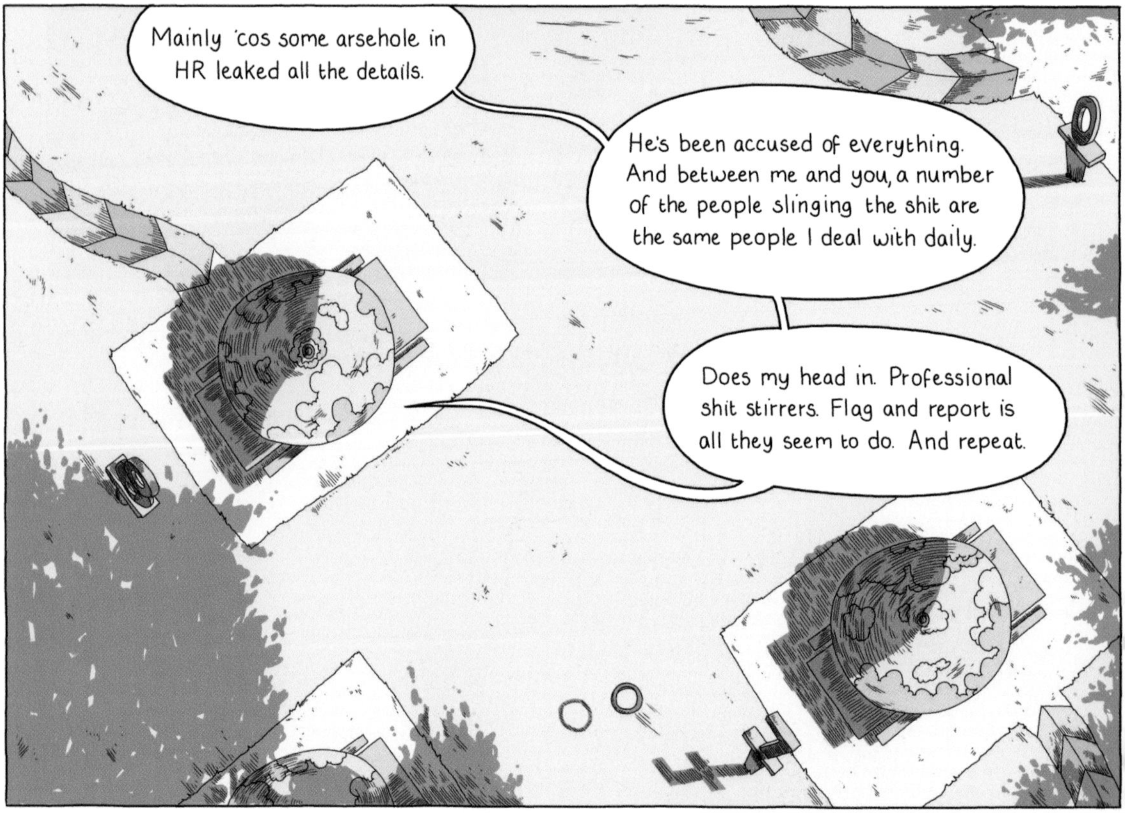
Mainly 'cos some arsehole in HR leaked all the details.
He's been accused of everything. And between me and you, a number of the people slinging the shit are the same people I deal with daily.
Does my head in. Professional shit stirrers. Flag and report is all they seem to do. And repeat.

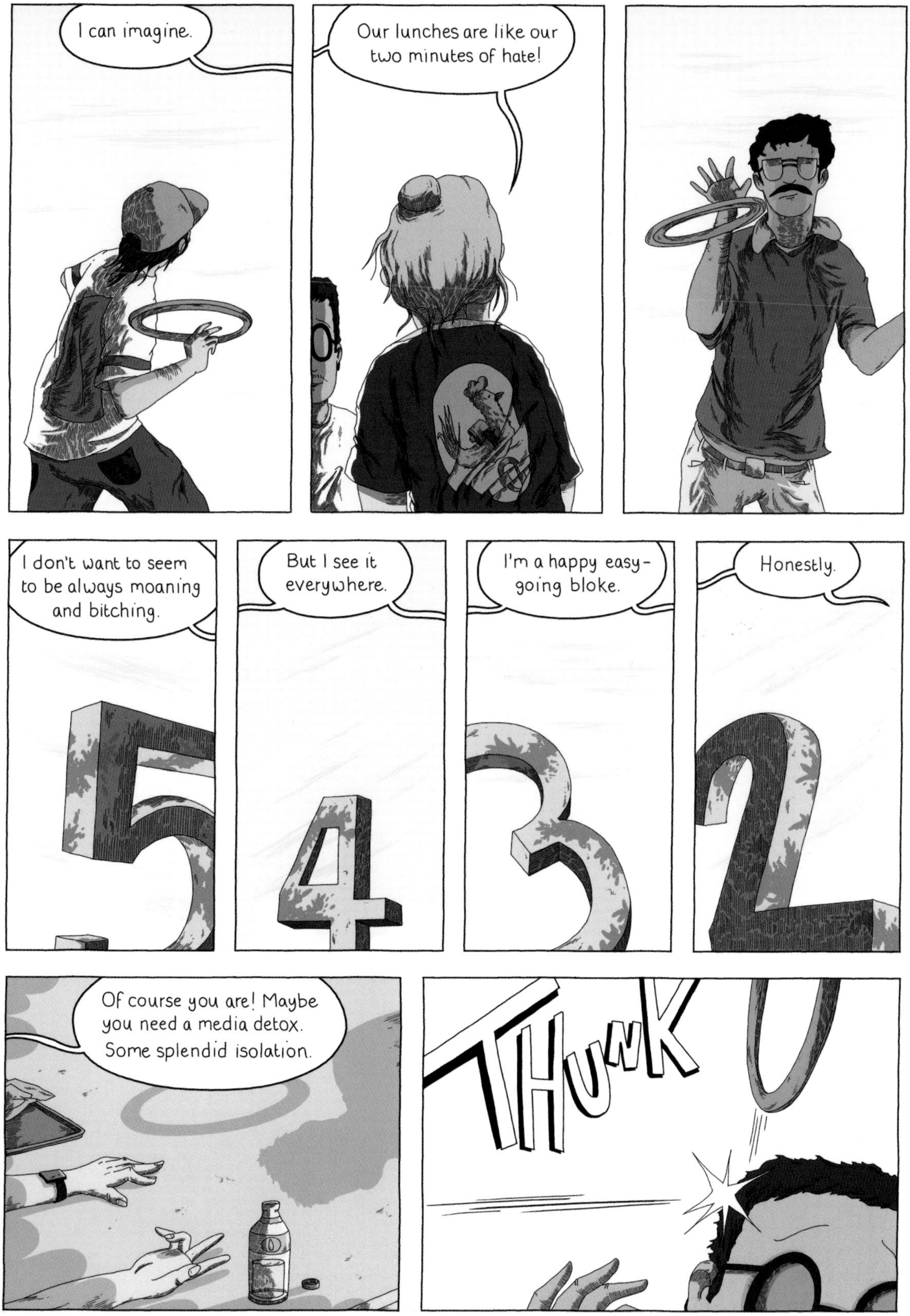
I can imagine.
Our lunches are like our two minutes of hate!
I don't want to seem to be always moaning and bitching.
But I see it everywhere.
I'm a happy easy-going bloke.
Honestly.
5
4
3
2
Of course you are! Maybe you need a media detox. Some splendid isolation.
THUNK

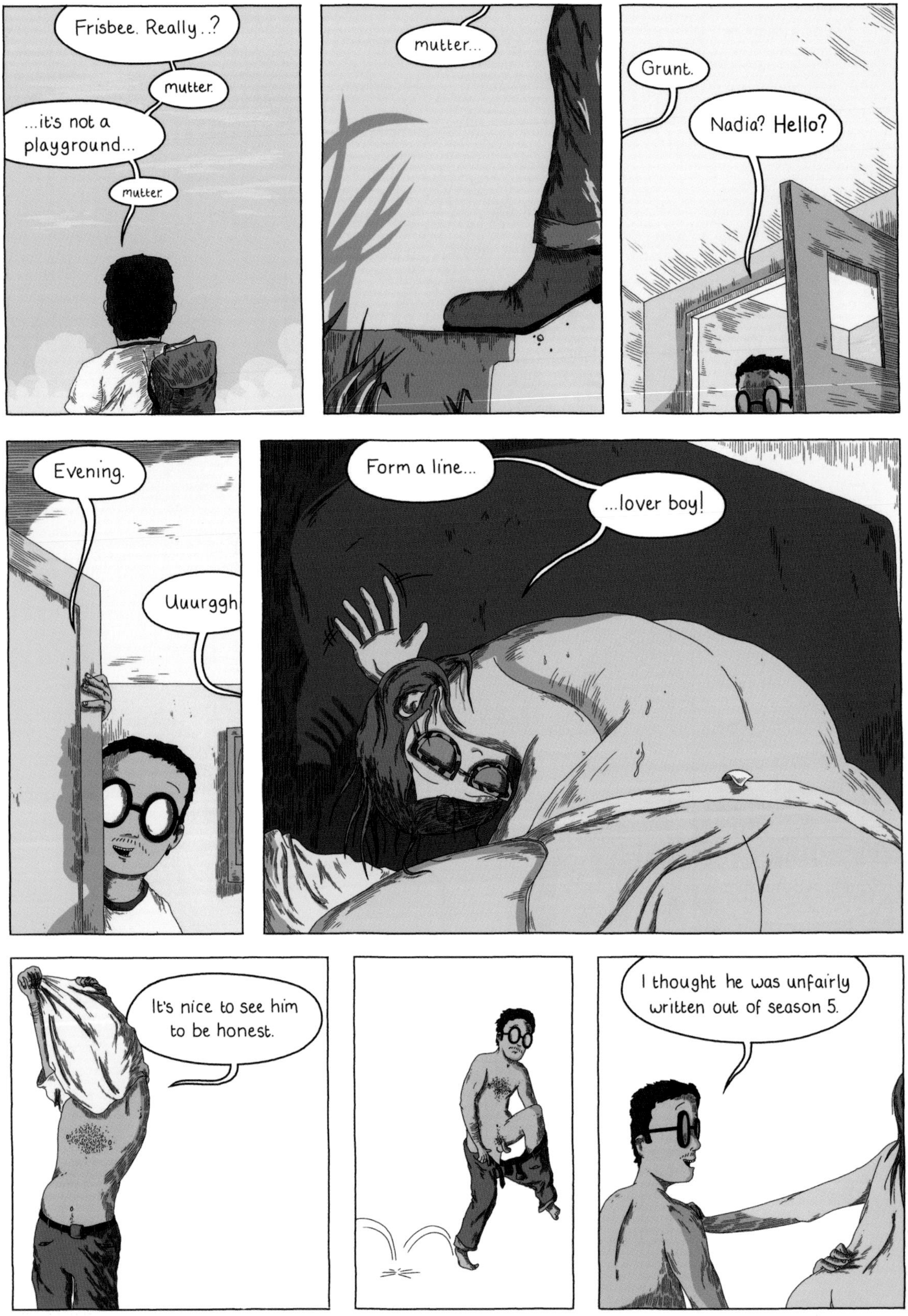
Frisbee. Really..?
mutter.
...it's not a playground...
mutter.
mutter...
Grunt.
Nadia? Hello?
Evening.
Uuurggh
Form a line...
...lover boy!
It's nice to see him to be honest.
I thought he was unfairly written out of season 5.

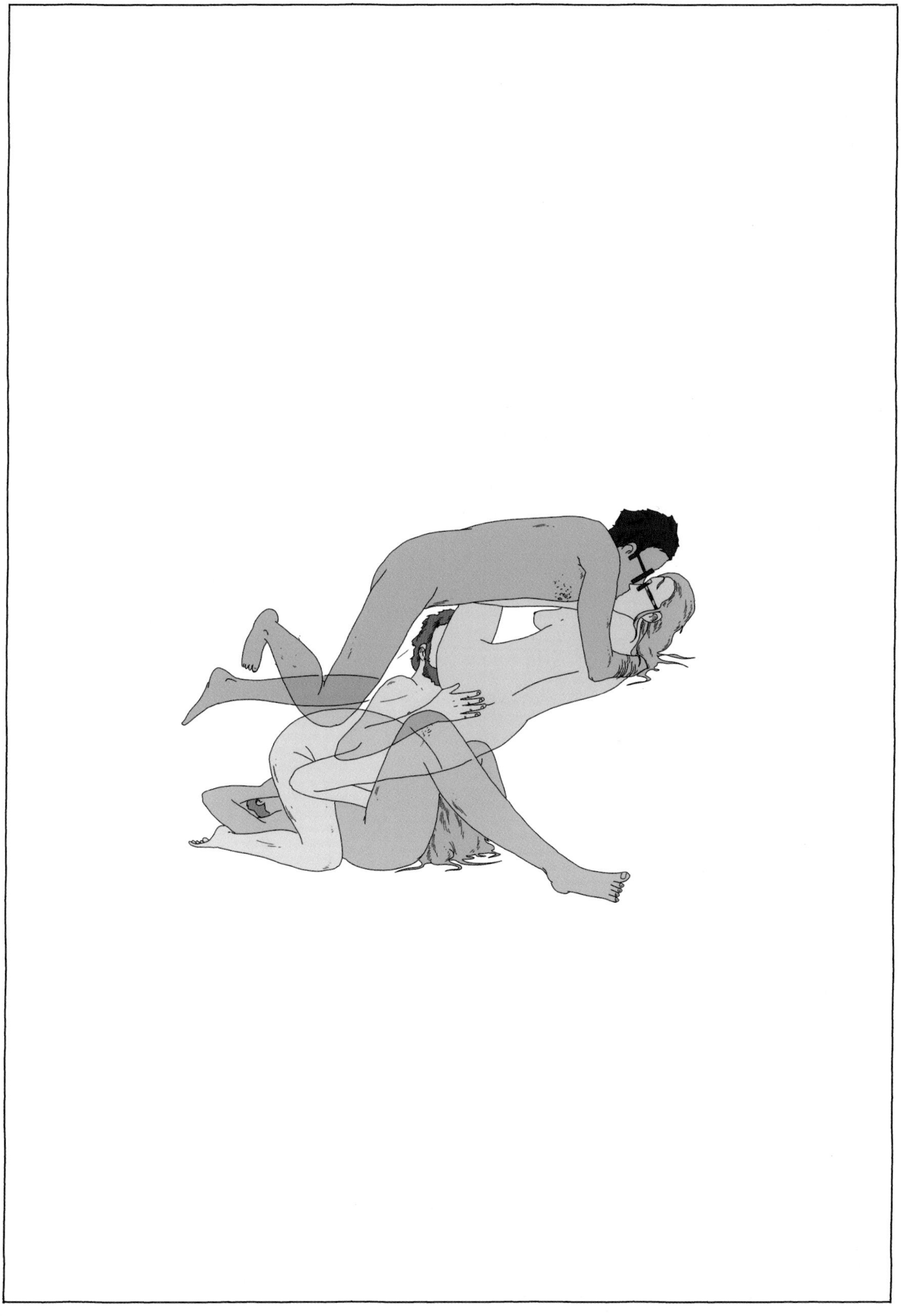

Welcome
To The
FWB
Arena

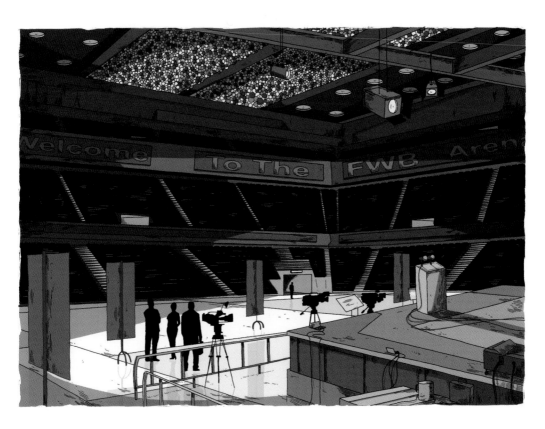

4 days to election.

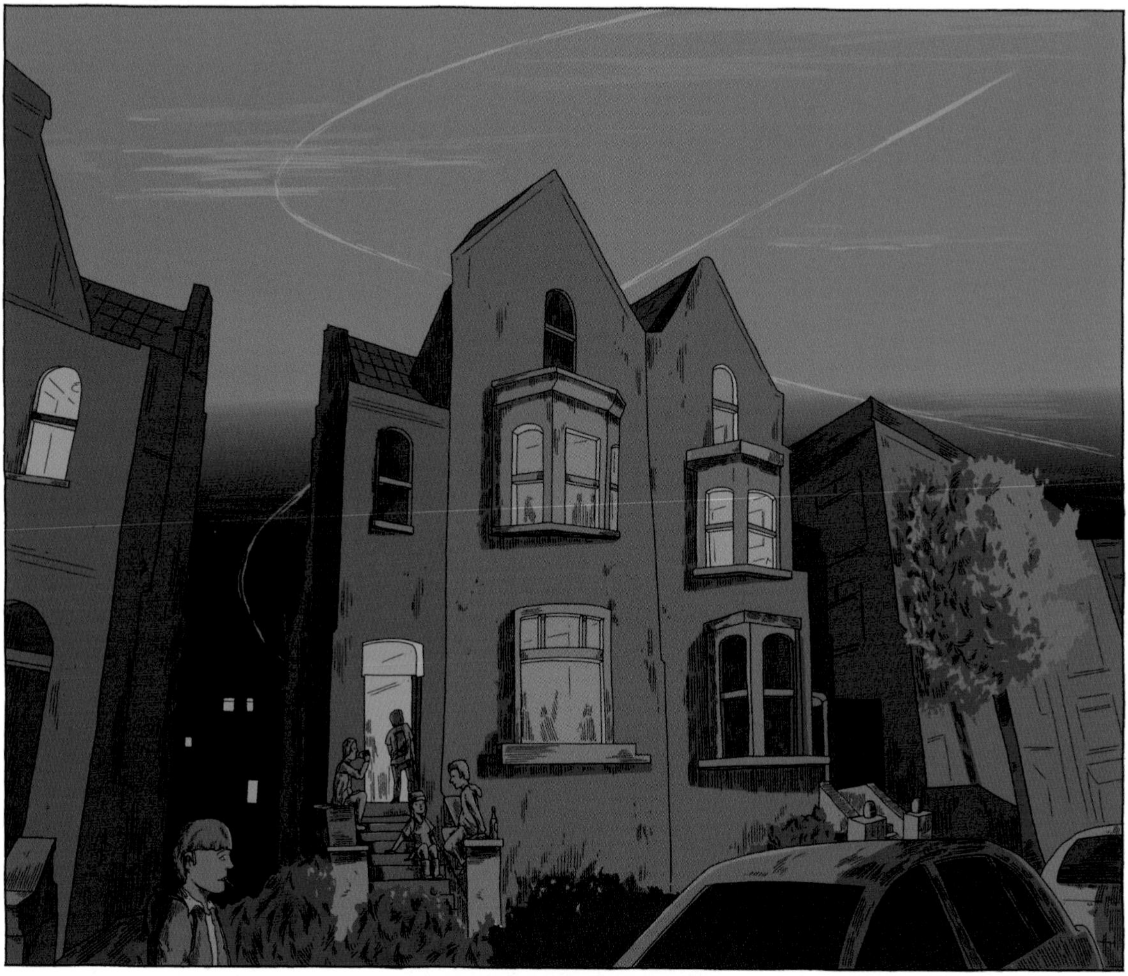

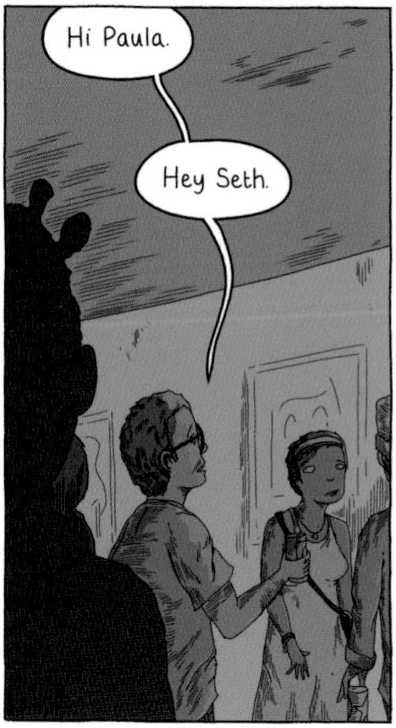
Hi Paula.
Hey Seth.

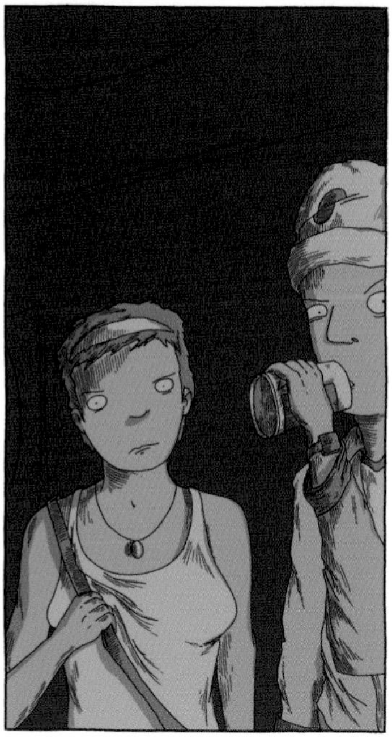

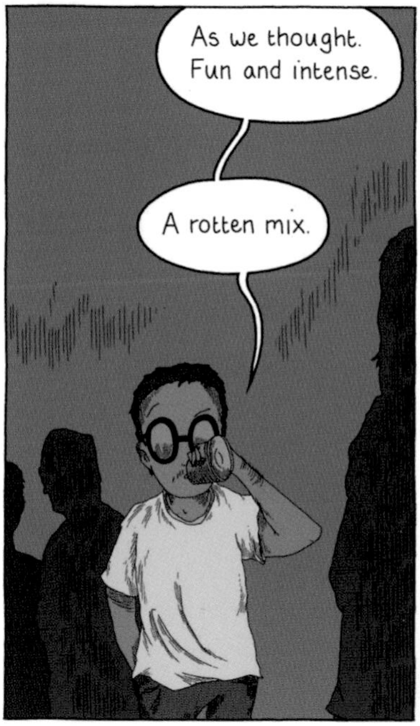
As we thought. Fun and intense.
A rotten mix.

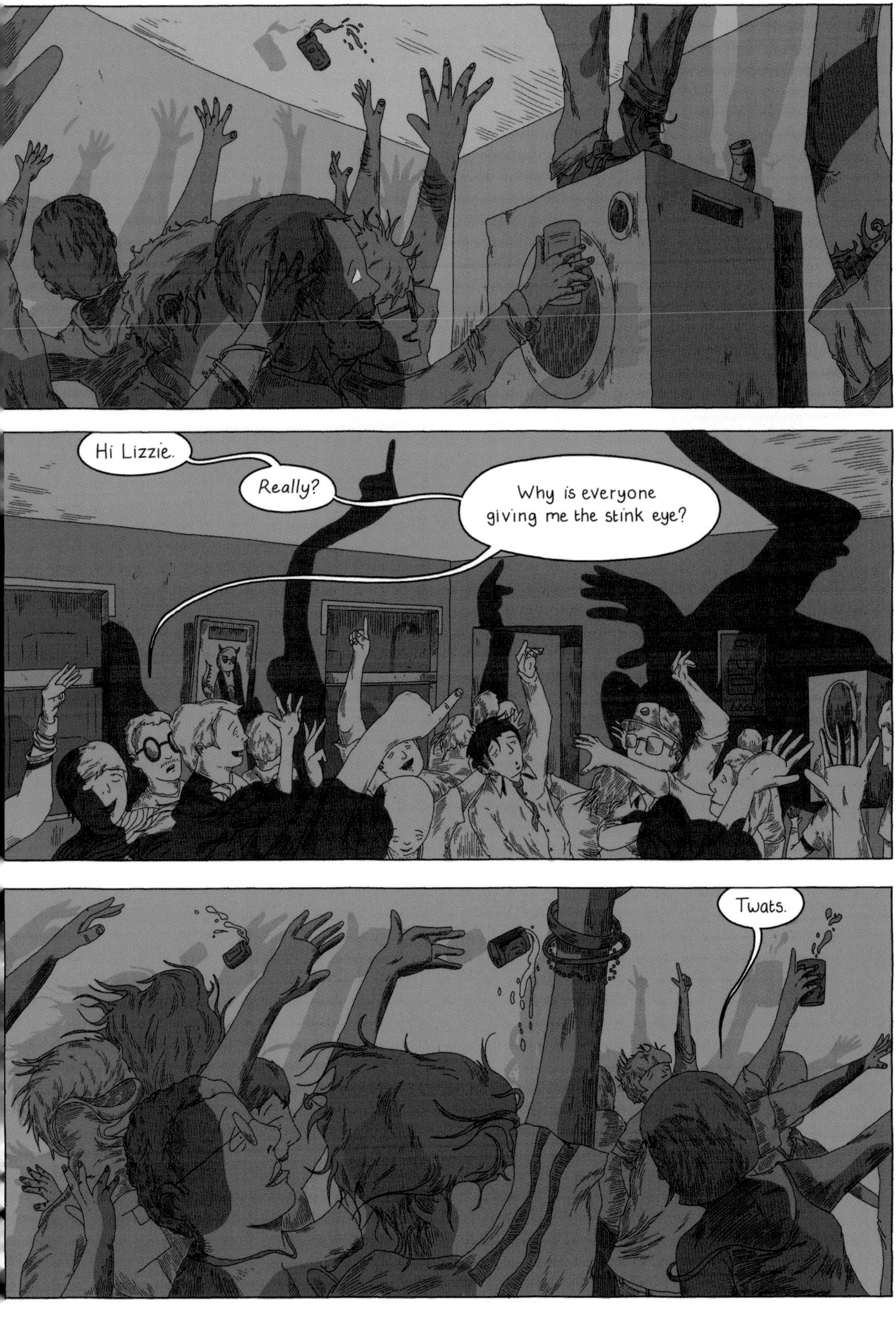
Hi Lizzie.
Really?
Why is everyone giving me the stink eye?
Twats.

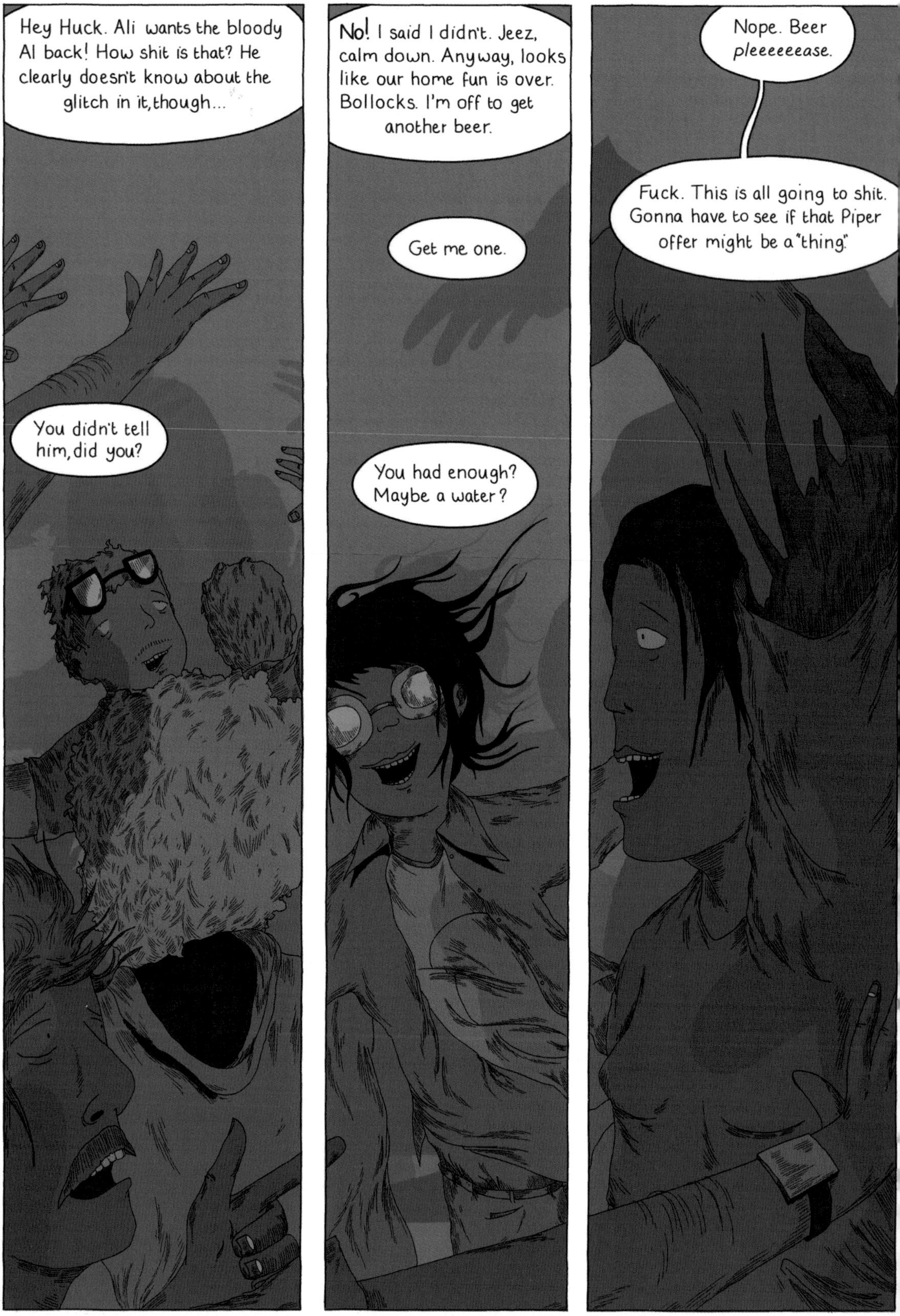
Hey Huck. Ali wants the bloody AI back! How shit is that? He clearly doesn't know about the glitch in it, though...
You didn't tell him, did you?
No! I said I didn't. Jeez, calm down. Anyway, looks like our home fun is over. Bollocks. I'm off to get another beer.
Get me one.
You had enough? Maybe a water?
Nope. Beer *pleeeeeease.*
Fuck. This is all going to shit. Gonna have to see if that Piper offer might be a "thing."

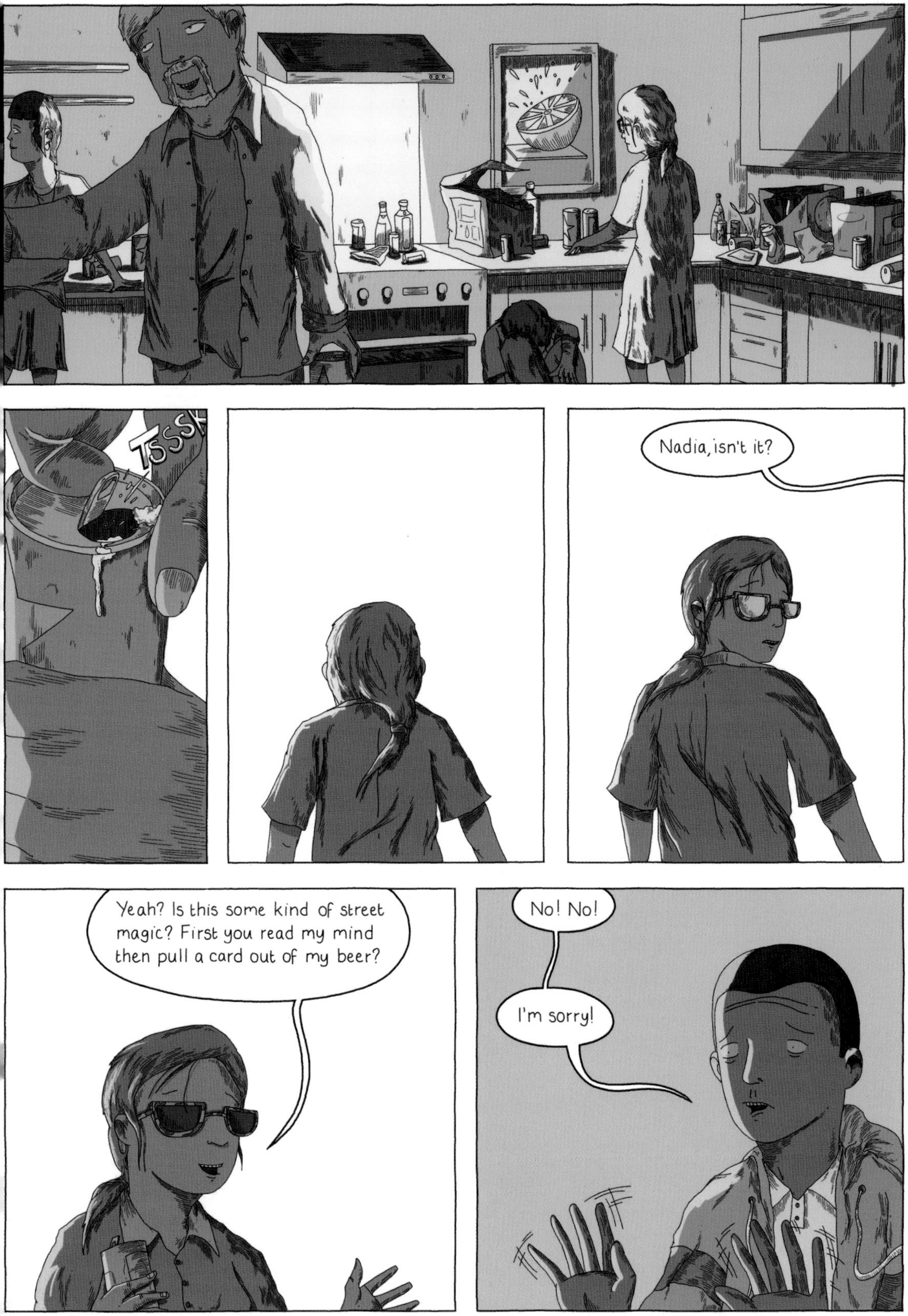
TSSSK
Nadia, isn't it?
Yeah? Is this some kind of street magic? First you read my mind then pull a card out of my beer?
No! No!
I'm sorry!

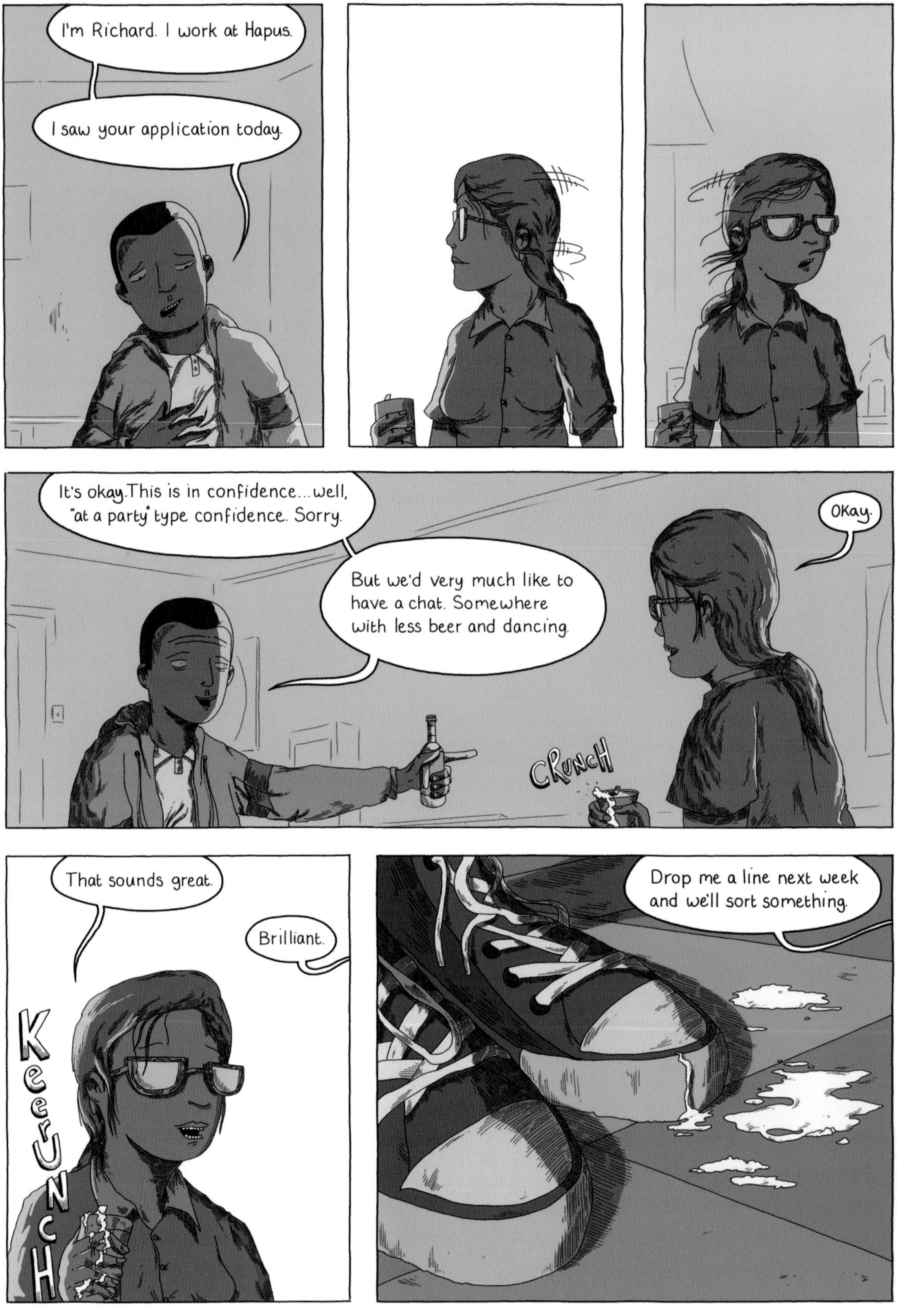
I'm Richard. I work at Hapus.
I saw your application today.
It's okay. This is in confidence... well, "at a party" type confidence. Sorry.
But we'd very much like to have a chat. Somewhere with less beer and dancing.
Okay.
CRUNCH
That sounds great.
Brilliant.
KeeRUNCH
Drop me a line next week and we'll sort something.

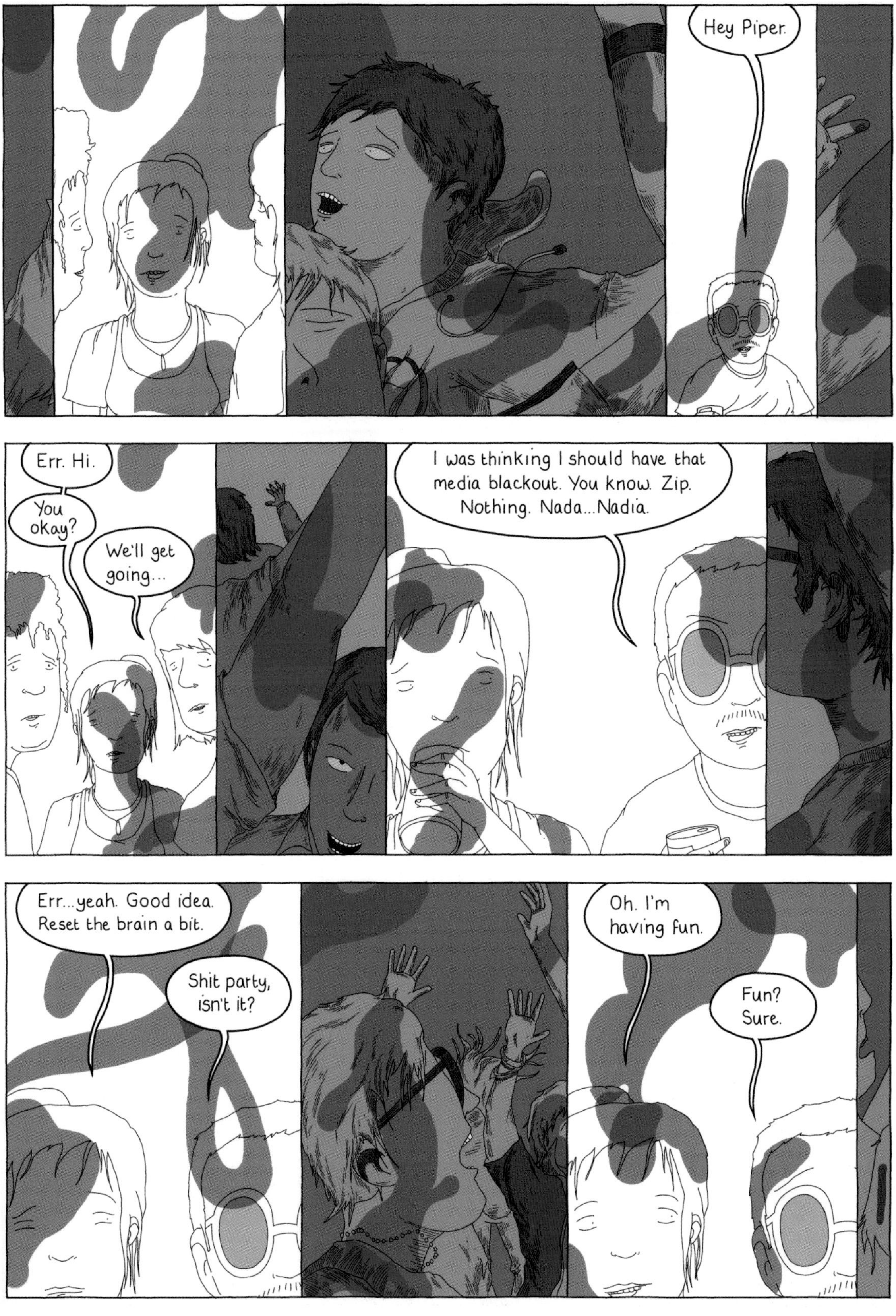
Hey Piper.
Err. Hi.
You okay?
We'll get going...
I was thinking I should have that media blackout. You know. Zip. Nothing. Nada...Nadia.
Err...yeah. Good idea. Reset the brain a bit.
Shit party, isn't it?
Oh. I'm having fun.
Fun? Sure.

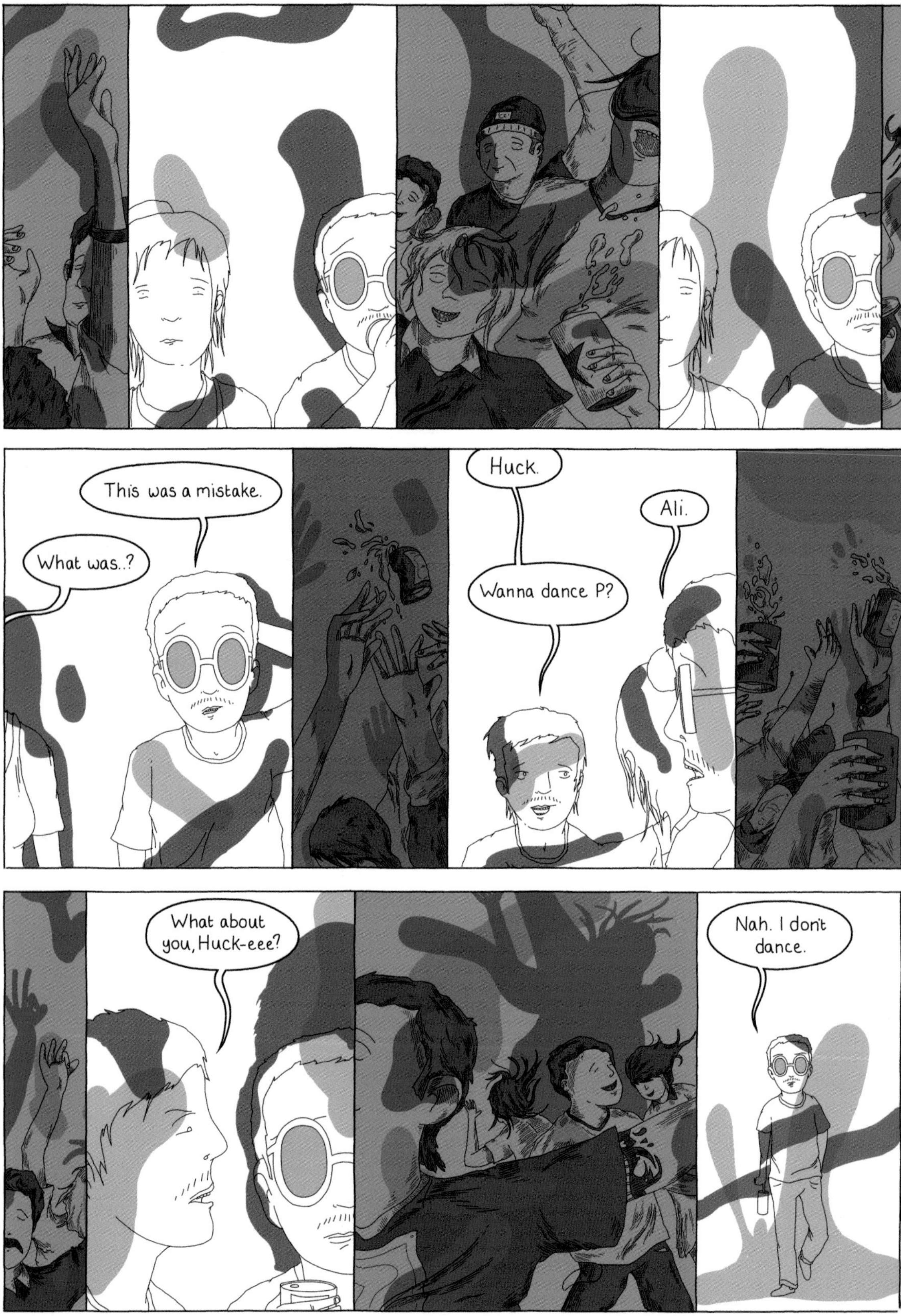
This was a mistake.
What was..?
Huck.
Ali.
Wanna dance P?
What about you, Huck-eee?
Nah. I don't dance.

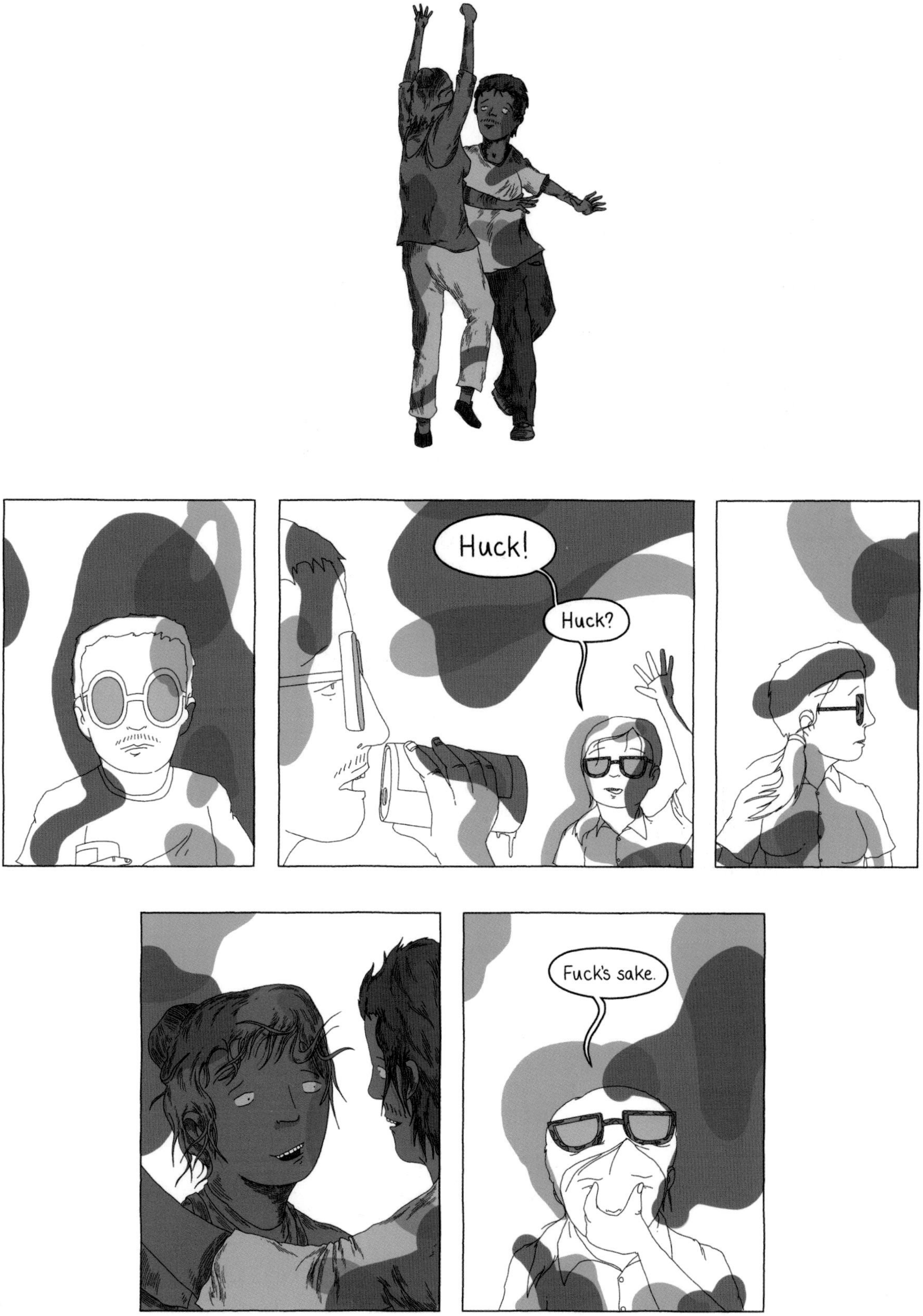
Huck!
Huck?
Fuck's sake.

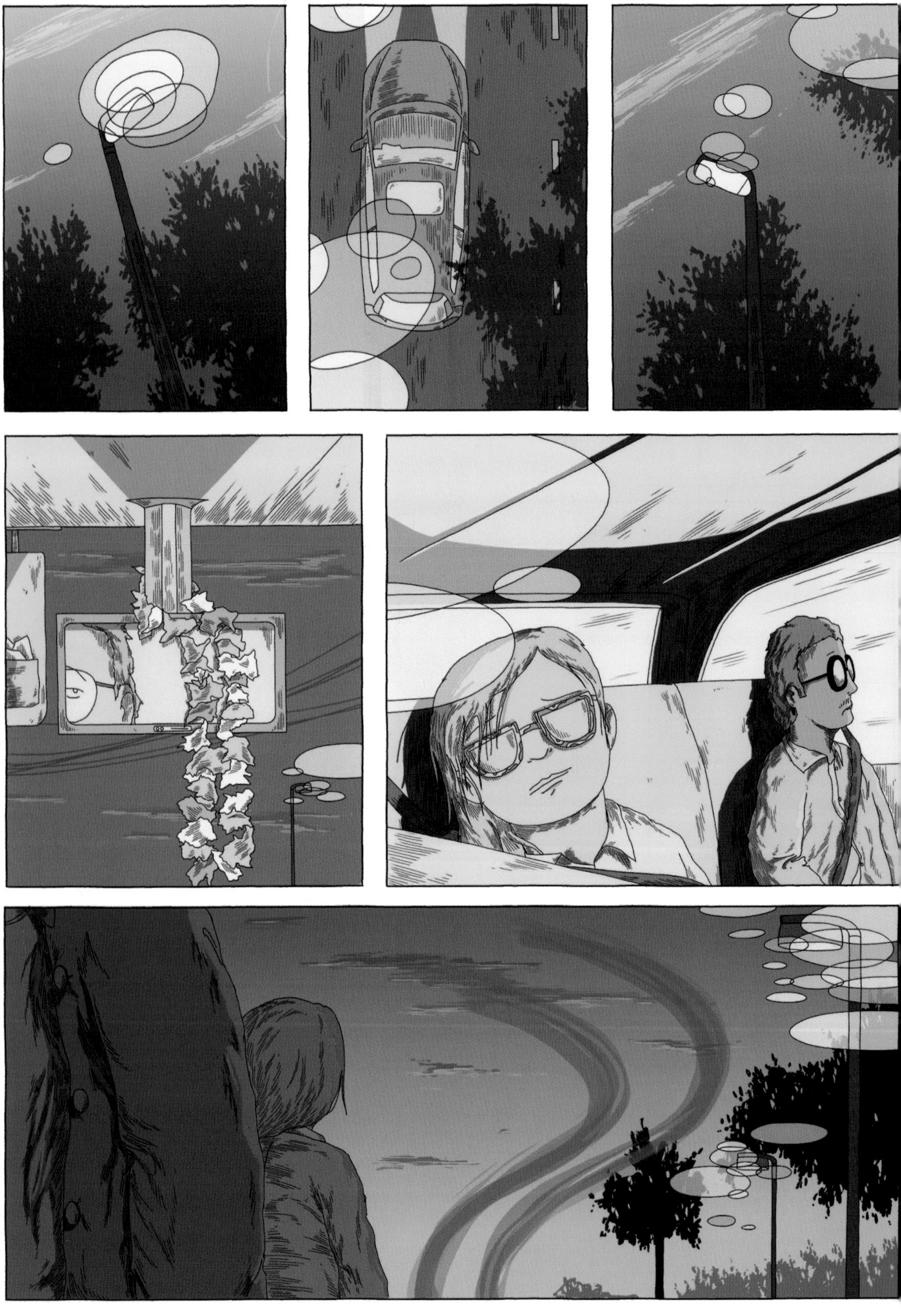

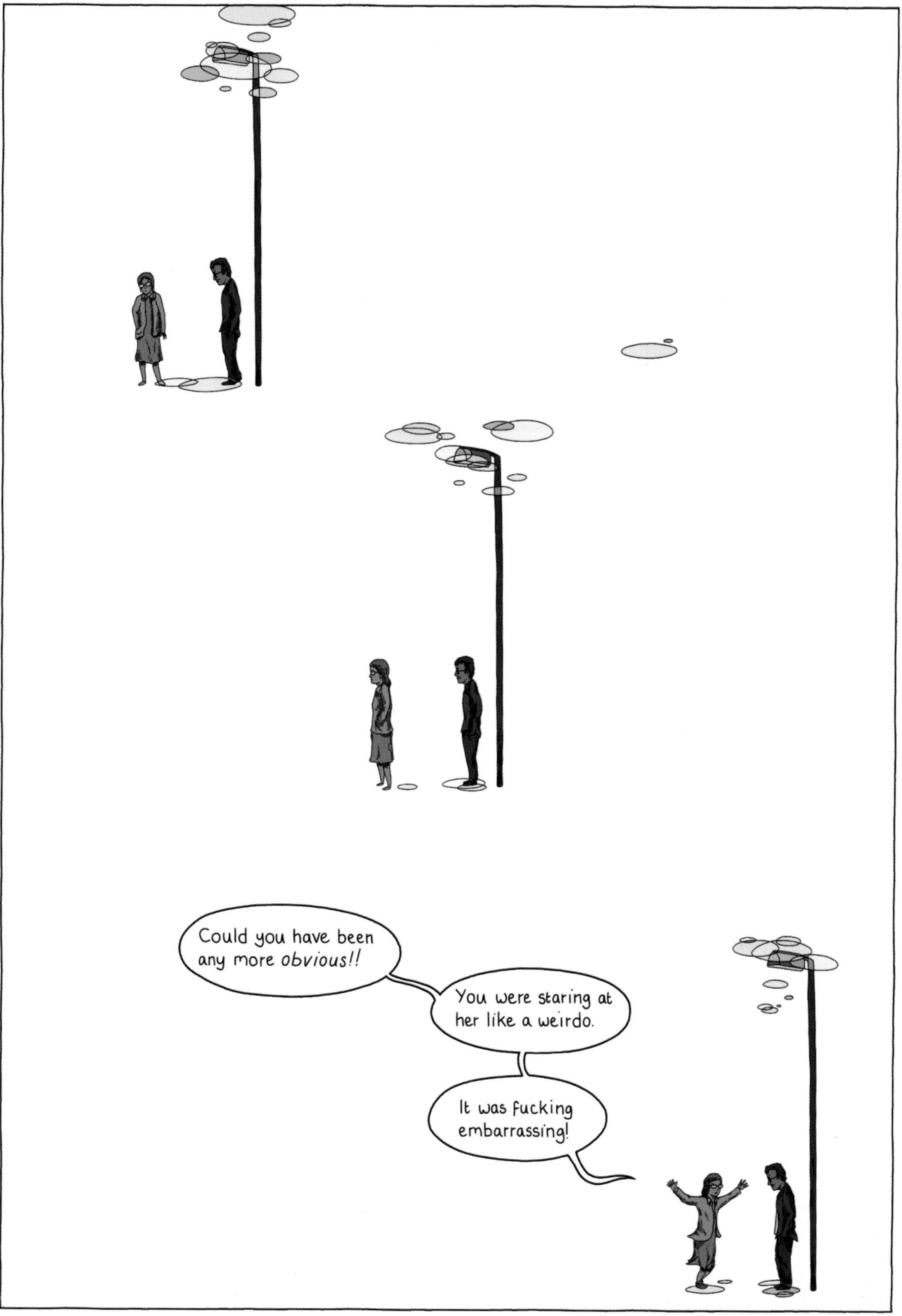
Could you have been any more *obvious!!*
You were staring at her like a weirdo.
It was fucking embarrassing!

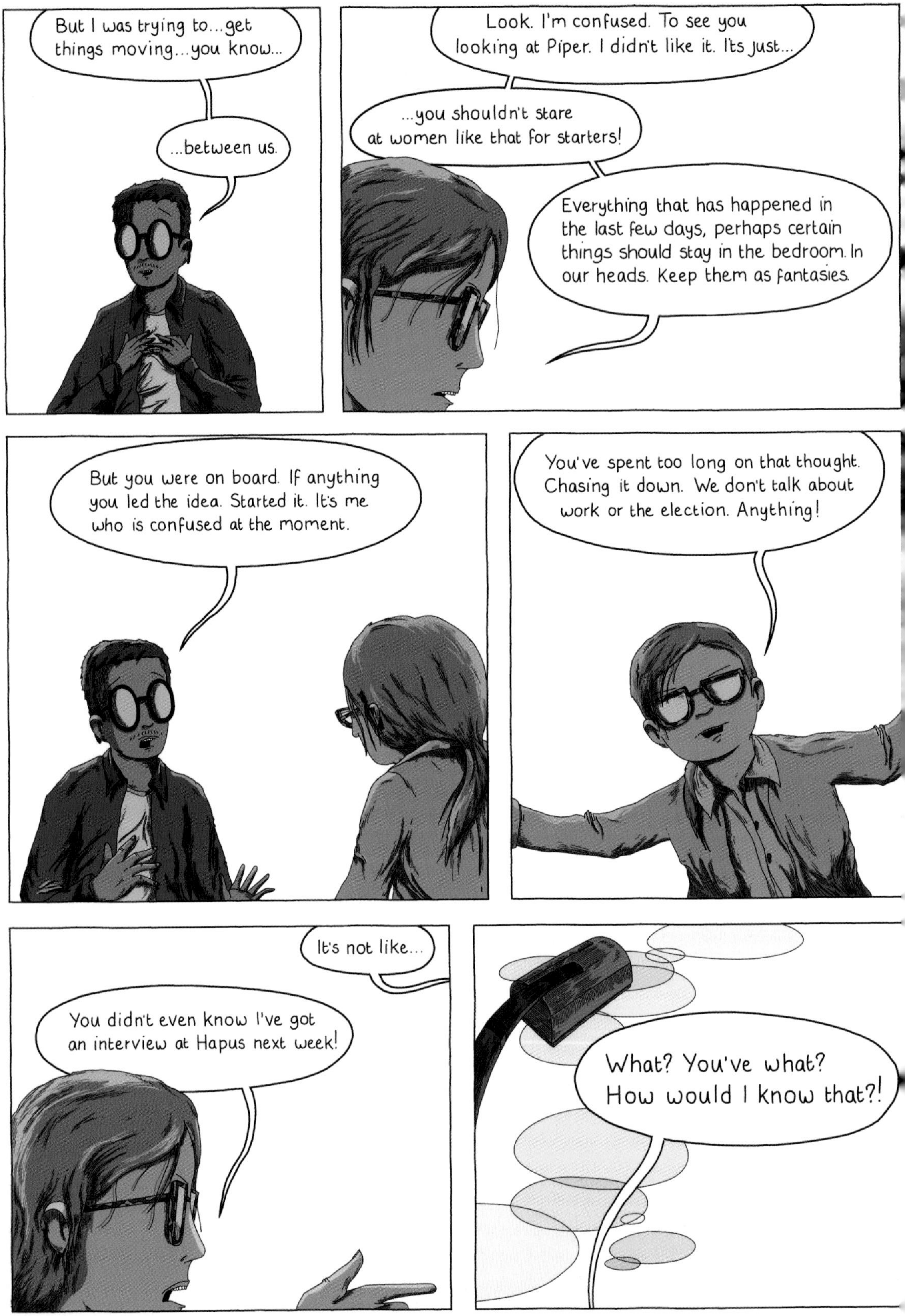
But I was trying to...get things moving...you know...
...between us.
Look. I'm confused. To see you looking at Piper. I didn't like it. It's just...
...you shouldn't stare at women like that for starters!
Everything that has happened in the last few days, perhaps certain things should stay in the bedroom. In our heads. Keep them as fantasies.
But you were on board. If anything you led the idea. Started it. It's me who is confused at the moment.
You've spent too long on that thought. Chasing it down. We don't talk about work or the election. Anything!
It's not like...
You didn't even know I've got an interview at Hapus next week!
What? You've what? How would I know that?!

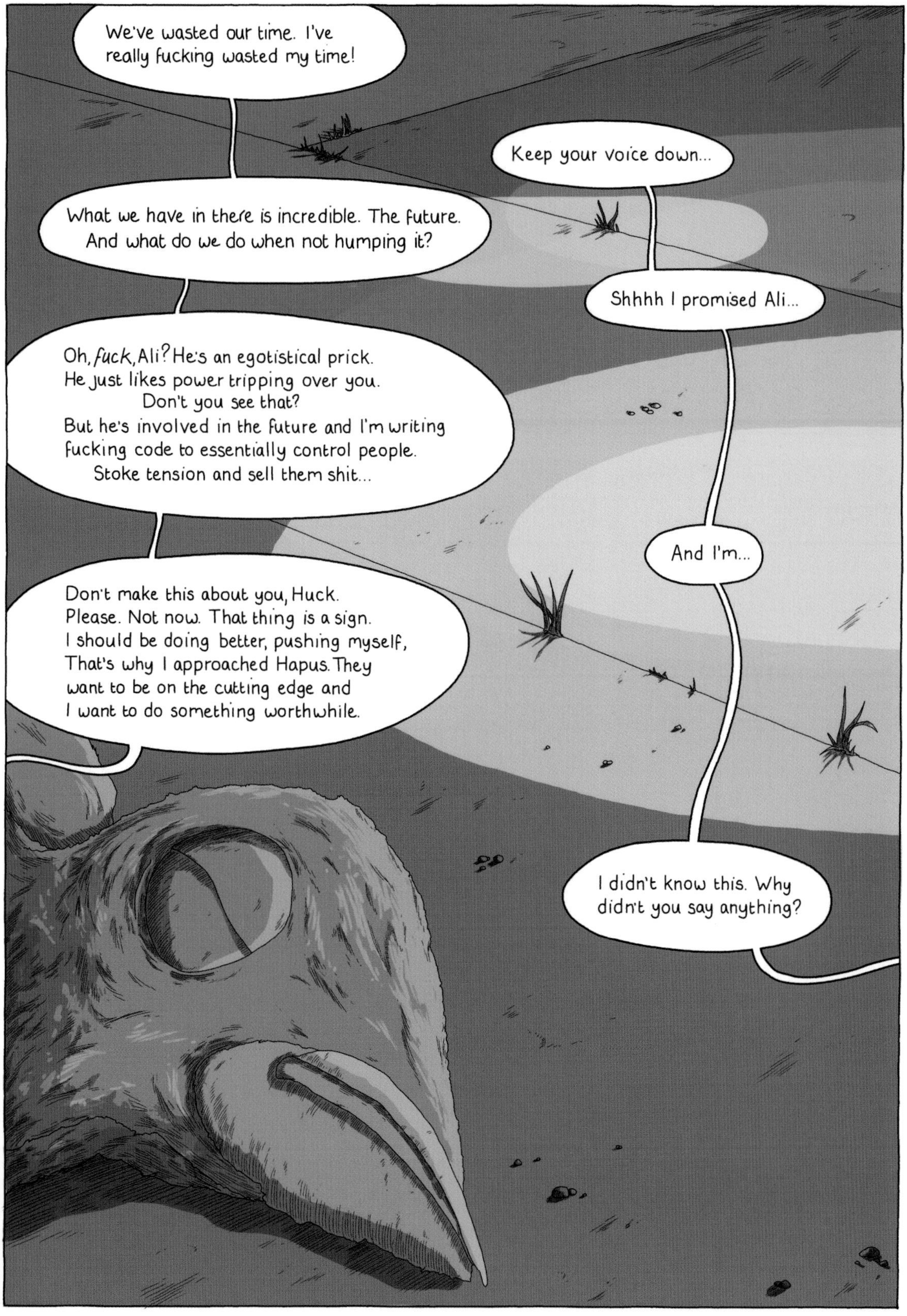
We've wasted our time. I've really fucking wasted my time!
Keep your voice down...
What we have in there is incredible. The future. And what do we do when not humping it?
Shhhh I promised Ali...
Oh, *fuck*, Ali? He's an egotistical prick. He just likes power tripping over you. Don't you see that? But he's involved in the future and I'm writing fucking code to essentially control people. Stoke tension and sell them shit...
And I'm...
Don't make this about you, Huck. Please. Not now. That thing is a sign. I should be doing better, pushing myself, That's why I approached Hapus. They want to be on the cutting edge and I want to do something worthwhile.
I didn't know this. Why didn't you say anything?

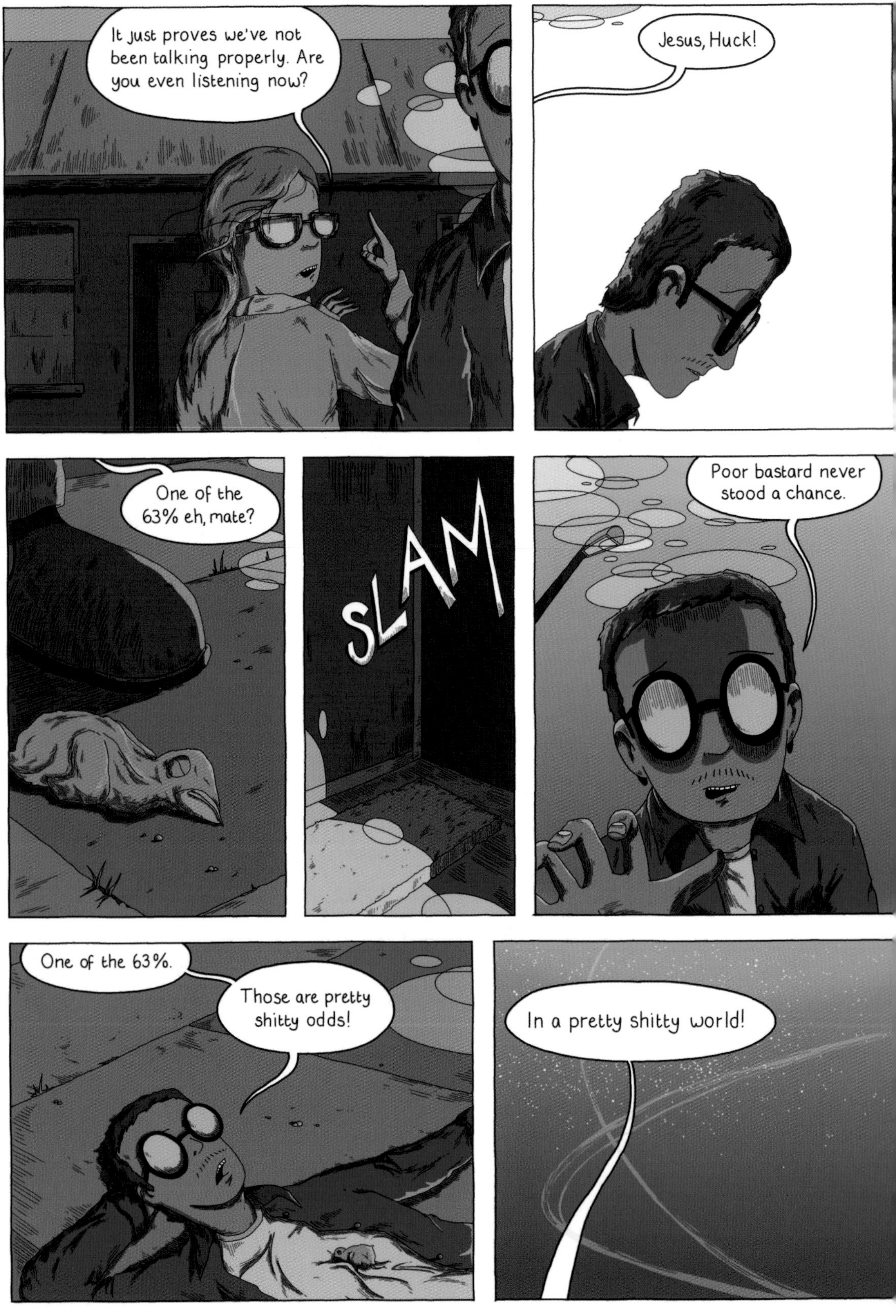
It just proves we've not been talking properly. Are you even listening now?
Jesus, Huck!
One of the 63% eh, mate?
SLAM
Poor bastard never stood a chance.
One of the 63%.
Those are pretty shitty odds!
In a pretty shitty world!

To The

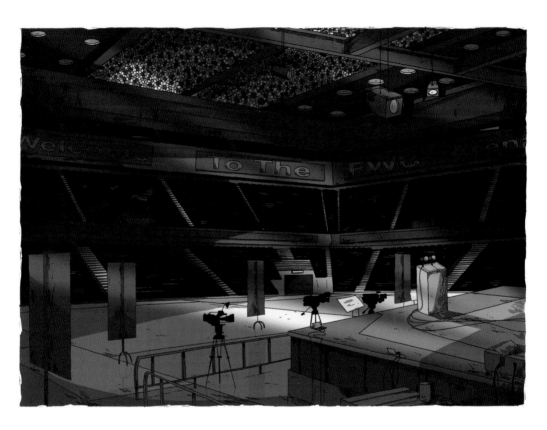

3 days to election.

Welcome
To The
FWB
Arena

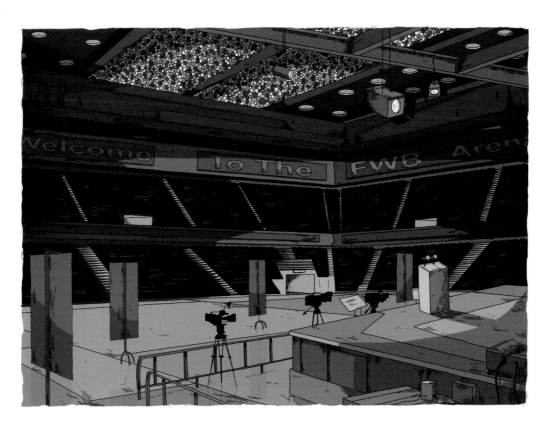

2 days to election.

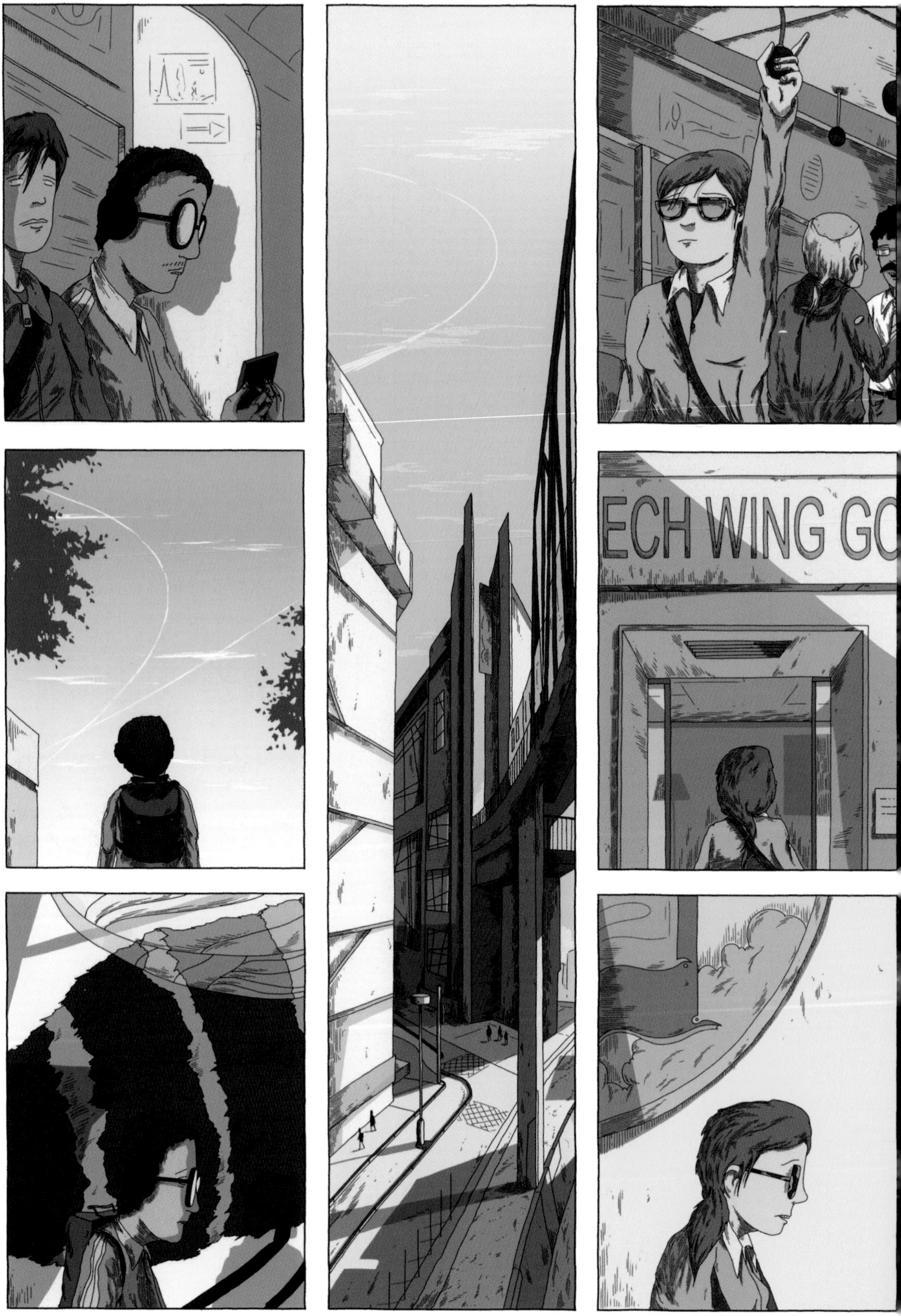
ECH WING GO

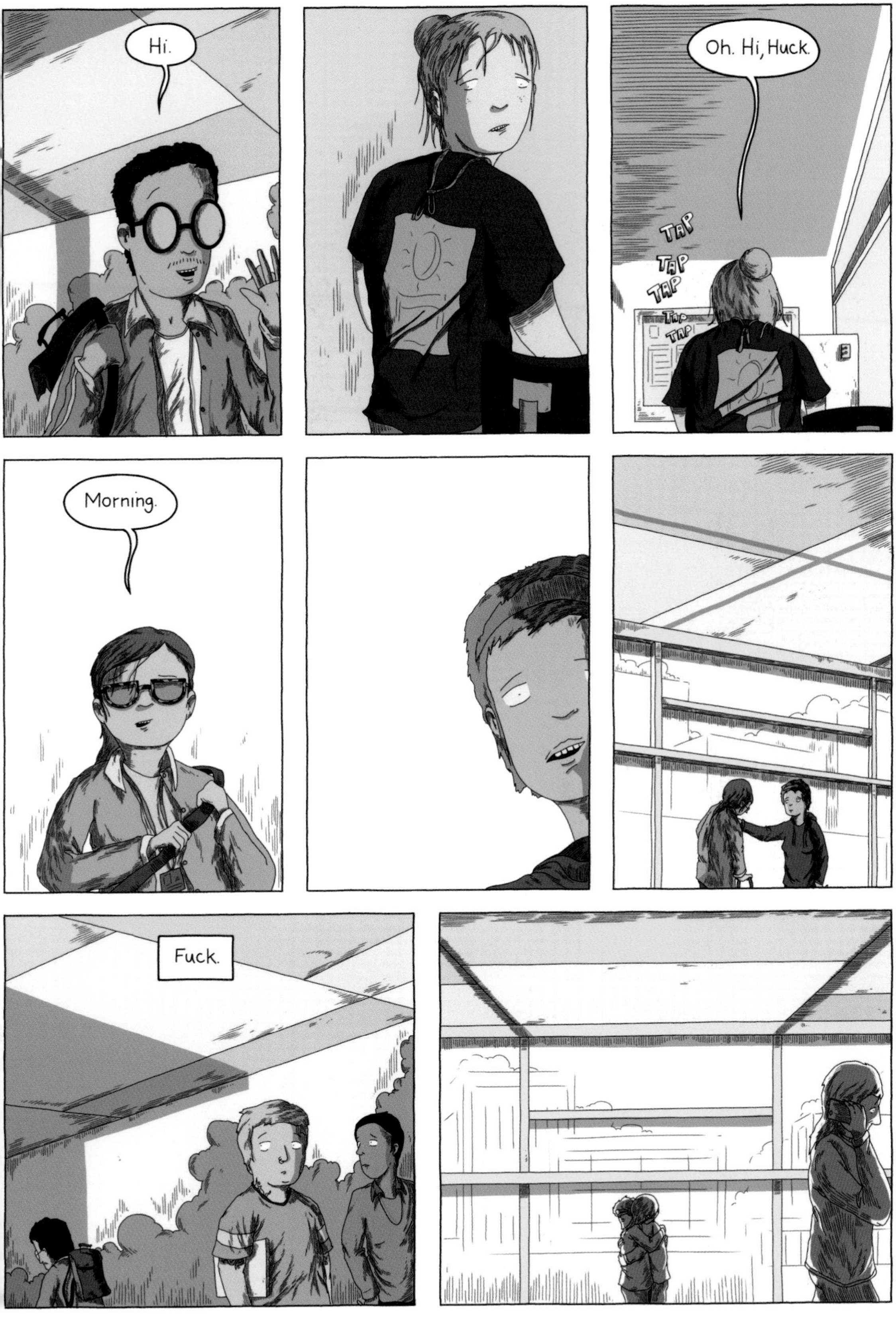
Hi.
Oh. Hi, Huck.
TAP
TAP
TAP
TAP
TAP
Morning.
Fuck.

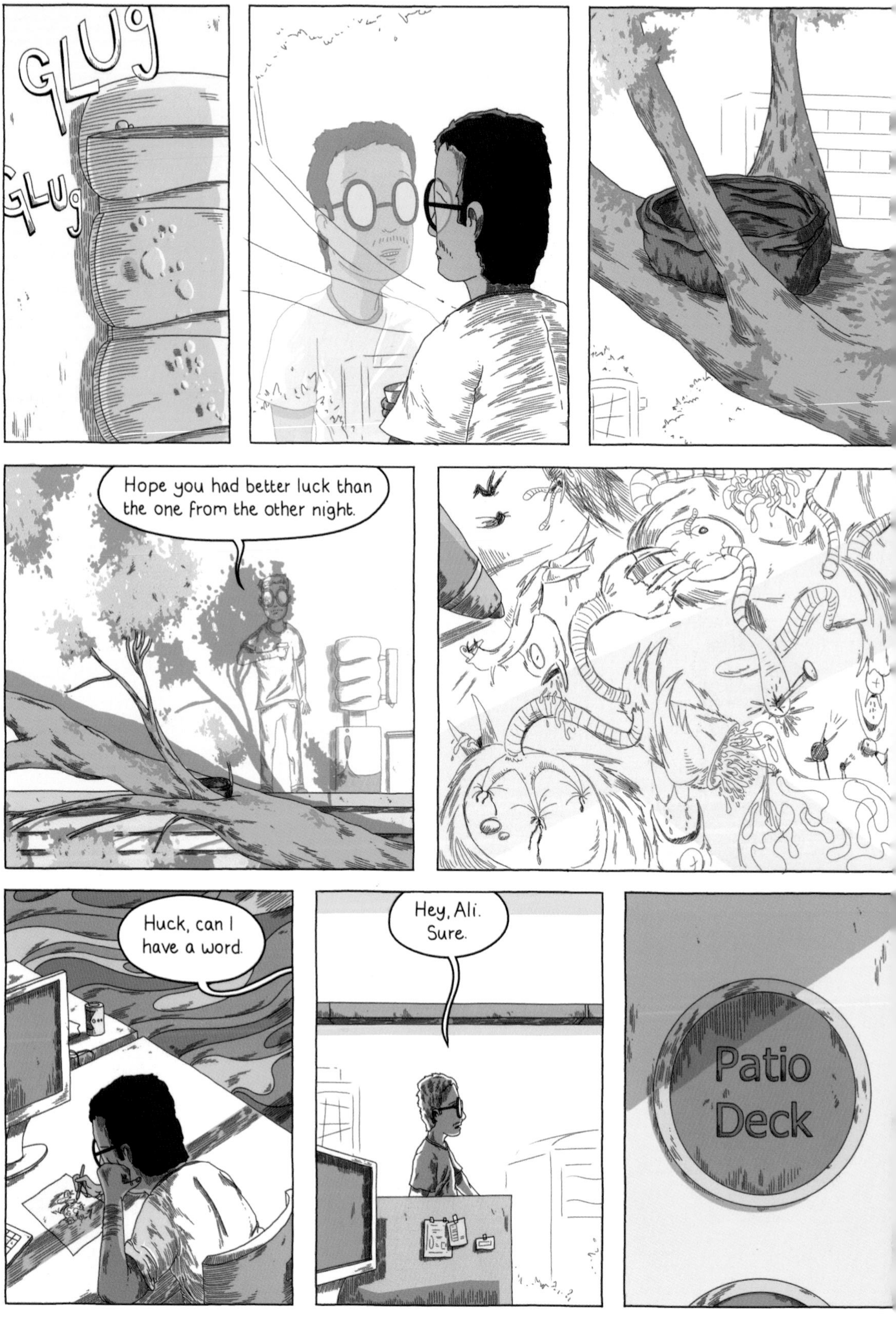
GLUG
GLUG
Hope you had better luck than the one from the other night.
Huck, can I have a word.
Hey, Ali. Sure.
Patio Deck

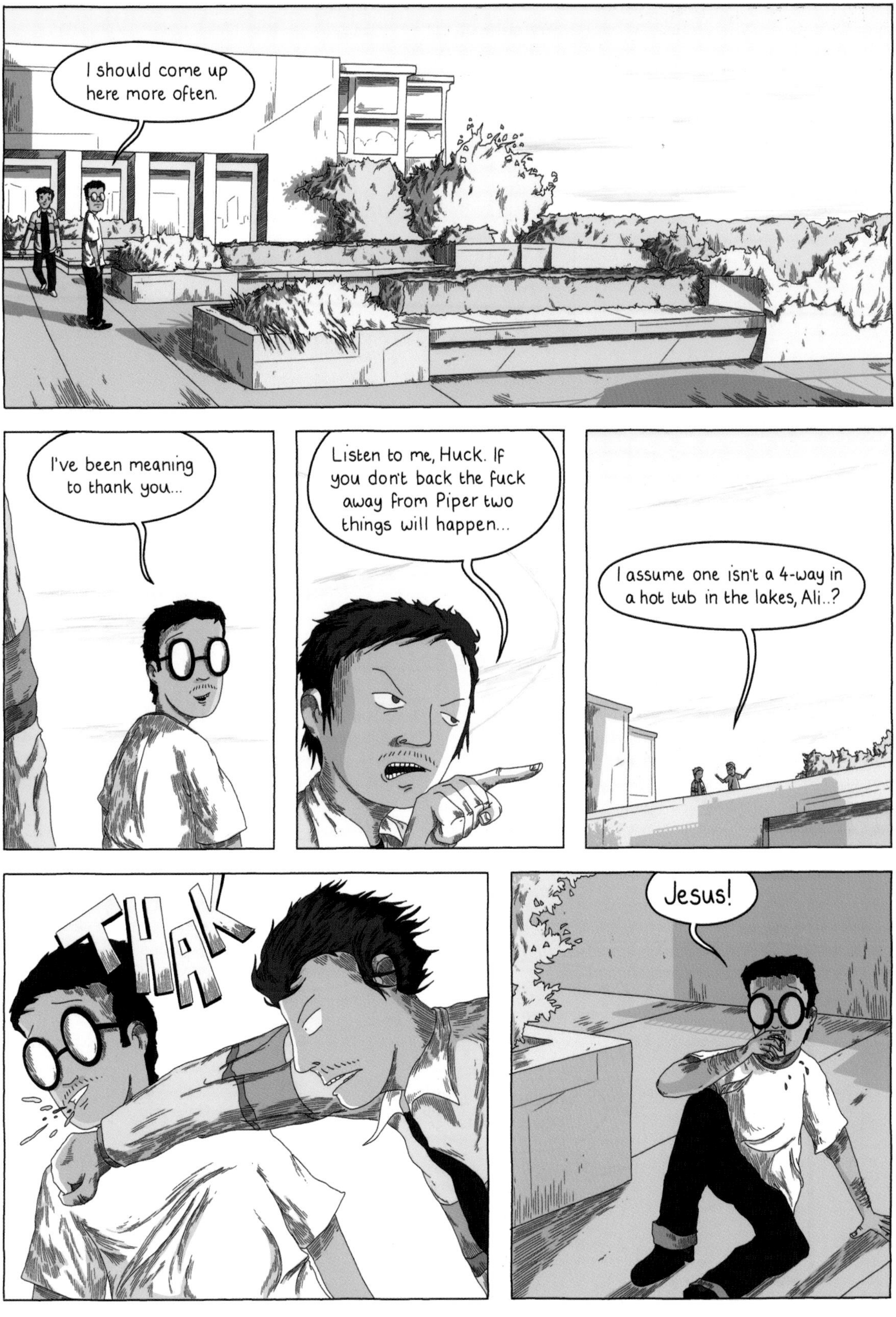
I should come up here more often.
I've been meaning to thank you...
Listen to me, Huck. If you don't back the fuck away from Piper two things will happen...
I assume one isn't a 4-way in a hot tub in the lakes, Ali..?
THAK
Jesus!

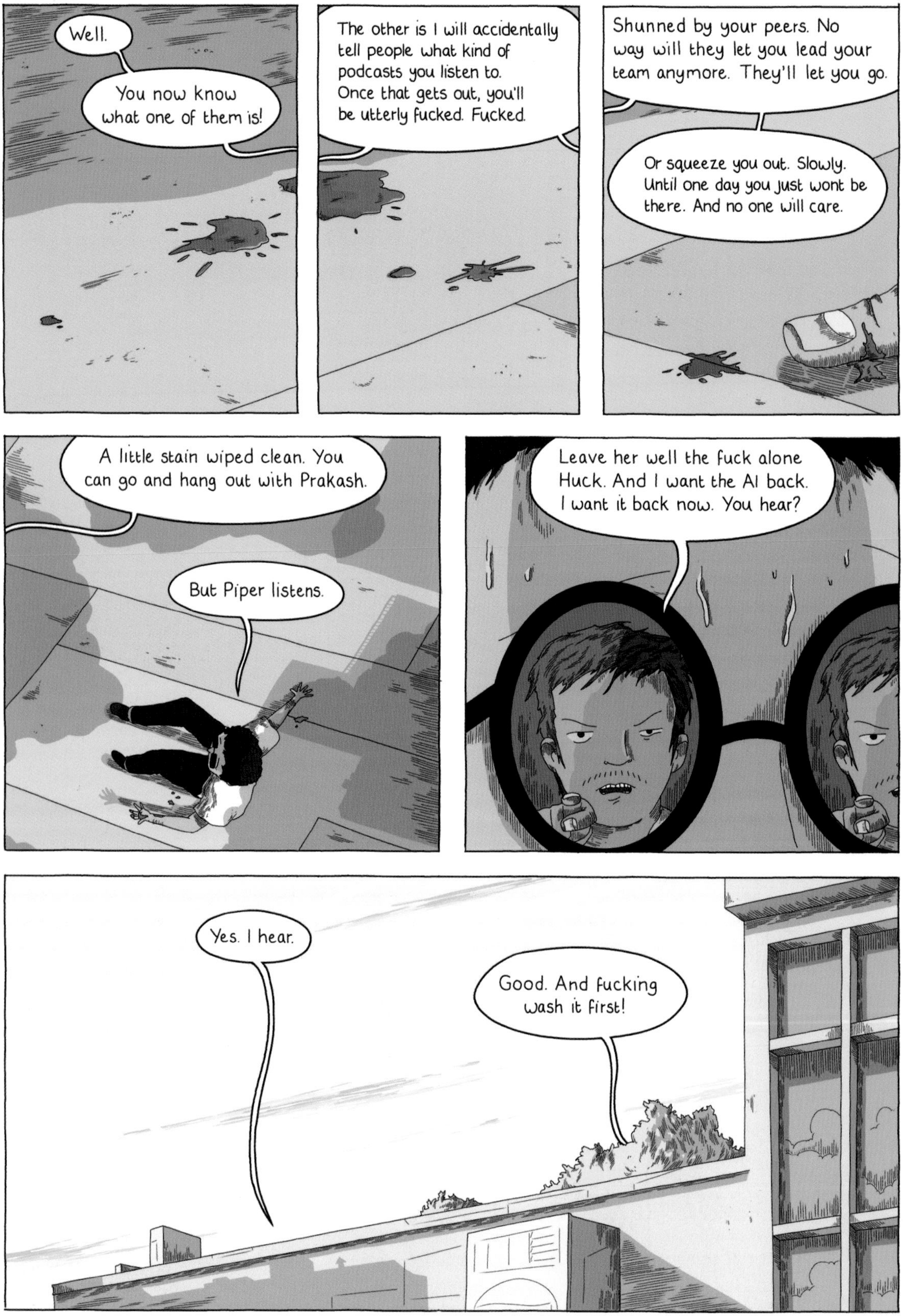
Well.
You now know what one of them is!
The other is I will accidentally tell people what kind of podcasts you listen to. Once that gets out, you'll be utterly fucked. Fucked.
Shunned by your peers. No way will they let you lead your team anymore. They'll let you go.
Or squeeze you out. Slowly. Until one day you just wont be there. And no one will care.
A little stain wiped clean. You can go and hang out with Prakash.
But Piper listens.
Leave her well the fuck alone Huck. And I want the AI back. I want it back now. You hear?
Yes. I hear.
Good. And fucking wash it first!

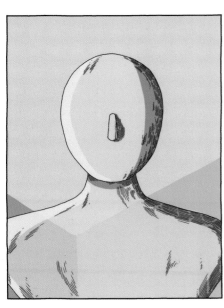

Okay. Let's pack it up and send it back. The party is over.

Are you okay, Huck? You've gone all quiet.

Yeah. I guess we knew this would happen. Not just this.

What else? Hapus?

Yeah. I'm okay with it.

I really am, as I said at breakfast. I think it will be good for you. It's change I have trouble dealing with.

The future seems to be happening so fast lately. Sorry. I was selfish.

Seriously, you don't need to keep apologizing. It is appreciated but we sorted it at breakfast. It's all good.

TAP
TAP
TAP

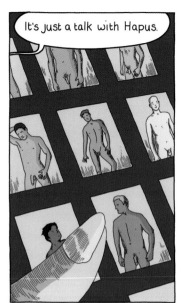

It's just a talk with Hapus.

I'm entering into the marketplace of ideas!

Ha!

Yeah. I should probably learn to code. You think?

You be you, and we'll be fine. But we do need to talk more. Opinions. Ideas. Don't hide them away.

You were right. I asked the first question all those weeks ago, that evening that set all this in motion.

BLIP

I know my Boolean from my CSAT.

I have an above normal sex drive.

But more importantly. I love being with you.

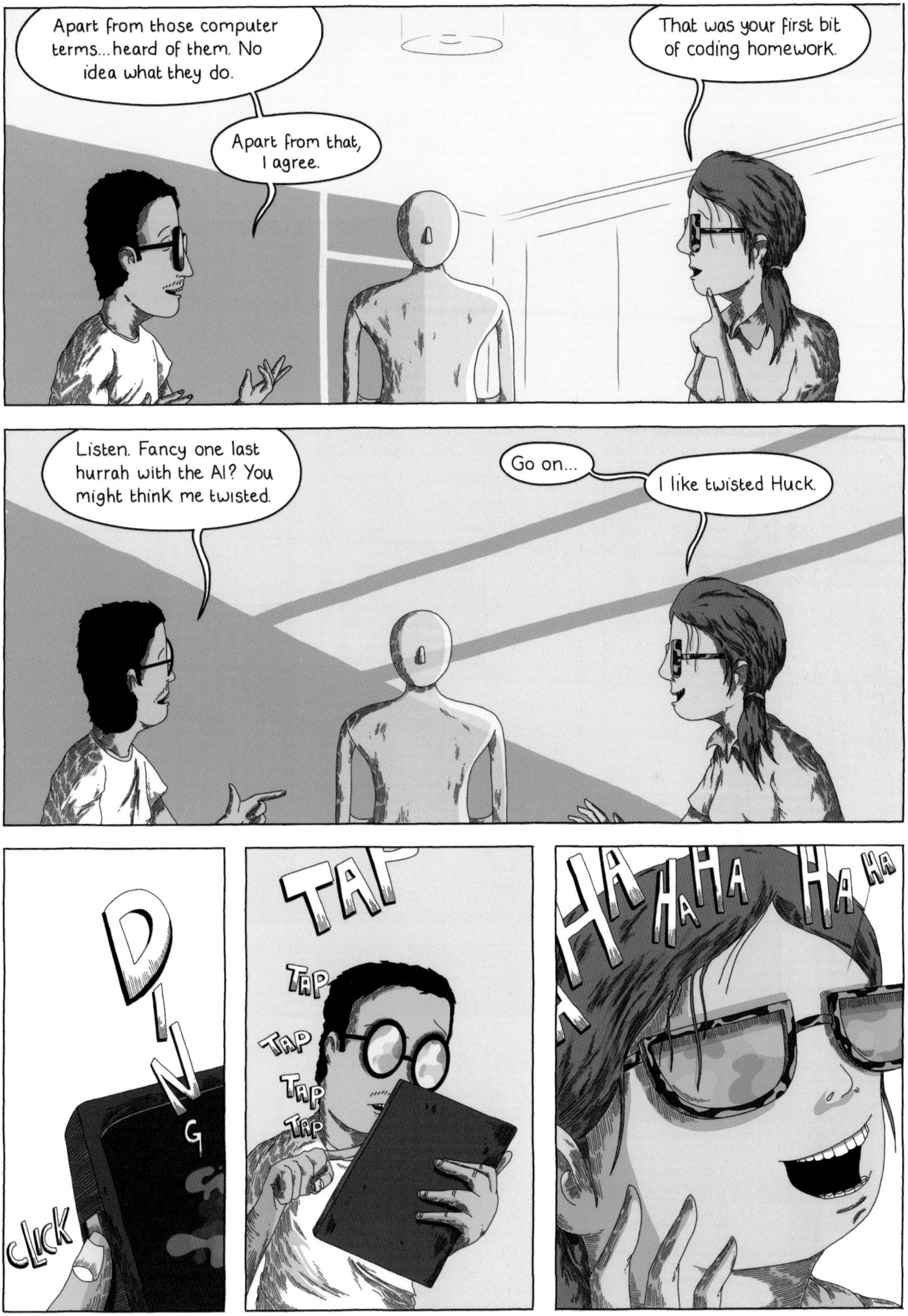
Apart from those computer terms... heard of them. No idea what they do.
Apart from that, I agree.
That was your first bit of coding homework.
Listen. Fancy one last hurrah with the AI? You might think me twisted.
Go on...
I like twisted Huck.
DING
CLICK
TAP
TAP
TAP
TAP
TAP
HA HA HA HA HA HA HA HA

You literally want me to fuck him?

Ali?

I would.

But it's utterly up to you...

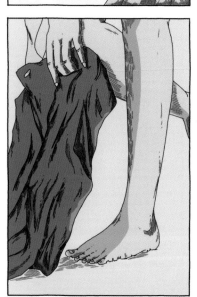

Love you!

Love you too, honey!

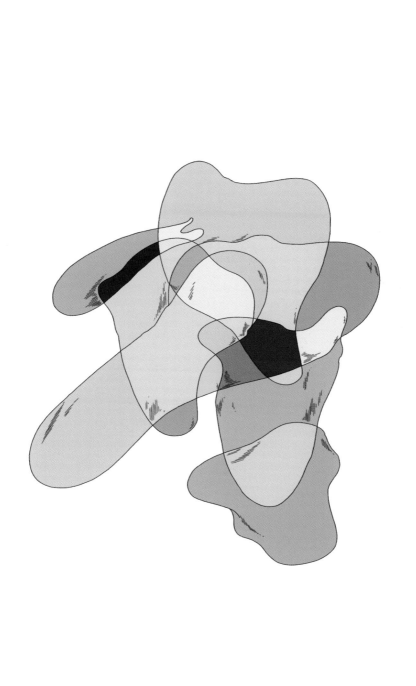

1 day to election.

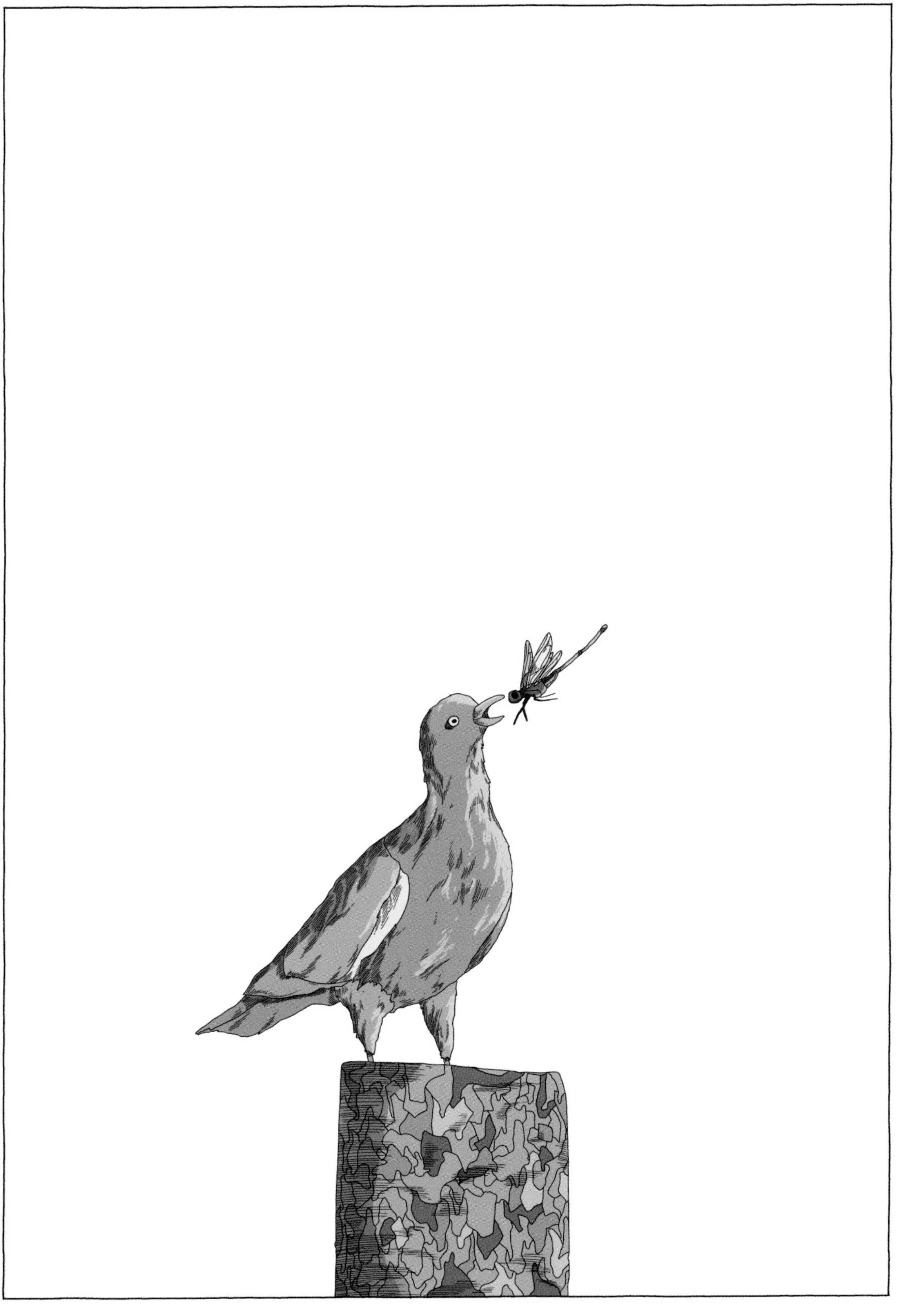

Welcome
To The
FWB
Aren

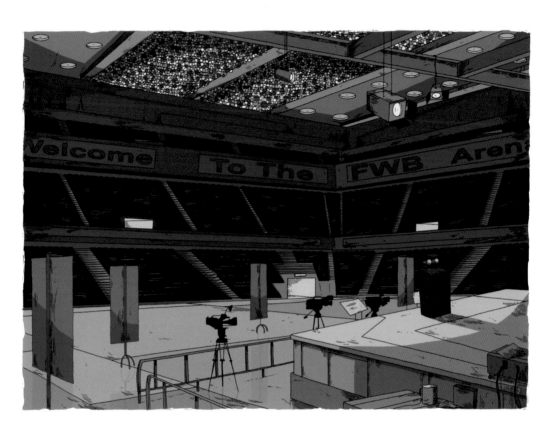

Election day.

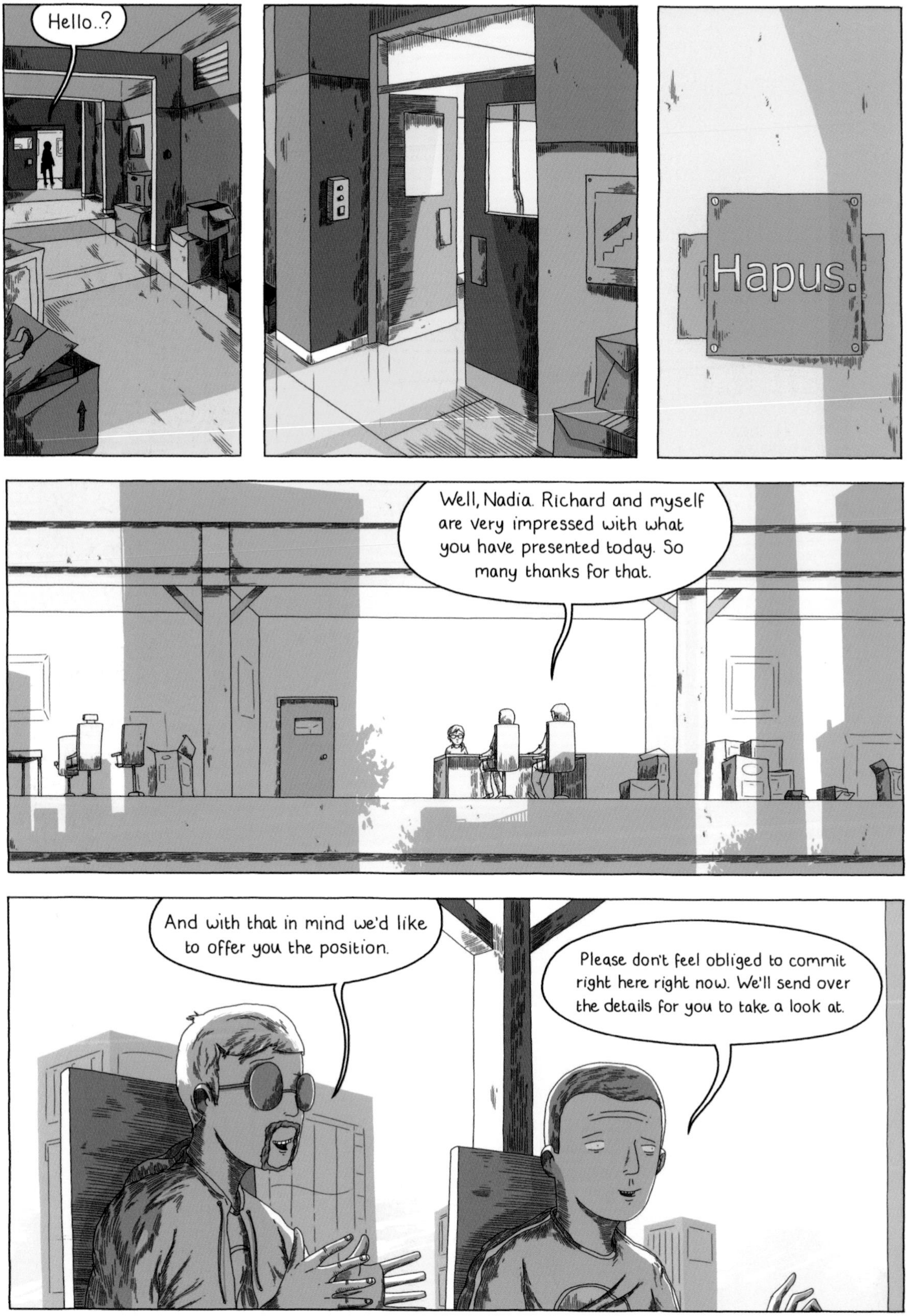
Hello..?
Hapus.
Well, Nadia. Richard and myself are very impressed with what you have presented today. So many thanks for that.
And with that in mind we'd like to offer you the position.
Please don't feel obliged to commit right here right now. We'll send over the details for you to take a look at.

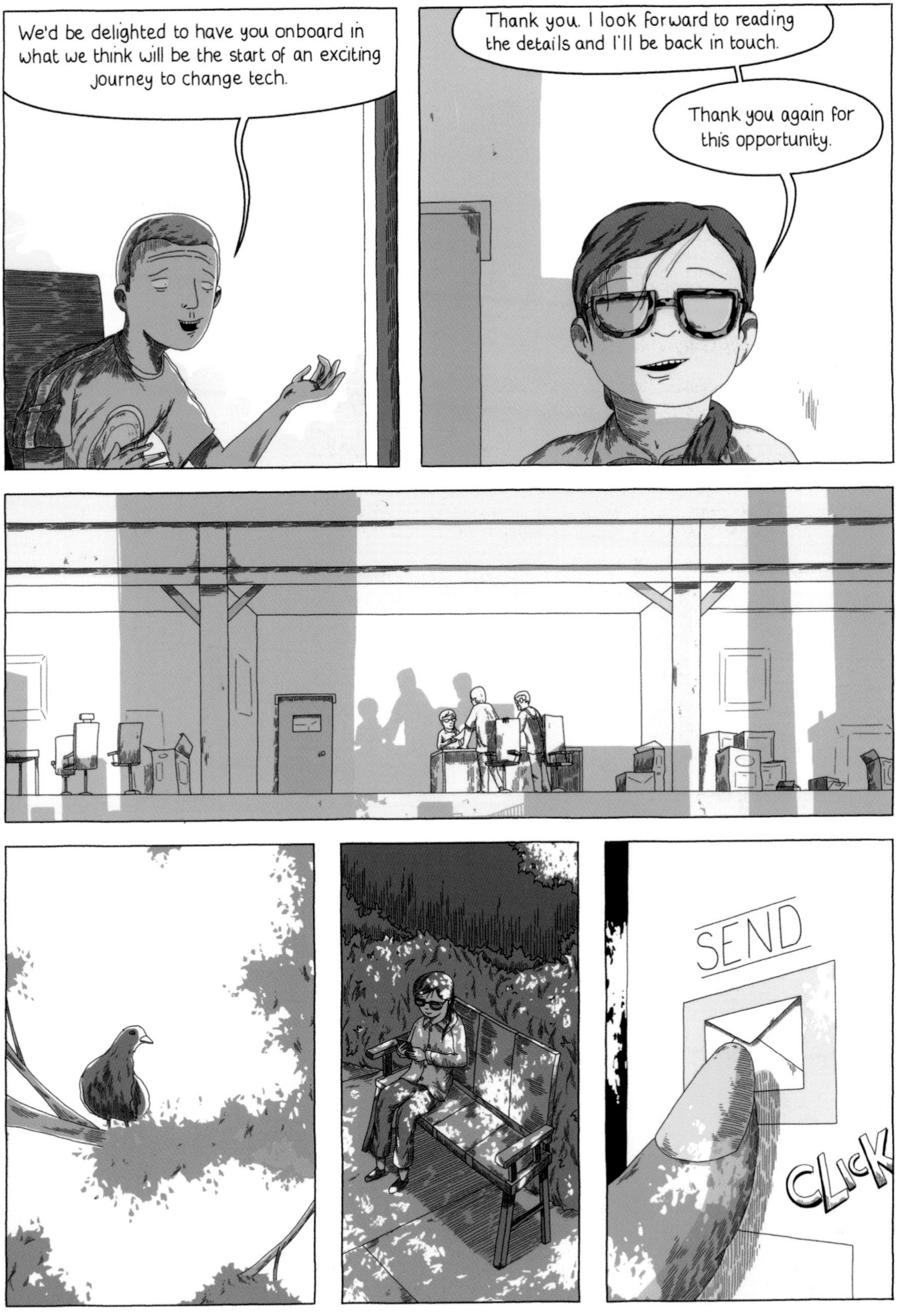
We'd be delighted to have you onboard in what we think will be the start of an exciting journey to change tech.
Thank you. I look forward to reading the details and I'll be back in touch.
Thank you again for this opportunity.
SEND
CLICK

PING

Nadia

Yes!

I've got the job! If I want it.
See you at 7? xx

CONGRATULATIONS!!
Absolutely. Love you! X

DON'T. FORGET. TO. VOTE!

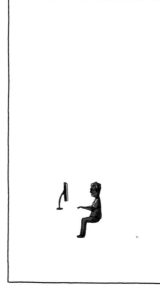

BEEP

Huck
Berninger

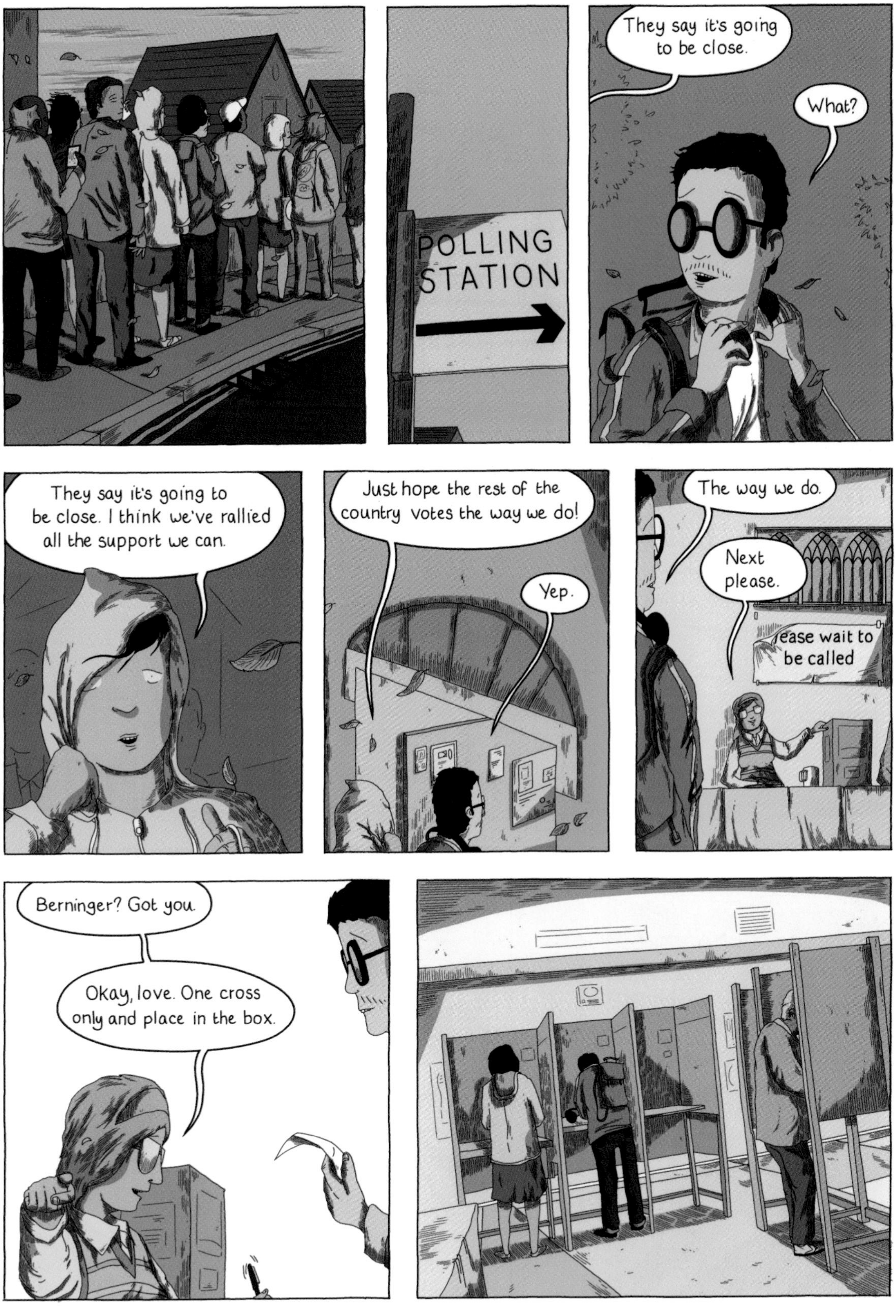
POLLING STATION
They say it's going to be close.
What?
They say it's going to be close. I think we've rallied all the support we can.
Just hope the rest of the country votes the way we do!
Yep.
The way we do.
Next please.
ease wait to be called
Berninger? Got you.
Okay, love. One cross only and place in the box.

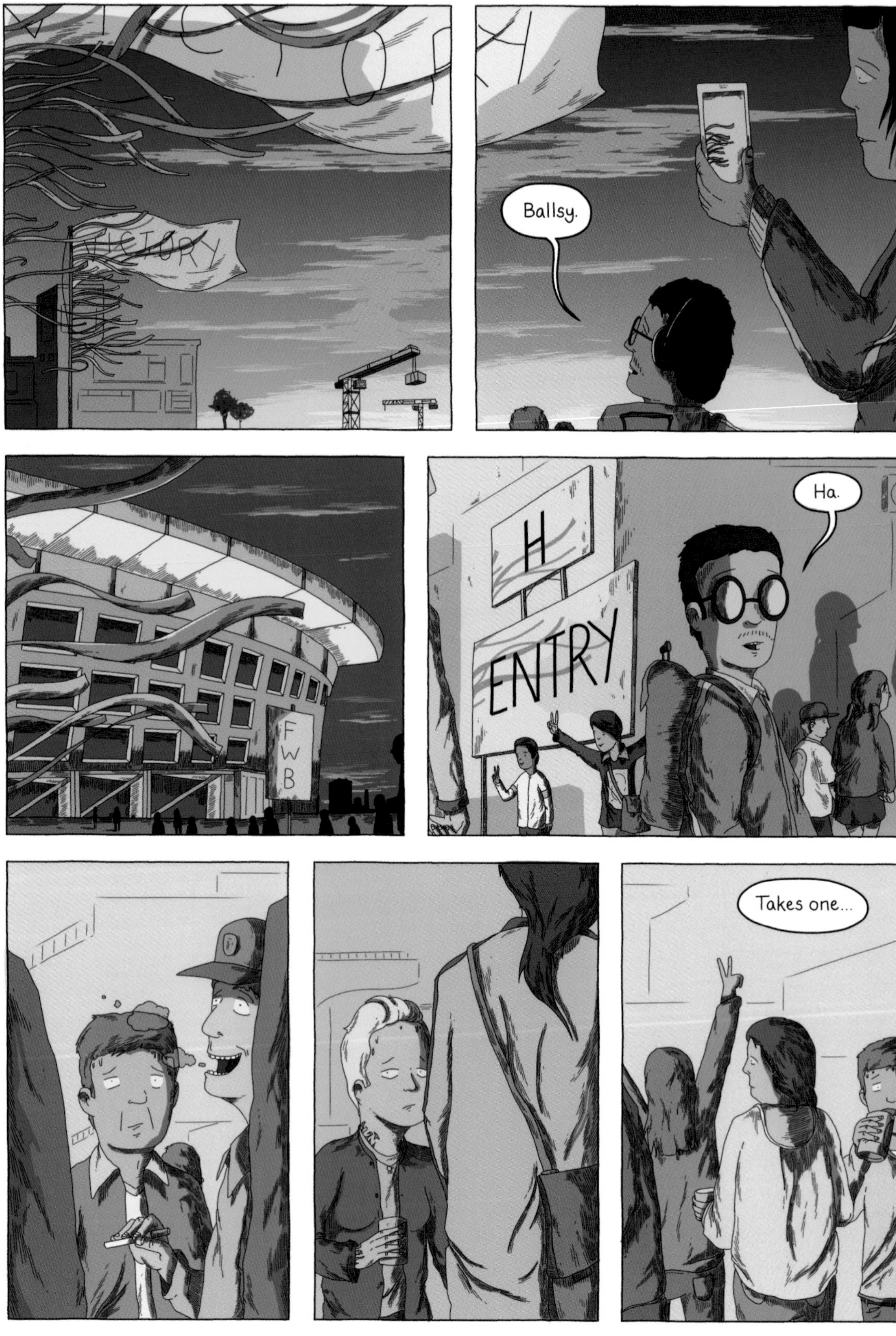
VICTORY
Ballsy.
FWB
H
ENTRY
Ha.
Takes one...

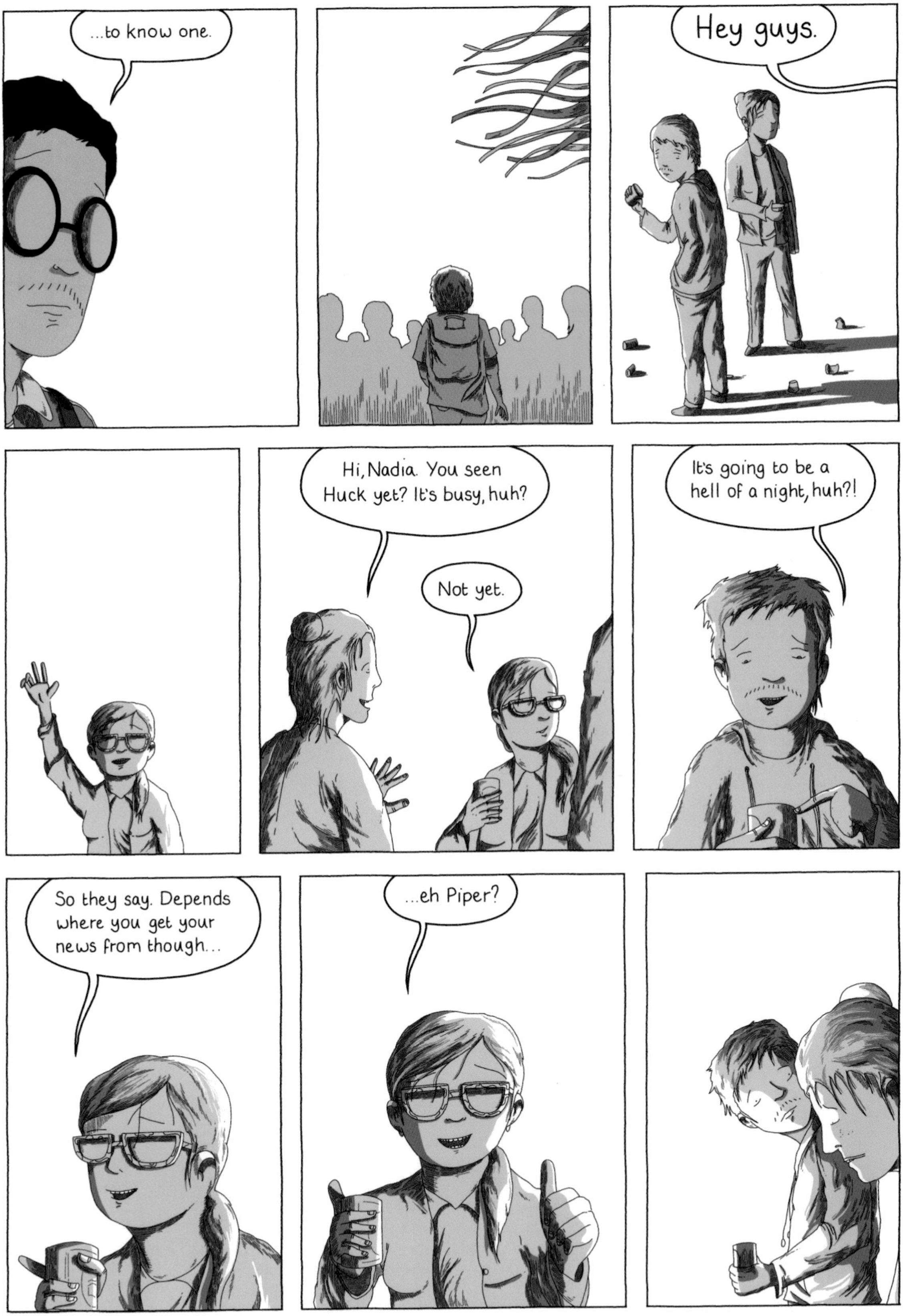
...to know one.
Hey guys.
Hi, Nadia. You seen Huck yet? It's busy, huh?
Not yet.
It's going to be a hell of a night, huh?!
So they say. Depends where you get your news from though...
...eh Piper?

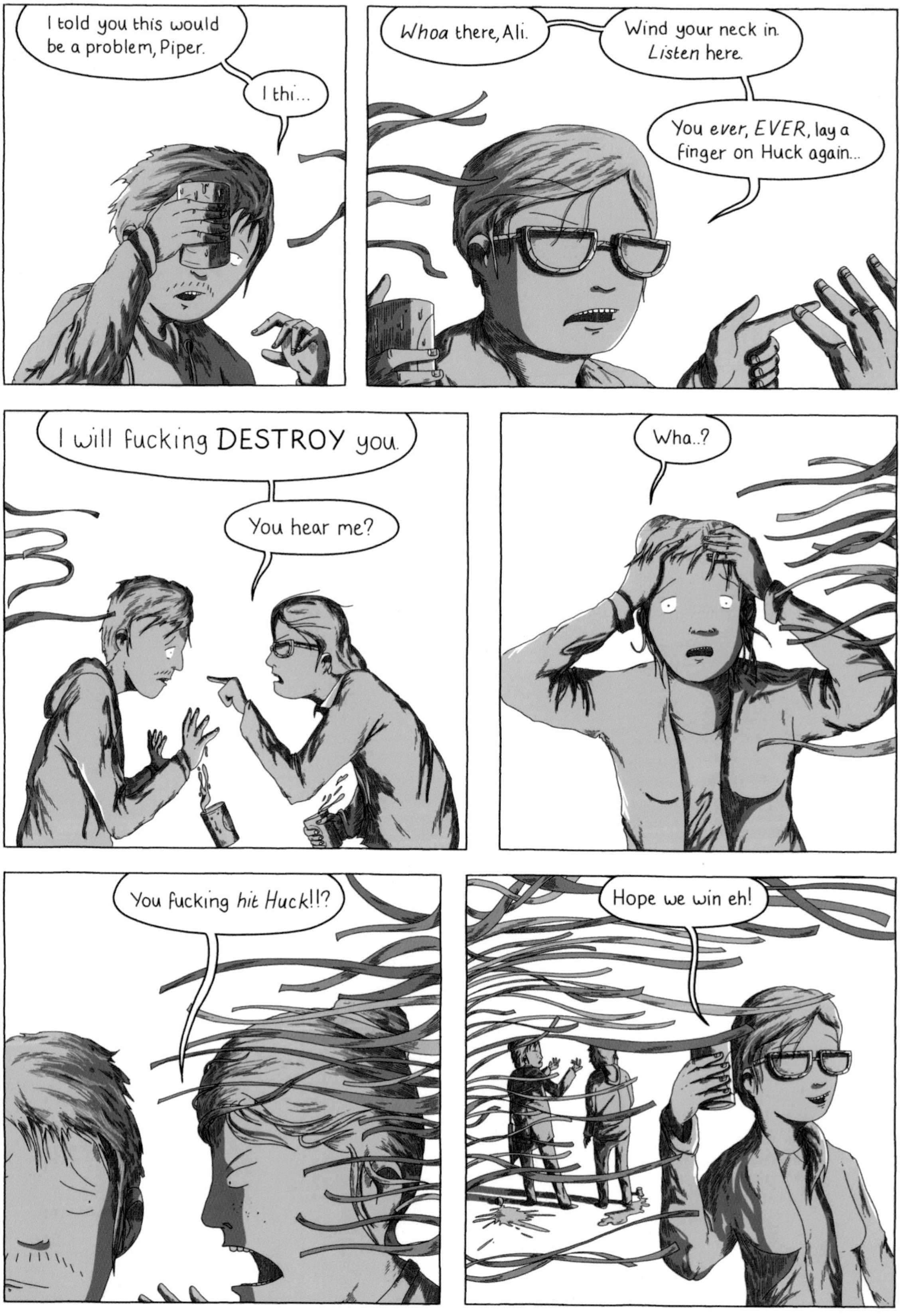
I told you this would be a problem, Piper.
I thi...
Whoa there, Ali.
Wind your neck in. *Listen* here.
You *ever*, *EVER*, lay a finger on Huck again...
I will fucking **DESTROY** you.
You hear me?
Wha..?
You fucking *hit Huck*!!?
Hope we win eh!

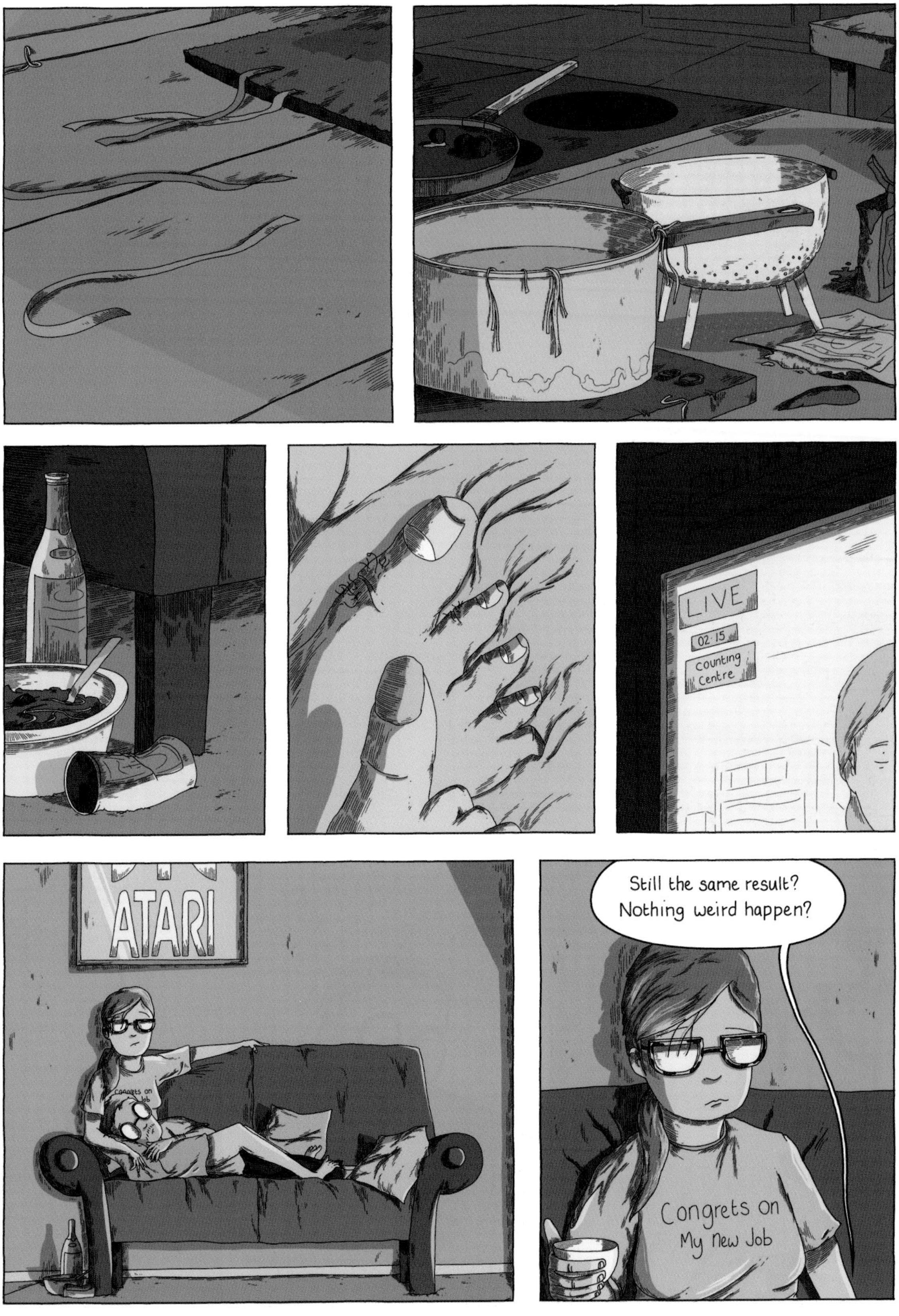
LIVE
02:15
Counting Centre
ATARI
Congrets on My new Job
Still the same result? Nothing weird happen?
Congrets on My new Job

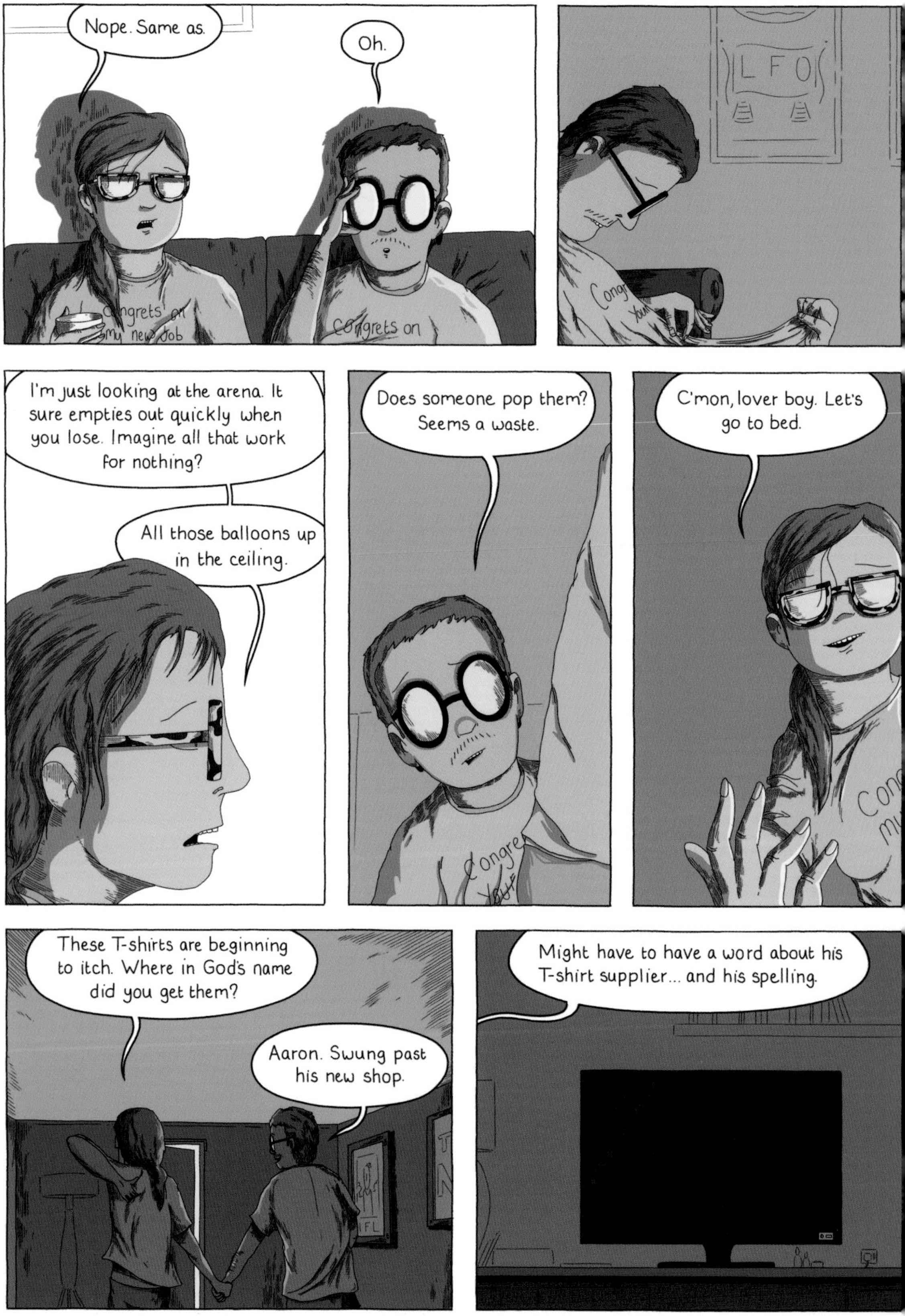
Nope. Same as.
Oh.
I'm just looking at the arena. It sure empties out quickly when you lose. Imagine all that work for nothing?
All those balloons up in the ceiling.
Does someone pop them? Seems a waste.
C'mon, lover boy. Let's go to bed.
These T-shirts are beginning to itch. Where in God's name did you get them?
Aaron. Swung past his new shop.
Might have to have a word about his T-shirt supplier... and his spelling.

One year later.

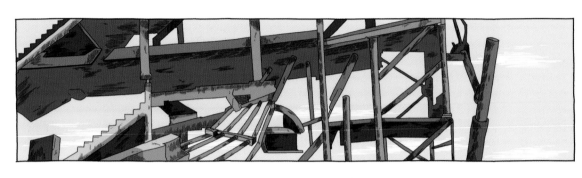

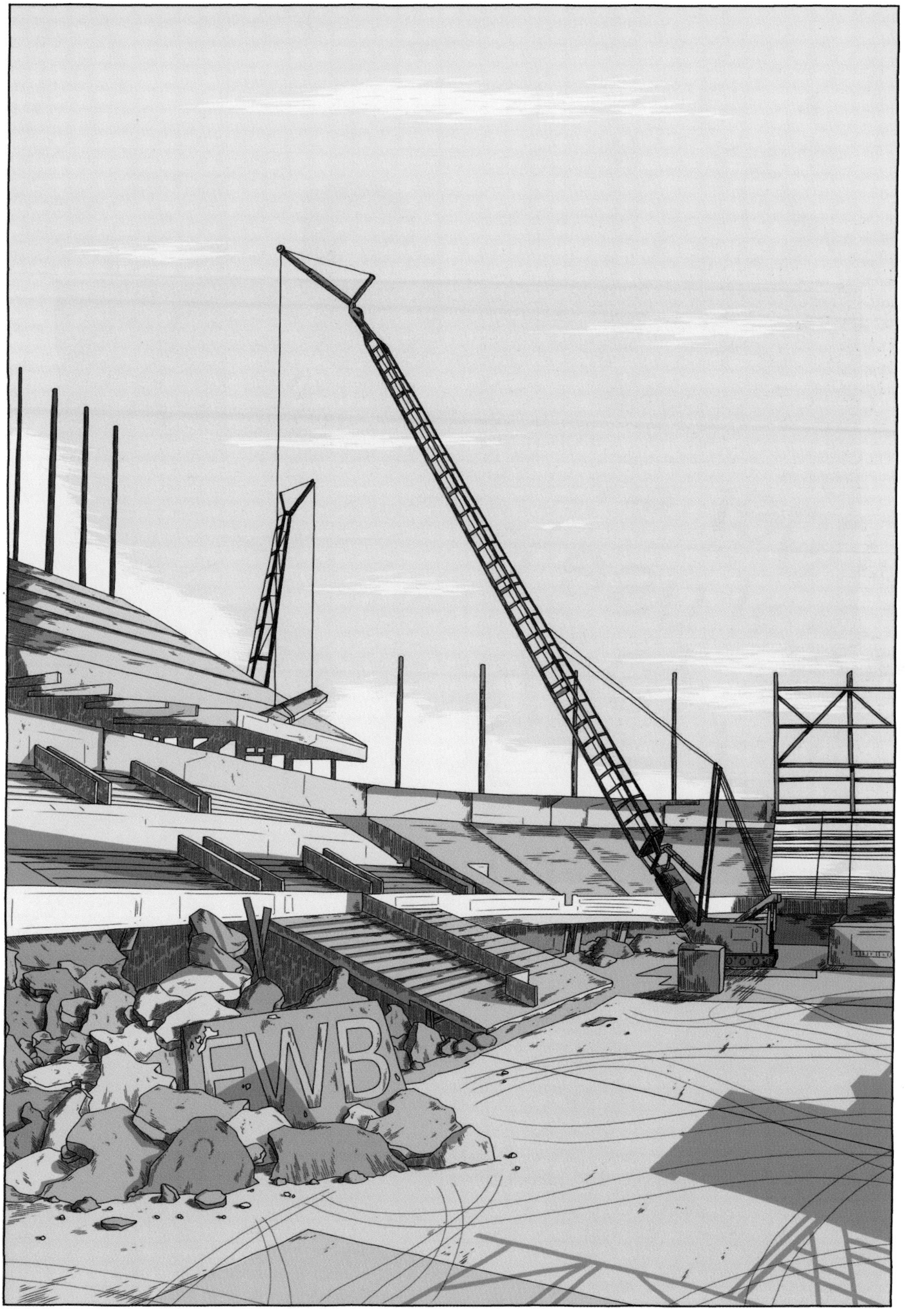
FWB

anger a
cal use o
Big Tech
a rise i
Election i
new energ

Right. I'm off.

Have a good day.

You too.

Oh. Can you tell Prakash I'll phone him later. Cheers!

Will do. See you after work for a bite to eat.

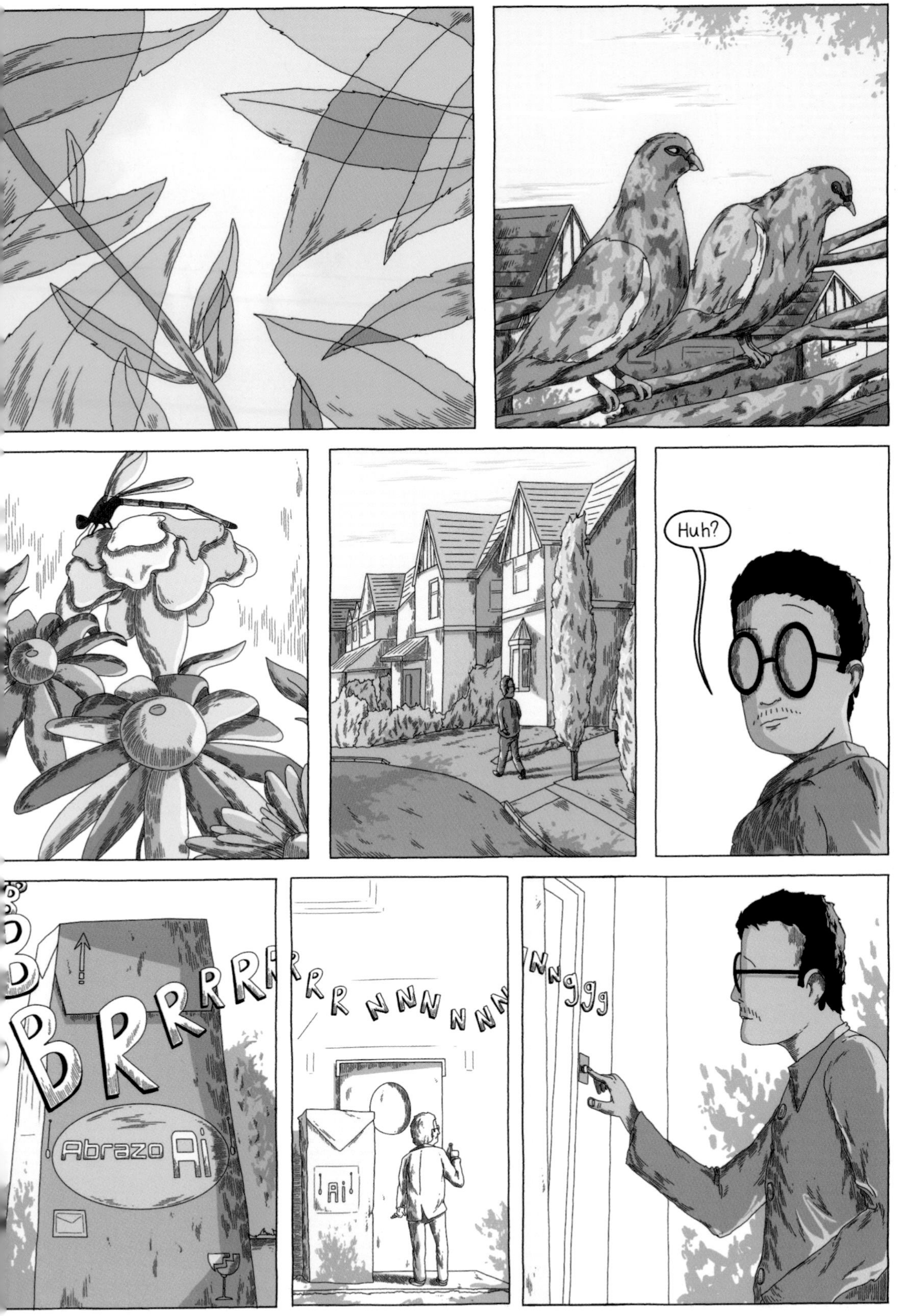
Huh?
BBBRRRRRRRRNNNNNNNNNgggg
Abrazo Ai
Ai

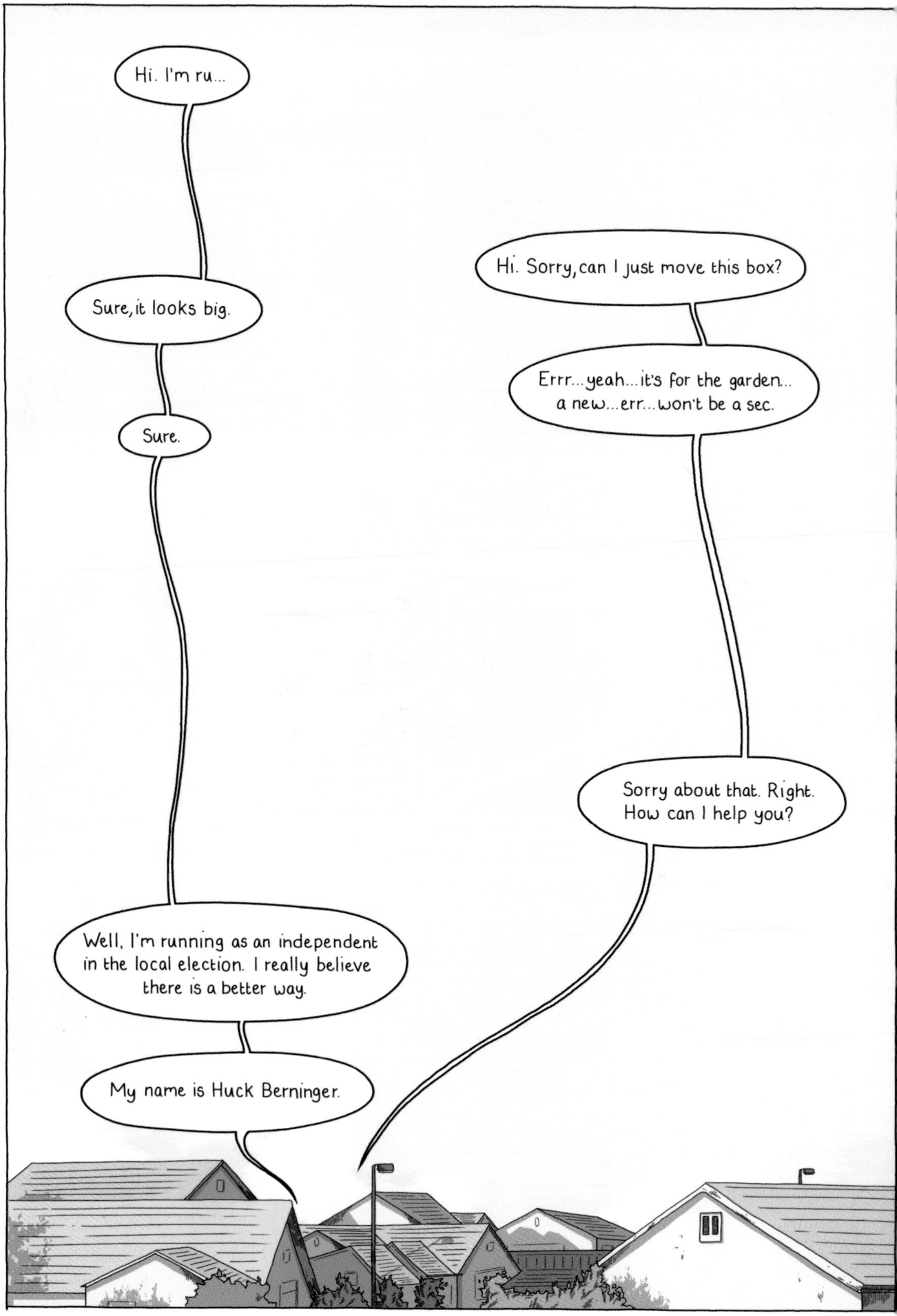
Hi. I'm ru...
Sure, it looks big.
Sure.
Well, I'm running as an independent in the local election. I really believe there is a better way.
My name is Huck Berninger.
Hi. Sorry, can I just move this box?
Errr...yeah...it's for the garden... a new...err...won't be a sec.
Sorry about that. Right. How can I help you?

Thank you

Sarah Faith. Linda & John.
Ravi & Rick. Irene. Krent Able,
Diane & Rory.

Published by Top Shelf Productions, an imprint of IDW Publishing, a division of Idea and Design Works, LLC. Offices: Top Shelf Productions, c/o Idea & Design Works, LLC, 2765 Truxtun Road, San Diego, CA 92106. Top Shelf Productions®, the Top Shelf logo, Idea and Design Works®, and the IDW logo are registered trademarks of Idea and Design Works, LLC. All Rights Reserved. With the exception of small excerpts of artwork used for review purposes, none of the contents of this publication may be reprinted without the permission of IDW Publishing.

IDW Publishing does not read or accept unsolicited submissions of ideas, stories, or artwork.

Editor-in-Chief: Chris Staros

Design by Nathan Widick

ISBN: 978-1-60309-505-1   25 24 23 22   4 3 2 1

Visit our online catalog at topshelfcomix.com.

Printed in Korea.